THE PHENOM'S WIFE

how a caregiver lost and found
herself in her family's trauma

JENNA MILLER BOOKS
MILL VALLEY · CALIFORNIA

THE PHENOM'S WIFE
how a caregiver lost and found herself
in her family's trauma

by
Jenna Ann Miller
www.thephenomswife.com
thephenomswife@gmail.com

ISBN: 979-8-218-43669-8
LIBRARY OF CONGRESS CONTROL NUMBER:
2024912166

COVER DESIGN:
Jennifer Siddens
www.jenniferksiddens.com

COVER PHOTOGRAPHY:
Jim Hughes Photography
www.jimhughesphoto.com

EDITING, PROJECT MANAGEMENT & PRODUCTION
D. Patrick Miller, Fearless Literary
www.fearlessbooks.com/Literary.html

Table of Contents

dedicated to

Steve, Aria and Payton

I love you.

CHAPTER 1

In the Blink of an Eye

"ARE YOU Steve Pelaez's wife?"

I have been afraid of that question for my whole life with my husband. Steve used to tell me he was going to die young. I hated when he said that but I didn't believe him. Inside my carefully curated world my husband was indestructible and besides, I would *never* let the father of my children die young. If I worked hard and smartly enough, I could choreograph my life to prevent bad things from happening. But the world was laughing at me. My husband's soul was obviously chasing death, despite my attempts to buffer Steve from Steve himself.

We live ten minutes north of San Francisco in the tiny town of Mill Valley, nestled between a bay, a mountain, and the Pacific Ocean. Waterfalls, parklands and coastal bluffs surround us. Our downtown is so charming it looks like a movie set with City Hall inside an English Tudor and a library that could be mistaken for a ski lodge. Our unassuming 1940s neighborhood has a few hundred original cottages sandwiched together, plus a sprinkling of new homes. It feels more cozy than crowded, especially with Mt. Tamalpais spreading herself in the distance.

Steve moved our family to Mill Valley to be close to her, where mountain biking was discovered. His spirit explodes barreling down her endless trails to freedom. Steve says he empties his mind and breathes life into his soul whenever he rides Mt. Tam, and he does so daily. Cycling is a family pastime. We mountain-bike with our children, who cycle to school and everywhere in between. To us, Mill Valley is paradise — and somehow we ended up here.

It's 9am on Friday April 21, 2017, another warm, sun-drenched day. I'm heading out the door to yoga when the phone rings. I pause for a moment and decide to turn around to grab it. "Hello."

"I'm calling from Marin General Hospital. Are you Steve Pelaez's wife?"

There are more words but I hear only "accident."

"Oh my God. Is he alive?"

She responds, "Yes, but you better come quickly."

"Payton, Dad's been in an accident! We need to go to the hospital right now!"

My hands shake as I dial. "Mom, Steve's been in an accident! I'm going to the hospital. Please call everyone and let them know."

My hands tremble as I drive to the hospital. Payton, twelve, is with me in the car and I am scared to death. I meditatively say the *Hail Mary* and *Our Father* out loud over and over.

Payton breaks the silence to blurt, "It's Dad. He's going to be fine. Dad's always fine…"

I stagger into the emergency room and see my friend Gillian, a physician's assistant in the ER. "Jenna, what are you doing here?" she asks.

Quivering, I whimper, "*Steve…*"

I collapse into her arms feeling weightless, like a sliver of myself. I've never felt this way before. My chest feels hollow, like it's stretching out to infinity. My heart is expanding as if it could fill the entire room.

Gillian ushers me through the ER doors and sits me down. She'll find out what's going on. Steve's friends John and Chris are here, and their facial expressions slay me: *It's bad. I'm terrified.* My head sinks toward the floor; it feels so heavy. I stare into space. My body is trembling but I'm not cold. My breath is slow and deep. A chaplain greets me. *Oh, is this a religious hospital?* I feel lost. What do I do? I'm so scared. *Does anyone know what to do?*

So many friends and family are with me but it's not comfort I feel, it's a mute stillness. *This is all a dream.* I feel like I'm peering out into the world from the back of my head. Everything seems far away. My body is suspended, floating six inches above the ground. *Please God, don't take Steve. I love him so much.* After repeatedly asking and waiting, my stomach drops as I nervously enter to see my husband.

Steve is buried beneath bruises, bandages and blankets. There are so many braces, tubes and medical devices that he looks like a robot. I see my husband's physical body but his life force has vanished. *Oh my God. How did this happen?* Steve is sound asleep but terror is stamped on his face. All I have to give Steve is my deep, abiding love but I cannot reach him. How can I save him if I can't reach him? I tremble looking at his frail body. I keep calling him *my baby boy.* My heart pounds from witnessing his severely damaged state.

The nurse says it's time for me to leave. Gillian shepherds me through the emergency room haze. I am drowning in agony and pain, drenched in love and helplessness, and she is an earth-side angel keeping me afloat. *Dear God, what are we going to do?*

Soon I am sitting quietly with friends, family. People keep coming. One of the police officers who responded to the accident walks in. He says he couldn't get Steve out of his mind. "Why? What happened?" I ask him.

He shrugs his shoulders. "She didn't look."

I look down at my phone; my Dad is calling. *"Jennifer, I'm so sorry."*

I'm crying. I say, "We had a perfect life, Dad. It was too good to be true. He's so badly hurt. There is nothing I can do. This is our life…"

A young doctor wearing light blue scrubs with operating glasses arrives. I say goodbye to my dad as the doctor leans forward in his chair. He tells me they've been resuscitating Steve all morning. I nervously ask, "When you say resuscitating, do you mean like on TV?"

"Not exactly. He's been getting lots of blood transfusions and fluids and is on blood pressure medication to keep his blood pressure up. There are three big things that we're worried about; bleeding is what we're focused on now. The brain is another concern. The third one is the lungs and breathing and for now that's stable."

I softly reply, "Okay." I sign the consent form for two surgeries, for the liver and the brain. I learn that the human body has five or six pints of blood; Steve has already received seven. Gillian tells me that out-of-town family members are calling the hospital and are being told to fly in immediately. My heart drops. *Oh my God. It must be really bad.* I am told Steve's stepfather, Mario, booked a red-eye. *Is he packing a suit?*

There is nothing for me to do except wait. I'm sitting here staring, not crying, not asking questions. I'm terrified, standing on the precipitous edge of a cliff, peering down into a dark void. The only thing available to me is surrender. I surrender to God — the only one who can save Steve.

The trauma surgeon Dr. Stahl is here. He's a young man with long dark hair and a goatee. He says, "I've talked to the Stanford Trauma Center and the plan is to send him there for a higher level of care. One is for the multitude of his injuries, and because of how severe the shoulder injury is..." Dr. Stahl says some big words I cannot process, but I understand that Steve's entire shoulder is separated from his chest, and they can't deal with that here: "... we need to get him to a level one trauma center, the highest level."

I whisper, "Okay."

Dr. Stahl adds, "They have to fly the helicopter here, which takes forty-five minutes or so..."

Barely taking it all in I softly reply, "Okay... okay," adding uncertainly, "Can I see him before he goes in the helicopter?"

Dr. Stahl replies, "Um, yeah I'm sure we can make that happen."

Looking down at my wedding ring I murmur, "Even if it's just to look in and say, 'Godspeed'..." my voice trails.

I feel dull. Broken. Empty. Everything is in slow motion. I only ask doctors what they are doing to keep Steve alive; I don't dare ask if he will die. The only way to avoid that thought is to stay right here, holding onto the Divine force deep inside me. That force whispers in my ear, *"Steve is alive. Steve is alive. Steve is alive..."* That's all I hear.

But my beloved husband of eighteen years is broken beyond

repair. His physical body is trying to die and I have no idea where his soul stands. I've seen images like this in movies; occasionally I hear about something like this happening to someone else. But it's happening to me. Right here in this dire moment, I am a stranger to myself. My voice is different. I'm toneless. I speak softly and slowly, using few words.

If I were simply in shock, I would feel numb. This is different. I feel a loving force taking over me, guiding me, holding me. I don't intend for this to happen; I didn't ask for it. It's just happening. I am gifted with love; I feel love for Steve, for our children, for the friends and family by our side. I feel love for God, and even for the teenage girl who did this. I have never felt this before. My husband is unreachable, yet for the first time in my life I am awake to a magnificent sense of love I have never known. Something is happening to my soul.

I can't explain how or why but from the moment the hospital called me this morning, a Divine energy has been holding me. I need to reacquaint myself with this force. It's been a while — or maybe never. I've always had an intellectual and fear-based connection to God, not an emotional or spiritual one. This feeling that holds my entire being is like nothing I have ever known. There is no separation between me and this feeling of Divine love. I don't know where this came from, but somehow I know it's my prescription for surviving the new nightmare of my life.

The quiet road where Steve's accident happened is Paradise Drive, which lives up to its name. Vibrant, lush landscaping hugs the meandering roadway as it winds up and down, curving along the sparkling San Francisco Bay. For years, Steve spent Friday mornings on

Paradise Drive with a couple of dozen cyclists on "The Chicken Ride"— named after the prize given to the first person who finishes. The so-called winner temporarily takes home the silly, stinky rubber chicken that's dressed like a cyclist. Although the chicken has camped out in our garage more times than I can count, this wasn't a training ride for Steve. He was there to be social. Afterward, the group sat outside Peet's Coffee and chatted. Nearly every Friday, my gregarious husband came home brimming with excitement about someone intriguing he met on The Chicken Ride.

On April 21ST the sun was shining as the cheerful pack of brightly colored cyclists hummed along a wide-open, flat stretch of roadway, seconds away from the makeshift finish line. A teenage girl was driving in the opposite direction, about to drop off her sister at school, when she abruptly turned left. She crossed the double yellow line, right into the stream of cyclists headed toward her, with Steve leading the strung-out pack. With only ten feet of roadway between Steve and her SUV, there was no time to react.

My husband's head violently smashed into the window of the passenger's side door. His crushed helmet landed on the backseat of the SUV and his body catapulted onto the asphalt, twenty feet away. As the riders who tumbled into the crash site picked themselves up, they saw my beloved lying face down, unconscious, bleeding from his mouth and ear. Steve had totaled a Ford Explorer with his body. The child who had carelessly turned her two-ton SUV was crying hysterically and screaming, "I killed him! I killed him!"

Three of the peloton riders that day happened to be medical professionals: Otis, Alexis, and Ross. Seconds after the crash, Otis and his daughter Alexis rolled up on their tandem bicycle. Steve wasn't breathing when Otis approached him. The protocol for a trauma victim with this level of injuries is *not* to administer CPR. Otis placed his hands over Steve's chest and pleaded, *"Come on Steve, breathe! Breathe!"*

As Ross, a nurse and our neighbor, was consoling the distraught teenager, Steve's chest finally rose. Steve took a breath and so did Otis.

First engine medic John, a friend of Otis, came on the scene. Otis pointed to my dying husband and said, "This is our patient," and John rushed him to the hospital, code three. Friends who had been on the ride came to the ER right away. I missed their messages. It took the hospital social worker an hour to find me. In the meantime, someone heard the doctors say, "We're losing him! We're losing him!"

The Chicken Ride meant so much to Steve because of his passion for connecting. On this fateful day, those connections were life-saving. The brutal accident was caught on a GoPro video that I will never watch. My Dad saw it and told me you can eerily see the exact moment — the true blink of an eye — between joyful life and the terror of near death.

I remember the last image I have of Steve, just an hour before the crash. He was standing in the hallway outside our bedroom, suited up in his bright white cycling kit. I recall his tanned, muscular legs, and how fit and strong he looked. Steve came back to the house because he forgot something. I asked, "When will you be back, honey?"

He didn't answer.

The Life Flight helicopter has waited at the hospital all day. After spending ten hours trying to stabilize Steve, the doctors are finally ready to fly him to Stanford, but Trauma Ambassador Gillian won't let my beloved go; Steve's intracranial pressure is elevated. Gillian asks the neurosurgeon, *"If this were your brother, would you send him on the helicopter now?"* The neurosurgeon repeats the CT to confirm no further swelling or herniation. All agree Steve can take flight.

As the sun is peacefully setting over Mt. Tam tonight, I say goodbye to my love. He is tightly packaged in a gurney, about to fly to Stanford, a world-renowned trauma center that offers Steve's only hope for survival. But the doctors aren't certain he will survive even the twenty-minute flight. Earlier in the day, one of the flight nurses, Becky, a pretty, petite brunette wearing a red jumpsuit, told me she would wait as long as it took for him to be stable enough to fly and she did. With her warm brown eyes, Becky also tells me Steve is going to survive the trip, and I believe her.

After spending all day watching over Steve and me, Gillian offers to drive me over an hour to Stanford. I need to go home to see our children, Payton and Aria. Somehow I have to explain what's happening and kiss them goodbye for a little while. Friends and family are with them, so I can be with my love.

Seated on the sofa, Payton and Aria think it's just another bike accident. I long to preserve the innocence in their eyes. Their distance from the truth brings me comfort; their lives are not yet ruined. I say, "Dad is badly hurt. I don't know what's going to happen, but it's Dad we're dealing with, so we are going to remain positive. He's being flown to Stanford in a helicopter because it's a world-famous hospital and will take good care of him. Gillian is driving me to Stanford so I can be with Daddy."

Aria asks, "What happened? Who did this, Mommy?"

Emotionless and factual, I reply, "A teenage girl turned her car without looking to park at her school and hit Dad."

Aria asks, "Is Daddy going to be okay?"

I reply, "No matter what happens, I know we are ALL going to be okay. If anybody can get through this, it's Dad. I am going to the hospital and spending the night. Call me anytime. I love you both."

I hug and kiss them goodbye, grab my things and hop in Gillian's car. As I gaze out the car window peering at the rolling hills and expansive sky, I pray, *Please, God, save Steve.* I feel God's presence wrapped around me as I press my tired head against the car window. This feeling is my only source of hope.

Before entering the Stanford ER, I see three familiar faces. It takes me a second to register them: our house cleaners Bertilla and Marcelino and their son, Brian. Confused, I ask how they got here. I'd texted them earlier saying, "Please don't clean tomorrow. Steve in hospital." They called my sister Michelle and insisted on coming to the hospital. I am deeply touched. I hug them, thank them for coming and shuffle into the ER.

The ER doctor looks like *his* husband was fatally injured, not mine. He is talking to me in another language, medical and technical. I can't make sense of what he's saying so I interrupt him and ask, "On a scale of one to ten, with ten being catastrophic, where is Steve?"

He hangs his head low and replies, "He's at ten." My knees buckle and I sob and sob and sob. My dear friend Kelly, who was with me all morning at Marin General, and Gillian wrap their arms around me and tell me to let it all out. I scream at the top of my lungs. I've been containing myself all day and I finally release the pain. "Dear God. Please save Steve! Please, please, please save him! He has so much more to give. I love you so much, Steve!"

CHAPTER 2

On the Brink

STEVE WAS born in the Philippines and moved to the U.S. at thirteen. We met in college, where he captured my attention. Standing six feet tall, he had long, thick, dark hair and an easygoing smile. He had a distinctive style, blending classic J.Crew with an edgy twist, wearing a small hoop earring. His frat brothers nicknamed him Johnny because of his resemblance to Johnny Depp. Wherever he went, Steve brought his bicycle and a warmth that was magnetic.

Steve was attracted to my curly blonde hair, tanned legs and playful demeanor. I laughed a lot and was always up for an adventure. I was also a workhorse and devoted student — a wise investment. We quickly became each other's world. I fell in love with him, and he was lovable. Together, we eased into what felt like the American dream. We were married in my small hometown, inside a quaint century-old chapel. After our intimate ceremony, we strolled from the chapel to the firehouse reception, and into a blissful life together. By age 25, we bought our first home and soon welcomed two children — a boy, then a girl. We were madly in love and inseparable. Our family joked that we lived in a bubble; we were the picture-perfect couple.

Eighteen years into marriage, our kids, now eleven and twelve, are the light of Steve's life. I work as a remodeling consultant and house flipper during evenings, weekends, and school hours, making it a priority to be home with the children. It's been a joy to watch them flourish with extraordinary experiences on the Food Network, dining at the White House, and giving a TEDx Talk. Our homes — and even our family — have been featured in magazines, commercials, and on HGTV. While my work has given me a creative outlet, my heart is rooted in being a wife and mother, pouring my energy into what brings happiness to Steve and the kids. I create family activities to be prolific. Our Facebook game is on fire.

Diminishing who I am as an individual, my family comes first. Being the one primarily responsible for our home, raising our children and working two jobs is exhausting, but Steve's pleasure comes first. He had a traumatic childhood and struggles; I empathize with him and want him to feel happy. Because Steve feels like he had no childhood, he wants to feel like a kid again, as he often says — hungering for freedom and play. Once Steve started hitting his head frequently, I begged him to stop riding but he couldn't. Cycling is my husband's medicine; it takes his mind away from his painful past. I agree to our unconscious arrangement because I want to keep the peace and I enjoy being the master of the "western white woman playbook" — rather than doing personal development work to figure out why I focus on everyone but me.

I feel like Steve is the kids' favorite parent — the fun, cool one who took them out for ice cream before dinner, taught them to ski, is ready to jump in the car and drive to Disneyland on a whim. I am the mother who makes them chug kale shakes, holds them accountable for their challenging behaviors, and ensures they keep their rooms tidy. As I witness my husband fighting to come back to life, my biggest fear is that my children will lose their epic father and be stuck only with me.

Steve's signature personality trait is that he loves to improve himself. He meditates daily and is a chronic self-help quoter. A few months before the accident, Steve started dragging the kids and me to church on Sundays. I went to church because my husband was adamant. It was unusual for him to be insistent about anything, so his request got my attention. Not only had I lost sight of my spiritual relationship with a higher power, I didn't really have one with myself. I was intellectually attached to the concept of God, believing the virtues espoused at Sunday services were good values. But I lived life inside my controlling mind, in a practical, physical manner. I did not read spiritual or self-help books, despite Steve's vast library spread all over the house. I practiced yoga for the workout, not the meditation. I thought meditating would be good for me, but never got around to it.

One time Steve asked me about my calling. "You mean besides taking care of the kids, working full time, and running this household?" I barked defensively. "My calling is keeping this family in order!" While my husband quoted Rumi and attended mindfulness retreats, I was creating financial spreadsheets, paying bills, and planning our future. I was a million miles away from my husband's soulful queries into life — overwhelmed playing the busy, martyred wife. Steve was the bright shining star, and I was his behind-the-scenes manager. I didn't appreciate how luminous his spark was until the accident smothered it.

My handsome, mid-40s husband has smiling eyes and makes friends everywhere he goes. They describe him as curious, authentic, and passionate. He loves fedora hats and peanut brittle. Steve has a successful career in tech but dreams of starting a non-profit.

He is also an elite amateur athlete. From 2007-08, Steve raced center stage in the *Track Cycling World Cups,* vying for a spot in the '08 Olympics. From 2013-14 he suffered Post Concussion Syndrome (PCS) after receiving multiple hits to the head snowboarding, skiing, and cycling. After the PCS diagnosis, he slept in a dark room for weeks and saw a variety of specialists while initiating his recovery. He listened to neuroscience, concussion, and functional medicine audiobooks. Steve meditated, took brain-boosting vitamins, exercised, fine-tuned his diet, and strived to be a "better man," as he used to say. After fully recovering from PCS, Steve posted this on December 4, 2014, on Facebook: "This Post Concussion Syndrome has been hell. And, I am thankful it happened. It was a gift. It was my wake-up call. I am AWAKE now and intend to live mindfully and be present as a husband, father, brother, son, and friend."

Steve has discovered truths about the meaning of life through his suffering that many people haven't. On one hand, he prioritizes giving back and is interested in deep connections with people rather than surface-level relationships. On the other hand, he is a relentless force when he wants something. He perseveres under challenging circumstances, able to summon great achievements seemingly out of thin air.

My friends Gillian and Kelly are with me in surgical waiting at the Stanford ICU, huddled together in the windowless, empty corner. Hours go by but there's no sense of time. I thank Gillian for her relentless devotion and convince her to go home. I am scared and anxious to see Steve. It's almost midnight. Finally, it's time. Kelly asks, "Do you want to go alone or do you want me with you, hon?"

Shaking, I confess, "I can't be alone. I am so scared. Please come with me, Kelly." She holds my hand. The heavy doors to the surgical ICU slowly swing open. We nervously turn the corner and are motioned inside the small room. Machines are tethered to my barely alive husband. The nurse standing next to him looks stoic. I scan Steve's body in silence. He is too large, doubled in volume from the transfusions. His swollen brain cannot drain its cerebral fluid, and his body cannot regulate its temperature. Both can be death sentences. Comatose, Steve cannot speak or see, and every machine-induced breath is another take at life.

Dark pools of fear, sorrow and despair quietly spill from my wounded heart. Cushioned by love, I am heartbroken and heart-open all at once. Instead of focusing on Steve's annihilated body, I cling to hints of life. I know the chances of his survival are slim, but I feel him in there, fighting to come back. I take a deep breath and say, "I love you, Steve. I've got this. Don't worry about me or the kids. All you have to do is get better. You can do this. You can get yourself out of this mess. Please come back to us. I love you so much." Wasted, I turn to Kelly and say, "Let's go to my sister's."

Kelly and I climb into bed together, but I can't sleep. I lie down on the floor and open my laptop. It's the middle of the night and I'm typing in the Caring Bridge blog my friend Lauren created. It's day one of the worst time of my life, and I'm desperate to share it. I need help. I must get the weight of this awful mess off me. I want to know I'm not alone. I finish typing and climb back into bed crying.

All I can picture are funerals. I know it's the wrong thing to imagine. Steve needs a miracle to survive, and I don't know where we can find one. *What are we going to do? God, tell me what to do! I'll do anything. I promise. Just tell me! Where can we find a miracle?*

It's 7am on Saturday. Neither Kelly nor I slept a wink. My friend Leslie calls. We are neighbors and our daughters are friends. "Good morning, my love. I have something to tell you. Steve's soul talked to my friend Meghan last night."

"Who's Meghan?" I ask. I don't recall who she is.

"You met her at our Halloween party. She's my Bowen therapist."

"What do you mean, Steve's soul talked to her?" I ask. I don't get it, but I'm open to anything. I say, "Text me Meghan's number."

Meghan tells me Steve's spirit came to her last night. I ask, "What do you mean? He came to you in your dreams?'

Meghan says, "Not exactly. It's hard to explain."

"What did Steve say to you?"

"He said, 'Tell Jenna not to worry. I am stoked and I have amazing things to do here!' His message was the Irish symbol of heart-in-hands. He was halfway turned to the other side. I know this sounds crazy! I don't know what this all means…"

I snap, "I do! I know exactly what that means! It means we can turn the odds in our favor. Steve took a picture of Aria making that symbol in Maui last week. Last night, he and I booked a trip to Europe. It was inspired by our favorite vacation before the kids, when we cycled all over Ireland. We loved connecting with the Irish culture, nature and people. We talked about wanting our children to feel like we did on that trip all the time. The Irish symbol means Steve wants to come back!"

Meghan seeing the Irish symbol leaves zero doubt she is connecting to Steve. I plead with her, "He is the love of my life. Will you please drive to Stanford to help him?" I feel a flurry of hope in my chest. *Please, God. Are you sending Meghan to help us?*

As I anxiously wait for Meghan, loved ones stream into the hospital — family who flew in, folks I haven't seen in twenty years, some people I don't know, all gather together with our dearest friends. The lovingkindness of these caring souls is more vital to me than food and sleep. We cocoon in the waiting area, sharing memories, dreams and prayers, filling up Steve's hospital wall with evidence of it all. Their love fills me with hope, instead of despair. I am grateful they are here.

Meghan and our friend Daniel emerge from the elevator. Daniel, a tall, handsome black man with a broad smile and loving eyes, is an old cycling friend of Steve's. We became close after living on the same street for a couple years. Daniel towers next to tiny Meghan — a beautiful, petite brunette with glasses and a glowing smile. Despite the circumstances, Meghan shines. I hug both her and Daniel and usher Meghan to Steve.

She looks down at my husband's horrific body, grins and says, "Hi Steve… You are beautiful." She closes her eyes and meditatively moves her hands back-and-forth above Steve, without touching him. He feels cold, dark and absent of light. She asks me to lay my hand on him, using me as a surrogate to energetically work on Steve's brain. While touching my physical body, she tells me the energy is going through my arm and hand and into Steve, although I am too numb to feel anything. She returns to Steve, placing one finger over his heart and another at his feet. She is calling in Universal Energy to connect to his life force. With outstretched arms, Meghan's body flows back and forth. She sees a faint stream of energy pulsate up and down his body; once the flow becomes brilliant taking on a life of its own that Steve can maintain himself, Meghan removes her hands and says, "He's got a lot of life in him."

Scared, I ask, "Is he going to be okay?"

Meghan replies, "I think so."

She tells me Steve's soul spoke during the entire drive to Stanford. Meghan gave him a pep talk, saying he's the love of my life and the kids and I need him, even saying, "Let's do this!" Steve's soul agreed and joined her in saying, "Let's do this!" repeatedly. Then, my romantic husband told Meghan to grab my face and kiss me all over when she meets me. I laugh and tell her that is "so Steve." I thank her for coming and hug her goodbye. No kisses, but I feel I've had my first experience witnessing an angel on earth.

My inner voice tells me to invite everyone to church tomorrow to pray but my mind is nervous about the turnout, given the short notice. I know we can't afford to wait, so I pull out my laptop and post on the blog: "This is Jenna. The love of my life is fighting for his life. Please join us at Mt. Tam Church tomorrow to pray for my darling, Steve."

DAY 3. It's Sunday morning and I'm speaking to Meghan. She says: "Steve came to me again last night. He says this is hard, not like he was giving up, but just stating the facts. Early Sunday morning, if you imagine facing his hospital bed, on the left there was a rope with knots every couple of feet. The rope was hanging from the sky and Steve climbed down. He entered his body but he insisted on entering it face first, even though he is lying face up in the hospital bed. It was as if he hugged his whole body once inside and then he flipped over so he matched the presentation. I asked him why he flipped over this way and he repeated the motion. He was wearing a burgundy shirt."

I've heard of people's spirits returning to their bodies after a near-death experience, but I don't know anyone who's done it. Despite my lack of experience, I wholeheartedly believe Steve climbed back into his body as Meghan saw it. I feel detached from the physical world myself — the place I vigorously worked to create a perfect life. In that world, I was the master of my future, planning and predicting everything… everything but this. I'm barely eating, sleeping, or moving. I give all my energy to Steve while sitting bedside — speaking to him, loving him, praying. Somehow I know that this loving state of being is keeping me from collapsing onto the floor.

I feel called home to spend time with Payton and Aria and attend the prayer service I organized. I'm shocked. Hundreds of people are at the church — standing room only! I can't believe how many people care. None of it was planned.

I receive incredible news: Around 1pm today, Steve reached for his breathing tube and raised his upper body and opened an eye. Dr. John got excited and yelled out, 'There you go Steve!'" This first physical movement since becoming comatose occurred a few hours after Meghan witnessed Steve climb into his body. I feel the energy of hundreds of people calling Steve back to life and it seems like he does too. I feel hopeful.

From neighbors to church members to strangers, hundreds of people are supporting our family. Prayer flags hang in front of our house, while prayer vigils are held worldwide. Bags of food, flowers and cards blanket our doorstep daily. Payton and Aria have multiple families caring for them, while I stand vigil next to Steve. To be cared for so deeply by so many gives our family tremendous energy and hope in a time of desperate depletion. I am humbled and in awe.

When the prayer service is over, I'm anxious to get to Stanford. Payton is ready to see his Dad for the first time. We've done such a good job warning Payton, it's not as bad as he pictured. The emotional response is another story. During my son's visit, we cry, laugh, decorate the room and talk to Steve and each other. Payton says going to school is grating on him because he is overwhelmed by kids comforting him non-stop. We talk about needing diversions and space from the pain. Payton is a brave boy, but he is shutting down.

I am crushed by my children's pain. Aria repeatedly says, "I can't do this. I can't hold on any longer. How much longer, Mommy?" Her needs and comforts are dramatically different from Payton's. Aria receives a bounty of gifts and cards from friends — expressions of love for her. Furious, Payton scoffs, "How could you profit from Dad's accident?" I tell my distraught children that each of us needs and expresses love differently and to try to respect each other's differences.

I have no idea how to parent through this.

The children and I pile into bed together. I suggest, "Let's listen to this song cousin Mark recorded for Dad, *Fix You* by ColdPlay." Hearing it with the kids tears me open. I release a deep, wailing cry. I scream at the top of my lungs, crying to Steve, "Please, we are so sad. We love you and we want to tell you to come home...."

Aria belts, "Daddy, please! I miss you. Come home. I love you so much. Please, please, please…"

Payton is silent. Depleted, the kids and I pass out in bed together.

CHAPTER 3

Love Enters the Room

DAY 6. Steve's shoulder is being reattached to his chest. Rather than worry about the surgery, I tell myself, *You are in one of the top hospitals in the country. They've got this.* Letting go of fear during the operation, I focus on love from friends and family.

By tuning into Steve's spirit and the spirit of those who care for our family, I am untethered from his crushed physical form. It is here that I find solace and freedom, unexpectedly transporting me into a quiet state of bliss. The Source of all living things burrows inside me, blanketing me with trust in our painful new life path, reassuring me that everything is as it should be. Loving energy is all around me, nourishing me when food and sleep cannot. I see signs of hope and healing constantly.

But my children are livid. Aria screams, "I cannot stand how you are finding all these positive things at a time like this. Daddy is so badly hurt. There is nothing good that can come out of this! *Nothing!*"

She has a point — my beloved is as close to death as he is to life, and I am blissed out. I could imagine countless scenarios that this desperate situation could produce, but for the moment Steve is alive. So I cling to that. I don't worry that I am blind to reality. Even if the father of my children doesn't pull through, I know we will be okay because I trust in the Divine path we are on. Heavenly Light floods Steve's lifeless body and radiates love through me and all those who surround him. I hold on tight. No matter what, I stay with the Light.

I thank God for the new person who stands before Steve. I see my old self watching, impatient with this agonizingly slow and uncertain process. The new me says, "Take all the time you need, honey." Our loved ones' boundless support and care allow me to feel patience and acceptance.

I am humbled by the people who grace us each day. It's like a reunion. Our oldest San Francisco friends, Fabio and Katherine, are bedside, reading their friend an endearing letter. A man I don't know walks in holding a book of poetry. He smiles at me and says, "You must be Steve's wife?"

I say, "Hi. I'm Jenna."

He replies, "Hi Jenna. I'm Josh. I'm sorry about Steve. May I read him poetry?"

Touched, I respond, "Thank you, Josh. How long have you known him?"

"I met Steve once." My heart swells.

Aria is ready to see her Dad for the first time. She stands outside his room, peering through the doorway. She approaches her Dad with stillness and hesitation, like he's a bird she doesn't want to fly away. She inches toward the hospital bed with a faint whisper, then turns toward me and says, "I can't connect the dots, Mommy. When I see Daddy I miss him because I feel like it's not Daddy. I know it's him, but I can't connect the dots. I want the

Daddy I know."

A week before the accident, when Aria and I discussed spirituality, she was on the fence. Since her father's accident, Aria sees God and the spirit of her Dad everywhere. She says, "God told me, 'Your Dad is going to be okay. This happened so you can learn a lesson, Aria.'"

I think to myself: *A lesson? What does that mean? She's a child — pure and innocent. Why would she have to go through something horrific like this to learn a lesson? It makes no sense.* I can't respond to her so I just listen. She speaks like a poet: "I am an egg. My shell has been cracked in a million pieces and I can't put myself back together. I was a perfect little heart. I was stable and perfect. And someone pushed me over and broke my heart. You can't imagine the pain I am feeling. I'm just eleven years old and going through this is so hard for me."

The decision to bring Aria to Stanford was spontaneous. It had been five painful days and I wanted her included. What I didn't think about was the weight her new pain would have on me. It's hard to manage my own suffering and that of the kids. My heart breaks for Steve, it breaks for my children, and it breaks for me. I didn't realize by having Aria distanced from the reality of her Dad's condition, I lessened my own burden. I cry myself to sleep each night. Nighttime is the hardest because the distractions are void. I only have my bottomless mind to wander into the darkness, into the sadness. This is hard. This is so hard.

Despite the heartbreak I feel, I cannot deny the bounty of blessings and signs of hope. They are everywhere. Balancing joy and pain is a new field I am mastering. When I'm buried in the red triangle of pain, I think of Steve. He taught me to control my mind.

We often spoke of helping our children do the same. *I'm giving it my all in your place, my darling.*

Pouring my heart out into the blog drains the pain from my soul. Reading words of comfort, love and hope from loved ones warms my heart and soothes the feeling of numbness that has taken up permanent residence in my frightened body. Spending time with friends and family at the hospital softens my fear and allows tender memories of Steve and even moments of laughter to fill the fissures that have cracked me open.

My adorable friend Jenny has short dark curly hair, twinkling eyes, and a smile that exudes childlike wonder. We enter the hospital chapel, a small, simple room with sacred writings and prayer books. There's a journal for handwriting letters, resting on a lectern. The children were here earlier. I am curious what they wrote. I see Aria's handwriting:

Dear God, *April 26, 2017*

You are the Divine. You fill my heart with love. You are the water we drink, the food we eat and the shoulder we lean on. We thank you for all you have done. We thank you for saving my dear Daddy from a terrible accident. Thank you so much. I love you so much. Please, we all pray for you to help the loving, kind, strong-hearted Dad he is and more. Please help my Dad get through the complications and surgeries he is going through. Please heal my Daddy. I love him so, so, so, so, so, so, so much. He is my world, my heart, my soul and more. I love you, God. I will give. I promise. Please heal my Dad.

DAY 7 of the hardest week of my life. While being driven to the hospital, I learn Steve's fever is climbing; this can be deadly for a traumatized brain. The Tylenol and ice blanket aren't working, so they're waiting for a high-tech machine called the Arctic Sun, which monitors ice pads placed directly on his skin.

When we arrive, I ask the attending neurosurgeon about the fever. He wants to see the fever more controlled, Steve breathing more on his own, and less output from the tube coming out of his head that releases excess brain fluid. The doctor also wants the neuro exam to improve. Right now, Steve's command-response movements are subtle or imperceptible. Each time the doctor asks Steve to move his fingers or toes, or open his eyes, I will them to move. When they are motionless, my shoulders slump.

Steve needs a tracheotomy to remove the uncomfortable breathing tube from his mouth and throat. They want to connect his feeding tube directly to his stomach too. Sometimes when Steve coughs, he reaches for the breathing tube. I'm hopeful this indicates an increasingly active brain.

The only person who could drop everything to step into my shoes is here; I can't survive another moment without my selfless mother. A mix of Mary Poppins, Martha Stewart and Bob Vila, my mom can make mundane tasks a blast and has workarounds and protocols for nearly everything. Given the generous length of her stay, I am genuinely surprised she came without her horse hair broom. She is driving us home from the hospital. I need her badly; I think about how tired I am. I also think about my friend Howie, a meditation teacher. He said one minute I will be a mess and next I will be laughing; I should embrace all my feelings. Last night, I spent hours in tears trying to soothe my broken-hearted Aria and myself. Tonight, my mom is here laughing with my children, gently guiding them away from the sorrows that blanket our home. They are thinking of other things. Nothing is permanent. When I'm drowning in heartache and pain, I remember what I tell my children: *everything will be okay*. It's a simple reassurance but to believe it takes immense courage and strength.

On the spiritual front, signs of love and healing keep pouring in. When our friend Fabio came to read a letter to Steve, we sensed him listening. His left eye slowly but consistently opened and shut, while shedding a tear. A friend, who is an artist, texts me saying that when she started a painting in honor of Steve, his recovery song, *"Fix You"* came on Pandora. Her heart burst. She felt him in the room.

I am nourished by our community's love and support, and my senses are heightened. The farm fresh eggs from Aria's friend taste incredibly rich. The rice and beans we devoured last night for dinner were exquisitely delicious. The flowers that fill our home have magnificent vibrance. The birds sing the most incredible songs each morning. I am awake. I am awake. *I am awake.*

DAY 8. The church service ends and I receive amazing news from Steve's stepdad whom he calls Uncle Mario. He asked Dr. Staudenmayer the question I couldn't: "Is Steve going to live?" She answered, "Yes." I am overwhelmed with gratitude! *God, Thank you!* We know there are risks of the unknown but he has come this far and we are holding onto hope. Doctors are ready to speak about my husband's injuries and future. I know Steve's life force is larger than his injuries.

I think back to last week while vacationing in Maui. Steve asked, "What are you searching for when you travel, that you can't find at home?" Unfortunately, I replied with a blank stare. I've changed since then. I know and feel God and pray I get the chance to show my spirit to Steve when he wakes up. My heart aches thinking about how connected to God my sweet husband was, and how I didn't have the time or interest to share that with him before now. Why did it take something so awful for me to meet him here? I'm training myself to surrender to the path I am on now — living life day-by-day, trusting this is the plan.

Today, I walk from the car toward the hospital seeing the world around me anew. There are trees, flowers and fountains that did not exist in my limited vision until now. Knowing Steve survived allows my vision to broaden. Entering the building, I am struck by the enormous, multi-story windows lining the long walkway to the ICU. Light floods the hospital through this gigantic wall of glass. They were invisible to me before today. I realize my physical senses dimmed as the world around me collapsed into nothingness. There was a tunnel with Steve's face at the end of it and I saw nothing more.

As I enter the ICU, Victoria, a friend who comforts hospice patients, tells me Steve reached out to her before his accident. I wonder why? Did he sense this accident looming? She recently bought a Claddaugh ring — the traditional Irish ring representing love, loyalty and friendship. Victoria read my post about Steve showing this symbol to Meghan and realized why she bought the ring. Holding my hands in hers, this thoughtful soul gives me her ring. It fits perfectly next to my wedding ring.

My sisters each gave birth two months ago. They are tending to their babies, as am I. While waiting in a conference room for the doctors, I notice the resident is named "Miquell Miller." I comment that her name is close to my sister's name, Michelle

Miller. The social worker turns to me and says, "That's my name — Michelle Miller." The Universe is telling me my sisters and I are together in spirit.

Today, I'm told Steve survived his initial injuries but they do not know for certain if he will awaken from his coma, or what his functional deficits will be if he does wake up. Once Steve is out of the acute ICU, it's likely to be a long wait with nothing visibly happening. Coming back from unconsciousness could take weeks or months; it's a slow awakening. Doctors predict that somewhere between six to twelve months, he will have functional limitations like not being able to find his way to the bathroom, or brush his teeth. There will be gaps in understanding and recognizing people; Steve will likely be confused for a long time. But the doctors' bleak predictions aren't sticking to me. I drift away from it all for a fleeting moment. *Is this a dream?*

A group of guys called the "Thursday night riders" are here. Steve mountain-biked in the dark with them every week before heading to a bar. The first time my night rider wasn't home by midnight, I thought a coyote got him. When I see them in the hospital I joke that I'm glad the Thursday night riders are not a cover for Steve's girlfriend. Steve told me cycling was his mistress. Look how that turned out!

My friend Ruthie organized a "meal train" to feed our family daily. I have given meals before but thought of them as fulfilling an errand, rather than a source of emotional comfort. On the receiving end, I feel loved, not just nourished, receiving food on our front porch. My friend Lily reminds me that I launched a committee at Payton's former school, providing meal deliveries to families with a sick or injured parent. I started this committee in response to a dad who got hit by a car while riding his bicycle. I completely forgot; how chillingly synchronistic.

I arrive home to a delicious dinner from a neighbor and am hungry for the first time! The good news that Steve is going to live allows me to notice my surroundings, accept food and envision a happy future. I feel God's blessings all around me, especially through loved ones who are embracing our family.

I am heading to Payton's school for a "gospel singing revival" hosted by a magical music director named Grace Renaud. She conceived of this gathering to energetically support Steve in making a decision to either return to his body or cross to the other side. Instead, we are celebrating the news that Steve survived.

Loving parents turn the school into an ethereal sanctuary filled with candles and flowers. Surrounded by earth angels, I feel held and whole. Looking toward the floor, I grasp my love's wedding ring in my hand. I long to lie on the ground and feel the earth. I look over and see a mom lying down to photograph at an angle. That's my invitation! I run to her and lie down too, holding her hand. When I rise, these magical earth angels hug me, creating a loving cocoon around my heart and soul. *I love you all.*

Then I'm at home, lying in bed crying. Steve's cell phone receives twelve calls from "unknown" starting at one in the morning. He's calling me and I am here for him.

CHAPTER 4

On the Internet
We Are the Perfect Family

PEOPLE used to say, "With his resume, Payton will have no problem getting into college" — when he was ten! Or they'd say, "With everything your family does, it's like you're a tiger mom, except you're not." If you Google our names, our lives look exciting. We've each done a thing or two that's somewhat extraordinary, but those experiences didn't fill us. Despite our good fortune, something was missing. Payton was born searching while Steve was leading the search. Aria's search was stymied by typical, age-based challenges. And, I was sprinting to catch up, asking, *"Where's everybody going? Get back here and clean the kitchen!"*

Payton was the first to demonstrate a desire for greater meaning. As a kid chef who started his own baking business, *Chez Pay,* at age nine, he's been in the public eye the most, and the least interested in it. He never volunteers that he was on the Food Network or gave a TEDx Talk. Payton sought those experiences to share messages with kids like "stay true to yourself" and "help others"— not for the limelight. You can imagine how much he pleased his parents.

Before the accident, Aria's heart hid behind the convoluted onion layers of a tween. Steve and I wanted our daughter to rely more on meaningful connections to fill her heart. We never suspected that trauma would be the pathway to fulfill that desire.

A few weeks before the accident, Steve announced our upcoming summer vacation to France and Switzerland. Our friends Amy and Jeremy, whom Steve met cycling to work before we had kids, are dear friends of ours. They now live in Basel, and offered to lend us their house, car and bikes to experience Europe like locals. It sounded thrilling and adventurous, yet I felt a dark undertone: *Why does this feel too good to be true?* Steve bought the plane tickets the night before the accident.

Before this tragedy, we spent our time fine-tuning our house, editing our careers, polishing our children. We were scratching our heads trying to figure out how to live more meaningfully in this tiring, demanding, physical world. After nearly "losing his mind" from his first head injury in 2013, Steve shifted to a heart-centered view of life. He worried less about life's physical stresses and focused more on his soul's purpose. Steve knew he was here to help people, but how?

Meanwhile I always operated at one of two speeds — 0 or 100. Steve suggested I land somewhere in-between, a place I had never been. I was either working my fingers to the bone, manning daily operations of our family and my business, and squeezing in work-outs or passing out. I could not fathom where Steve found the time to read books on mind and spirit and think about creating a non-profit.

Each time I tried to make an imprint on the world, I struck out. Payton and I prepared to grow kale in our backyard for homeless shelters but after building our urban farm, we moved. I was politely fired from my volunteer job delivering food pantry items to a family in need because I kept forgetting to show up. I could not merge giving back with the busy life I engineered for myself. My days overflowed with chores. It never occurred to me that I could find an opening to work on myself in order to *find* myself. I didn't even know I was missing! I knew my life wasn't right but didn't know how to fix it.

I share in my blog: "It's hard for me to write this but I can't deny I feel it. The accident had to happen. As much as I want to stop Steve in the hallway the last time I saw him whole, part of me knows he had to take that fall. We are uncovering why as we claw our way out of this. We are suffering so we can give back to the world — something bigger than ourselves, bigger than our family, bigger than our community. And the price of that opportunity is suffering. I don't know what we are supposed to do, but I am awake, I am searching, and I will find it. God Bless and Godspeed, Jenna"

DAY 9. Steve looks like himself today. His color is bright; the bruises are healing; his body is transforming. Who has great hair in a coma? My hot husband! The physicians removed a chest tube so he's initiating his own breaths, but needs the ventilator since he's in a coma. The brain swelling is subsiding. Today's downside is ventilator-associated pneumonia, but it's a straightforward fix with antibiotics.

I'm hanging out with a crew of bike racers, shedding tears over the accident and making Steve jokes. My friend Jenny bounces into the waiting area shouting vitality in her brightly colored outfit. She carries a basket of treats to lighten the mood: sushi, essential oils, art supplies, prayer books and a heart-shaped rock that reads "love." We all poke Steve, commanding him to move. I know Steve is happy we are being playful and joyful.

Driving home from Stanford I think about the love I feel. Over a thousand people are reading my CaringBridge blog; our home is overflowing with love and support as people come and go constantly. There's a meal train running and groceries are dropped off. Dishes are washed; the floor is swept. Every day when we pull into the driveway there is something waiting for us on the front porch: dinner, a gift, a loving note. And nearly every day whatever is sitting there is more than what it seems. I nickname the entry to our home "the magic front porch." I don't question any of this help. I am so physically, mentally and emotionally drained that all I can do is get myself to the hospital each day and get myself into bed at night where I lie awake crying. Maybe I sleep three hours a night. I turn to my blog for comfort and to flush out my heart, desperate to share this life of drenching pain and wonder.

People say I'm strong, but my strength is not my own. It's a reflection of what I learned from loved ones over time. My friend Ruthie prepared me for this tragedy when her husband Bill suddenly passed away from cancer. *How does Ruthie do it?* I pondered. Sara prepared me for this moment when her baby Eliot was diagnosed with cancer. *How does Sara cope with her baby being ill?* Dave faced his eleventh hour with optimism and focus, awaiting a double lung transplant. *How is Dave optimistic on the edge of death?* Thank you, dear ones.

Day 10. Today is another invigorating church service. I've never looked forward to going to church more than I do now. I have a personal relationship with God and attending services not only brings more magic but it comforts me. The constant synchronicities make me feel like God is speaking directly to me at church on behalf of Steve. A friend remarks, "Steve has gotten us to church two weeks in a row!" Another blessing!

Steve's brain drain output is still high. He's been hiccupping a lot and his body temperature still fluctuates, so he's covered in ice packs. His face looks more like himself, but there's no tracking or responses on command.

Open your eyes, Steve… open your eyes…

My dad John, who reminds me of Tom Brokaw with a full head of white hair and watery blue eyes, arrives from Maryland, ready to anchor this crisis. Despite his son-in-law's dire state, Dad chooses an optimistic outlook, uncharacteristic for an Army engineer of forty years. He points at Steve, turns to me and says, "He's going to wake up sooner than you think, smile and give us all a big thumbs up."

Day 12. I wake up blissed-out, draw the window curtains open and announce out loud, "The day is upon us!" Then I have a phone meeting about the accident and feel nausea coming on; I am entering the black hole that is State Disability Insurance. I pass out on hold until Dad wakes me with a start: "Jennifer! Pick up the phone!" Thank God the person who answered gives me a second to come to.

Our friend Megan, a nurse and the wife of Steve's best friend, Ray, texts me from the hospital that Steve's tracheotomy and peg tube operations are were canceled, after the doctors saw he has pneumonia and needs his lungs suctioned. I'm frustrated by this mistake, and concerned about the collaboration between the fifty or more doctors who round daily. I book a meeting for reassurance.

But when I get there, Steve looks good. His swelling is decreasing; his left eye opens more; his arms are tan, smooth, and trauma-free. He's even kicking his legs! He'd better not be cycling in his dreams…

When the day is over I'm gassed, despite starting on a magnificent high — the yo-yo swing of life under the dark umbrella of trauma. Good moments and bad ones are piled together in one spectacular, messy heap. The other night, my friends and I were sharing signs and blessings we've each witnessed. Thinking back to that conversation, I feel called to write a letter to the cyclists on the Chicken Ride:

Dear Cyclists,

Those of you who were there on April 21st carry heavy hearts. Haunted by the images in your mind, you ask questions no one can answer. Why was I saved? How could we have prevented this? Why did this happen? Deep sadness and fear linger, being so close to death, so close to Steve. I understand.

I want you to find the love buried beneath your pain to open your hearts. I'm speaking your language, riders. This is what you do. Cycling is about suffering. Then, you reach a certain state where you push through the pain and break free of it. When you push through the pain of this tragedy, you will be overwhelmed with blessings. I know because I have received more blessings than I can count.

Please, cyclists, find the joy that only pain can bring. Keep the air in your tires, and your love rolling.

God Bless & Godspeed,

Jenna

CHAPTER 5

Dance Class

STEVE AND I met in a college dance class. I was there to meet a graduation requirement; he was there hoping to meet girls. Our first date didn't go well — he thought I was a party girl, while I dismissed him as a typical frat boy. But when we reconnected after spring break, everything changed.

My college friend Kelly coached me on our courtship, even dressing me. Once we were a couple Steve dressed me, teaching me the art of layering clothing. Steve called me Bella Bambina in Italian, which was shortened to Bina. I called Steve Bino, short for bambino. I was a tennis player and we played often, but I was curious about cycling — a passion of Steve's that he secretly hoped I'd try. When we got on the same page, I began riding his old Greg LeMond bicycle– a seemingly innocent symbol of the team we were becoming. Looking back, it feels both prophetic and tragic.

On the night of December 4, 1995, our senior year, I was headed to Steve's dorm room around 10pm. Gearing up for the short bike ride, I placed a black knit hat over my head so that I'd look like a boy, since I was riding alone in the dark. I wanted to be safe, but I left my bicycle helmet at home. When I didn't show up, my concerned boyfriend rode to my apartment. There, he found a police officer carrying my mangled bicycle. I'd been hit by a bus crossing an intersection and suffered a broken collar bone, a cut in my skull, and moderate head trauma. I was delusional at the scene, and my siblings might jokingly say for a while thereafter.

My mom tells me Steve did not leave my side in the hospital, where I stayed for over two weeks. It was then she knew how much my boyfriend loved me. I remember lying on my parent's sofa saying, "Who gets hit by a bus and survives? All I have to do is get better! Life is wonderful!" This is where I first learned of the gift of trauma. It clears away everyday annoyances and distractions, leaving life simple and effortless. All that truly matters is being alive.

For half a year, I moved, talked, and thought slowly. My collar bone glued itself together in a big, ugly knot. Nobody paid attention to my brain so I was left to glue that back together too. I forgot basic words like *salt, glass, table*. My balance was off as I wobbled up and down the stairs, getting by without a brain recovery road map.

I slept a lot and missed the remaining semester. I resumed Spring classes and continued as a Sociology undergrad taking graduate classes to pursue an honors degree. While sitting around a table in one of my tiny graduate classes, the professor, a petite man with white, curly hair, called on me. I drew a blank and he got upset. I burst into tears saying, "I'm sorry professor, but I don't have any thoughts in my head." Not having thoughts in my head lingered for years. Even so, I completed my senior thesis, earning the distinction of high honors in my college, five months after being hit by a bus.

I remember all this today, recalling my healing and channeling it to Steve. I've long admired Steve's dedication to being a better husband, father, friend. (For some reason, he doesn't want to be a better handyman.) In his journey of self-improvement he's faced many setbacks, overcoming one obstacle only to be slammed with another. Never giving up, Steve put his head down and climbed out of whatever pit he was in next.

Yesterday's operating room misfire made me realize I've been leaning on Stanford's reputation and not doing my due diligence. I request a lay of the land. Dr. Miller replies: "There are four primary teams right now: Surgical ICU (SICU) team is 'the boss'. Other teams provide recommendations to SICU, who decides what to do. Neurosurgery manages Steve's EVD, the brain bleed. Neurocritical care prescribes the medicine to manage the brain injury. Acute care surgery service handles the tracheotomy and peg tube." There are other teams like plastic surgery, vascular, orthopedic, etc. but those listed above are primary because the brain injury is the top concern. Each team has one attending (big boss), one or two fellows who rotate every four weeks, one chief resident who's there for six weeks, two or three junior residents who rotate every four weeks, and medical students who are observing. This is why there are hundreds of doctors who see Steve weekly.

Today Steve's swelling has noticeably decreased. He's losing weight, being tube fed. I am shocked to see corn syrup is the number one ingredient in Steve's feed tube. How can this be? When I ask the woman administering it, she reassures me that he's getting the nutrients his brain needs. I research healthy tube feeds but feel too scared to advocate for this, given Steve's vulnerable condition. What if I bring in a feed tube that makes him sick?

They are giving Steve a neurostimulant, Amantadine, to wake him up. They think the fevers are caused by neurostorming, when the components of the nervous system have difficulty self-regulating. Symptoms include increased heart rate and blood pressure, tremors, increased intracranial pressure and fevers. By successfully treating the fever with the *Arctic Sun,* the storming has improved. The terrifying days of him being tachycardic, hypertensive or agitated have faded. He still has pneumonia.

Right now they are removing the other chest tube. The doctor performing this procedure says, "Wife! We've got a view of Steve's nipple!" I take a peek and laugh; his chest looks healthy and normal. Still no chest hair, which surprises me.

Steve has sacs at the bottom of his lungs, normal when you're not moving. Coughing pops them open. I realize it's Day 12 and no one has told Steve what's going on. I've read that comatose patients hear everything. I brief him on the accident, encourage him to meditate and think positive thoughts. I say, "There is no hurry to wake up, my darling. Just focus on healing. Your body will wake you up when it's time."

Tomorrow is Steve's birthday. I was hoping he'd give himself a draining brain but he isn't. He needs a VP shunt: a rubber tube that goes in his head, through the brain, down to his abdomen, redistributing excess fluid there. It's the most common brain surgery; I guess that's comforting. My sadness about the shunt lifts when I read sentimental letters written to him by loved ones, and Steve gently squeezes my hand for the first time.

DAY 16. Nearly two thousand people are reading the blog now! I can't imagine we know that many people. I feel so loved! I post on the blog: "It's May 6, 2017. HAPPY BIRTHDAY, my darling husband! Forty-five and alive! For this birthday, my love, you are given the love of family and friends, the will to fight, the best care in the world, and the ultimate gift — life. I know you will come back to us with a soaring spirit and heart of gold. I love you! —God Bless & Godspeed, Jenna"

I've never been happier to celebrate a birthday. While reading birthday wishes to my beloved, I receive my first *tight* hand squeeze. Now, the birthday boy is lifting his arm up six inches while wrinkling his nose and eyes! "Do you have an itch, Steve? Let me scratch it." Best birthday ever!

The next day, God is talking directly to me at church again. The service is about broken bread symbolizing how we are broken through pain, but in that hardship, God shows us life. The brain surgery to install a VP shunt is scheduled for Thursday. I'm worried and pray for it all to be okay.

Before this tragedy, I was distracted by the everyday tasks of life that mask its essence. Chores, playdates and pick-ups; games and performances; what's for dinner, what's for lunch? The routines drained me and seemed more important than making space for my spirit. The list was too long and the day too tiring; *I'll start meditating next week. I'll pray next month.* While I was putting off my spirit, Steve was growing his. He meditated daily at 5:30am and questioned the meaning of how we spent our time. He prayed for his friends' kids. Steve was awake and still is, even though his physical body is sleeping. And while he sleeps, I finally understand what being awake is…

I want to help other people feel how I do without the trauma. I am present to whatever is happening in each moment. I fill myself up with the joy of *right now*, instead of feeling anxious about the uncertain future. I celebrate the tiniest victories. I see and feel magic all around me. And, I have an impenetrable sense of knowing that my calling is to share this state of being with as many people as possible. It's one of the reasons I feel called to blog everyday. Connecting to my blog readers gives me hope for something beautiful to come out of something so horrible.

Can I help those who are coasting like I was? Can I bring them to this awakened place without tragedy? It's the happiest place to be because when you are buried in heartache, a new life becomes possible. But it's only possible through our connections to one other, leading us to the Source of all beings that binds us. This is something that I couldn't feel before the accident but is the only reality I know now.

But once we're all here, how do we stay? Will I stay?

Day 18. Aria wakes up crying: "I dreamt about Daddy."

I reply, "It's good to cry. You are lucky. You see Daddy in your dreams and spend time with him there!" I wish I dreamt about Steve more, but first I'll have to sleep. In one dream, he was in our bedroom with bike grease all over his hands. I asked how he could get bike grease on him when the bikes were gone. Then I shouted, 'Steve! You're awake! When did you wake up?' The dream ended before he answered.

A Mikes Bikes truck is here to empty the garage. No more bicycles ever. "What was, will never be again." We'll sell the bikes to pay for alternative medicines and treatments.

I know I can't control life but since I have this opportunity to be with Steve for another lifetime, I want it to last. There's so much to share when he wakes up but the most important thing I have to do is thank him for coming back. Steve formed an alliance with God and I promise to pay homage to it. In picturing this deal with God, I reflect on one mysterious miracle in particular. There was evidence of a spinal cord injury on the first scan but nowhere to be found on subsequent imaging. Before climbing into his body, I picture Steve up in heaven, renegotiating his soul's contract. "Alright, God, I'll return to earth in this mangled body with an even bigger calling. But, let's not put me in a wheelchair. Hook up my legs please!"

Steve continues moving his left arm, although not on command. He seems more tired today, or maybe it's me. I go outside the hospital to lie down in the sun. I jokingly text my friend Robin, who's on her way over, "Look for me in the 'cabana." I tell myself I'm staying at the "Stanford Resort and Spa." The helicopter landing on the roof is giving tours of the coastline. The cabana is poolside, not next to the bus line. The water fountain is in the swimming pool. The grasses are nestled along the beach. I nap here thanks to my precious friend, Kara, who introduced me to this sleeping refuge. Sleep is a gift.

The other day, I wiped Steve's face and chest with a washcloth, while rubbing wet, ice-cold swabs on his dry lips. "It was a soothing facial, wasn't it, Steve?" Sometimes when the pain digs deep without warning, I need to escape. Looking at an old photograph, witnessing my children's anguish, and imagining the accident are chronic triggers. Sometimes I want to forget today and savor life eighteen days ago in Maui. "I'll have a piña colada, please."

CHAPTER 6

We've Never Met, Though We Are Family

DAY 21. The blog has taken on a life of its own. Dozens of people comment each day and thousands are following. I am told people talk about the blog with each other out on the street! So many loving souls care about Steve and our family but it's more than that. They feel good reading my stories and helping our family. Some are even telling me they are finding God through my blog. This means there is purpose in our pain. This brings me so much joy!

Today's hospital visit has a steady rhythm. As I wonder about the tracheotomy and peg tube surgeries, in waltzes the surgeon, Dr. Spane, who will perform both. He wheels in a common plastic bin of surgical supplies and tells me he'll do the 60-minute surgery in the room. I grill him on whether this is a common protocol, and after feeling satisfied, release my anxiety. Steve's mom Lola and I anoint Steve with holy water, and retreat to our campsite — "surgery waiting." Just as I sit down, my gorgeous friend Lily appears with her luminous blue eyes and bright blonde hair, embracing me with a warm hug.

While Lily and I chat, a pretty woman from guest services named Karyn approaches. She gave me a duffle bag with a blanket and some parking passes on Day 2. I lost the bag. We chat about yesterday's blog post about the "Stanford Resort and Spa." A short while later, Karyn reappears with a replacement duffle bag, more parking passes, and a gift certificate for a hospital chair massage. Then she says, "Follow me."

We enter a fully stocked, private lounge with TVs, computers and comfy sofas. Lily says, "Jenna! This is the 'Stanford Resort and Spa' you asked for in yesterday's blog post." I'm speechless. Talk about manifesting! How did Karyn find me again? My old San Francisco friend Kira, whom I hadn't spoken to in years, had her friend Rachel reach out to "Spa Karyn," asking her to take care of me. Payton quietly does homework here now, avoiding talking to people. The respite is priceless as our family climbs out of the depths of despair with no reserves. The exhaustion, stress, and anxiety are catching up to us. I need more sleep, quiet time and a get-away. Voila! We are blessed.

I've been thinking about connections to people I barely know, or in many cases, have never met. I read a blog comment from a sweet soul named Cindy who says to Steve, "We have never met, though we are family..." Is she a cousin of his from the Philippines? I continue reading. "I heard about you through a letter your devoted and loving wife sent out in a school newsletter. Reading her unfiltered, unrelentingly optimistic, adoring words about you have made me feel as if I know you and her too."

We draw lines, create borders and boundaries, place ourselves in groups and categories. We forget that we are more similar to one another than we are different. We have the same overall hopes and dreams for our lives but get trapped in our differences and miss the connections. This painful journey has given me so much hope for my spirit and the spirit of those around me. I see how much power each of us holds to lift each other up and care for one another in ways that defy logic and reason. I want to give these gifts away to as many people as possible.

DAY 22. I've discovered a buried treasure, Steve's bike-racing blog from eight years ago. I've never read it before. At the time he wrote it, I was consumed with parenting our young children and, honestly, I resented cycling. It took my husband away from fully supporting me as a wife and new mother. Raising a family was not a co-creation. It was me poking at my elite athlete husband, shouting, *"Pull your weight at home, not just at the velodrome!"* I realize I lost my connection with God after becoming a mom, which seems counterintuitive.

I found the job of motherhood overwhelming, especially when my husband was too tired from training to pitch in, or off traveling for racing. Instead of turning to God for support, I turned to my to-do list. And I didn't tune into the wisdom and soulful longings my husband shared with others through his blog and Facebook posts, not to mention in person. Steve's insights were tied to cycling, which I ignored.

I've been asked by a few people, including my father, how I'm not pissed at Steve? After all, if he wasn't cycling on the dangerous open road, this tragedy would not have happened. I know exactly why I'm not resentful. From the moment I received that call from the hospital, God was with me. He literally flushed my mind, body and spirit with love, aligning my thoughts, words and actions to that frequency. As I beam love out to the world through my blog and connecting in person, it has the same impact on those people who receive it that the accident is having on me. We are swimming together in a love bath that increases in strength as more people jump in. I feel the immense power of this positive ripple effect, creating a sense of urgency, longing and purpose in writing the blog.

When I miss Steve, sometimes I Google him. Each time I do so, I find an article about him and his achievements I never knew existed. I was oblivious to my husband's athletic prowess and awakened spirit, running our household and planning for the future. I long to reconnect with who he was before the accident, but as the awakened person I am today. I have no idea if that's possible and it pains me. It feels like a tragic loss — a Romeo and Juliet kind of sadness. I table that heartache and bring myself to the present. The good news is that I can hear my husband now, ironically, when he cannot speak. While he can't communicate to me from the hospital bed, he is doing so through this eight-year-old post.

Posted by Steve...

VELOBISCUIT BLOG, OCTOBER 3, 2009:

Payton is wise beyond his years. I should be happy with my performance at Elite Track Nationals. I did a personal best in the 200-meter time trial and won the first omnium event. I should be happy we got bronze in the team pursuit, despite a disastrous team effort. I should be happy that I held my own against the young pros. But my mind is critical of all that went wrong. I am not happy and I am not present. My five-year-old son, Payton, brought the negativity to a screeching halt. His words liberated my mind and brought me back to the here and now. He gave me a gift. That's why it's called the present.

When I got home, I was happy to see my family. Joking around, I showed my kids my torn fingernails from crashing. Aria said, "Ewww, it's yucky," which it is. But when I asked Payton, he said, "I don't think it's gross."

Surprised, I asked, "What do you mean?"

Payton said, "When I look at your torn fingers, I don't see what you see. I see rainbows and clouds."

Impressed, I asked, "Why do you think that, son?"

He said, "Because I want you to feel happy!" His response choked me up and made me stop and think. I can't help but be proud of him and thankful for reminding me what I know to be true. Things happen, but nothing ultimately means anything. We make up our own meanings. Our reality is a choice we make. As I like to say, between stimulus and response is a choice. It's our ultimate freedom. Thank you, son, for your wisdom.

Praying for the brain surgery to be canceled, I draw on my husband for inspiration, visualizing rainbows and clouds all morning. Like every day, this day is full of winks from God, the greatest of which is the neuro doc saying the VP Shunt Surgery is out! Thank you, God! Rainbows and clouds!

DAY 23. Steve's pupils get examined with a piercing light every four hours. He endearingly frowns his eyebrows as doctors check for a response and pupil dilation. I'm praying the frown means he's inside there. His right eye does not open because the nerve that controls the movement of the eye and pupil was sheared. The physicians don't know if it's completely torn and therefore unrecoverable, or just stunned. If it's the latter, it may repair itself. Otherwise, he will need ophthalmology surgery. There is a slight improvement in eye movement to date. We measure Steve's healing in micro-changes.

The brain drain was removed this morning, another big step. He's also wearing a trach collar. Lying motionless, day-after-day, his thin body and deteriorating muscle mass are difficult to witness. Steve's sporty new vest is a back brace, which looks like a white, plastic shield on the front and back with thick velcro straps piecing it together. It's been three weeks since Steve's body has sat up. The brace was custom-made to enable therapists to move Steve by lifting his legs over the side of the bed while propping him up to sit. Although he opens his left eye while sitting, he's still "not there." A tear trickles down his right cheek. *Are you crying because you know what's going on and you're so sad? Are you crying because you're in pain?* It's hard to see him like this. My heart yearns to take his pain away.

This is the worst time of my life and the best. I feel Steve's pain and the suffering of those around me, especially my heartbroken children, but I am flooded with so much love and Light, it's impossible not to feel comforted by the Universal Energy that binds us.

Every day someone reminds me that I have a "long road" ahead of me. At first, I agreed and tried to picture the road, but it had no destination. Imagining a long, blank road to nowhere makes me feel lost and sad. I need a substitute image for what the next weeks, months, and years of my life could be.

So I'm not on a road. I'm planting seeds in a new garden. Some will grow into vibrant plants and flowers; others will die. Some will be harvested; others will be overcome by aphids. I will sow a garden that's colorful and vibrant. I will water it, the sun will shine, the wind will blow, and the garden will grow. When a new season comes, we will plant again and see what blossoms.

I post to the blog: "The love and support we receive feed my spirit. Our amazing community is doing it all — Costco runs, making dinner, sending flowers. Kind souls are caring for Aria and Payton, hosting prayer circles, bringing me food when I'm starving at the hospital. Thoughtful souls know what I need before I do. Robin told me she'd pick up my Mom from the airport before my Mom booked a flight. Kristine, John, and many others knew we'd need housing near Stanford before I did. It's impossible to thank everyone personally. I read every blog comment, every email, every card. Every gift we receive 'feeds our garden.' Our devoted community is helping me *grow my garden* and I can't wait to share the bounty with you. *— God Bless and Godspeed, Jenna"*

Waiting for me to come home, Steve's cousin Grace describes "a dozen men coming toward the house from all directions." They are Steve's brothers from the ManKind Project, which Steve participated in a couple of months ago. He spent the weekend alone in a forest with a group of men to clear trauma from his past to live a happier, freer life. I picture a self-help boot camp. Only one guy actually knows Steve. The rest come in support of a fellow ManKind "brother" to spruce up our overgrown yard. They are so kind and generous to help a family they don't know.

DAY 24. Today is Mother's Day. Serendipitously, the nurse who admitted Steve is caring for him tonight — his last day in the ICU as he "steps down" to an intermediate ICU in the trauma unit. Although unconscious, our miracle patient is animated. He puckers his lips, wrinkles his eyebrows, moves his mouth. He's actually smiling with his lips closed. When I move his leg, he grimaces. I am hopeful this is a pain response indicating he is conscious and coming back to me.

CHAPTER 7

Olympic Dreams

IN THE summer of 2006 Steve discovered track cycling, and he'd drive over an hour to race at Hellyer Velodrome in San Jose. He raced with his buddy Brian who came by the hospital, and posted in the blog today about their competition at track nationals. Brian wrote: "Steve was hungry to win. The Madison was the last event and we rode it as a team. We both dug deep and managed to win." The Stars and Stripes jersey from that race is hanging in the ICU room. I wistfully remember how Steve was riding a high from that week and said, 'I wish I could bottle up this feeling and drink it when things are not going right.'"

That year, Steve won loads of medals at *Elite Track Nationals*. During the summer of 2007, Payton was a toddler and Aria was a baby. Steve and his best friend Ray ran a remote online business and had loads of time and just enough money. We planned to live overseas for a year, and found a family to temporarily rent our home. It was also the year my 35-year-old husband secretly dreamt of racing for the Philippine National Team with the long-shot goal of competing in the '08 Olympics. Unbeknownst to me, one night from up in his attic office, he reached out to the Philippine

National Team. The next morning, Steve cautiously approached me and asked, "Jenna, how would you feel if we didn't move to Italy?"

I shrugged my shoulders, "What's up?"

He grinned. "I've received an invitation to join the Philippine National cycling team to try and qualify for the Beijing Olympics."

Pumped, I responded, "Are you kidding me? Congratulations! Go for it!" Just like that, Steve was chasing the dream of a lifetime. He spent the next year racing around the world. I nicknamed him *Velo Biscuit.* "Velo" means cycling in French and "biscuit" came from Sea Biscuit, Steve's favorite racehorse and underdog story. We laughed at Velo Biscuit riding his rollers solo in the attic, trying to compete in the World Cup. Velo Biscuit went from the attic to the Philippines, Sydney, Korat, Thailand, Los Angeles, Denmark and Manchester.

His Russian coaches, Vlad and Dmitry, trained him like a twenty-five-year-old, even though he was an "old man" at his age. This would later haunt him. This hilarious description of training with his coaches gives me a reprieve tonight as I lie in bed crying, remembering the amazing athlete I married.

Posted by Steve...

VELOBISCUIT BLOG, JANUARY 30, 2008

I hurt my back and could barely get on the bike. My coach had a Russian ointment and asked me, "Are you man or are you woman? If you man, you can take this ointment." Of course, I told him, "I am man." Ten minutes later, my back felt like it was on fire. A minute more, someone was pouring hot tar on it. Soon enough, I screamed, "I am woman! I am woman!"

My coaches frantically started yelling in Russian. One ran to the car, while the other searched his desk. Soon, they found what they were looking for: canola oil. It diffused the chemical explosion in my back. They said even though my back looked like a third-degree burn, it wasn't... just blood rushing to the skin.

Funny stuff like that keeps the training entertaining. But it's literally back-breaking work. It has to be since I'm competing against the best, while playing catchup with my fitness and experience.

Steve traveled to the Philippines to train with his team and started a fundraising campaign to raise money for impoverished Filipino children. An American Philippine news station interviewed Velo Biscuit, pegging him as the Phil-Am cyclist who would bring the Philippines to the Olympics. Steve traveled to Thailand, competing in the Southeast Asian Games where they won gold.

Steve's racing buddy Brian recalls, "Racing at that level was hard. These are the best-of-the-best. They are full-time athletes and younger. But Steve wouldn't quit. He gave it his all."

Day 26. After three weeks and three days in the ICU, Steve is in the Step Down Unit. He is far from being out of the woods but making progress. The device draining cerebral fluid was removed; he's breathing on his own through the trach; and, he has a feed tube in his stomach. There's still no response to commands. Physically moving in an agitated state, my husband chews on the C-collar like a baby. His body is skin and muscle; his mind is vegetative. Despite physically moving and opening his left eye, Steve is still not behind his eye. We pray to God for a miracle.

Nina, Steve's former work colleague from the dot com days and longtime friend, reminds me via the blog, "God is powerful and can lift your soul, and provide strength when your body has little to give. God did so with me in my paralysis at Stanford Hospital too! Honor each moment, trust in the journey, and celebrate each milestone, because the milestones are His wonder working through Steve." I turn to the blog, which miraculously is now read by over two thousand people, whenever I need a boost of faith and to share both the magic and heartache birthed from my circumstances. I am going through the hardest time in my life without my best friend, my husband. Somehow the intimate connection I feel with the blog readers, including strangers I've never met but post frequently, eases that empty void.

I step into Steve's new room and stop breathing. Terrified, I see an old white man instead of my husband! The posters, tchotchkes, cards, flags, ribbons, letters, and photos have vanished. As images of Steve dead flash before me, I run to the nurse's station panicking, "Where is Steve Pelaez?" The charge nurse explains he was transferred to a private room and takes me there. I am stunned to see that the nurses redecorated the new room with the mountain of memorabilia that took Steve's friend Funke, his wife Frances and me an hour to install.

I'm crying because I'm scared; crying because I'm happy; crying because the nurses are so kind. I'm crying about everything. And then I start crying about insurance. I say, "Insurance told me if he's not in a double room, I will have to pay the difference."

The loving nurse assures me that it's okay. "Steve needs this room," she says.

While Steve's progression to this unit is wonderful, it's also frightening. Instead of a dedicated 24/7 nurse, one stops by every so often. Who's going to unlock Steve's jaws from the C-collar when I'm not around? Steve's monster cough hurls loogies clear across the room. What if he chokes on one? I'm assured he cannot since he has a trach, but I still worry.

Steve twists up in bed, as his head hangs off to the side. He looks uncomfortable but I can't move him, given his broken back, neck, ribs, and shoulder. I wait for two nurses to safely move him to a comfortable position. Without communicating, we have no way of knowing if he is in pain.

DAY 27. I received an unlikely email from the CEO of Salesforce, a multi-billion-dollar San Francisco-based tech company. Steve was supposed to begin a new job with them, starting after the date of the accident. Clearly, that wasn't happening — but without being employed, he'd be uninsured. I reached out to his old company and the new one, asking for help. Salesforce offered to hire Steve in a coma to ensure he had benefits! His former company, FinancialForce, insisted on reinstating his employment to avoid switching coverage. I wrote the CEOs of both companies, Tod Nielsen of FinancialForce and Marc Benioff of Salesforce, thanking them for their immense generosity.

Marc responded by cc'ing a slew of contacts to help, including a world-renowned neurosurgeon, Dr. Geoff Manley, who calls me on a Saturday night from his cell phone. He's trained many of the doctors treating Steve. He offers to speak with Steve's physicians and call me. I am beaming with anticipation. I cannot wait to hear from Dr. Manley. Talk about blessings!

DAY 28. Steve's best friend Ray is here at Stanford, along with Payton and Steve's mom, Lola. We are talking to Steve, trying to make him laugh. My phone rings; it's Dr. Manley. Excited, I step away to take the call privately. He makes small talk, explaining what happens when a head gets violently struck.

"I'm sure there are people who will look at Steve's MRI and say, 'Oh my gosh. There are so many axonal injuries here. This guy is never going to wake up.' I talked to Dr. Staudemayer and all the folks who are taking care of him who have looked at the scans, and I have to be honest with you. We all agree it looks pretty ominous. That said, I've seen people who have had nasty looking MRI scans wake up. I'm not saying it's impossible, but to be fair and honest with you, he has some ugly looking stitching…"

My body is both numb and shaking. I feel shattered. This started with the miracle referral to Dr. Manley; I thought I'd been given a magic wand.

He continues: "Steve has a lot of axonal injuries — a profound amount. That's the reason he's not waking up. The real issue is how much of this stuff can reconnect? Currently there are no drugs, no treatment that's proven to fix somebody's brain and re-connect it. It doesn't mean it may not reconnect. Basically, what's going to determine how he does is time. There's no magic treatment we can do. There's nothing special that can be done. We're going to have to wait this out and see what happens…"

I'm crying. I say, "Thank you. I've been here twenty-seven days and I haven't gotten an assessment."

Dr. Manley says, "I apologize, Jenna. This comes from total empathy and my passion for curing this for everyone. I wish I were there to hold your hand. I didn't mean to have this talk with you. My assumption is somebody talked to you before. It's not to say there's no hope…"

I listen to some next-step suggestions and hang up the phone. My face feels numb; my eyes sting; my heart has fallen to the floor. Unable to stop sobbing, I step into the room to look at Steve and everyone there. I tell them what Dr. Manley said — even Payton. I have no willpower to hide my devastation from our sweet and innocent son, to protect him from this awful news. Steve's eye is wide open; he's been fixated on Payton the past hour. It's time to go and I barely say goodbye. I want to curl up next to my beloved and weep. I want this to be over. It's so hard. It's too much.

Aria is not with us, but when we arrive home, she tells me she's been crying. It's unusual for her to tell me she's been crying alone. I soothe Aria and collapse into bed. Tears stream down my face as I turn to the blog and write:

"My friends and family, neighbors and strangers — you're all I have and I need you desperately. Please, help me give Steve the impossible. He survived the initial injuries, despite having to be resuscitated multiple times. He survived the Life Flight, despite us being told he might not. He survived the first week of touch-and-go days in the ICU. Please help him come back. I need you at Stanford singing, talking and praying to him. You're all I have, and I promise you, he is worth it. God Bless & Godspeed, Jenna"

Day 29. My cell phone is blowing up after last night's post; texts, phone calls and dozens of blog comments are pouring in. The readers come from every direction — old bosses to childhood friends to strangers — and I love them all the same. I am blown away by how far and wide my call for help travels, from our hometown to the UK to the Himalayas. Ray's best friend from Maryland, Chris, booked a flight! At 9am my friend Kira's friend Rachel, whom I've never met, calls. All I know of her is that she gifted me with the VIP hook-up at Stanford. Rachel says, "I can't explain it, Jenna, but I have to see Steve now. I've never had this feeling before." I tell her to go for it.

Reading my blog, Steve's impact on people astounds me. A man in the UK whom I don't know, Marty, posts, "Hi, Jenna. Steve is constantly in my thoughts. We met when he was trying to qualify for the Olympics in Sydney. I was looking after Magnus Backstedt, and we became this little team of nations, or as Steve said 'Team Planet.' It is one of my fondest memories of my life in cycling. I was devastated to read of Steve's accident, but I'm sending all my love to him."

My cherished friend Mary posts, "Dear Jenna. Butter lamps were lit for your family in a tiny nunnery, nestled in a small valley within the Everest region of the Himalayas. When the butter lamps were lit, there were two hundred nuns and monks, saying your names, praying for you with laser-like focus. Your lights were shining from the rooftop of our world, lighting up the heavens and shedding love and wisdom into our world. I know with all that I am, and all that is Divine and good, that you all are in God's gentle and loving hands. We are all calling to Steve. We are lighting the way back for him. With oceans of love and care — Mary"

I am befuddled by what I see. The woman who called earlier, Rachel, is here. Rachel is strikingly beautiful— tall with long silver hair, radiant skin and hip, black glasses. She has one arm in the air and the other above Steve, speaking in a soothing, gentle voice while Mozart plays. His left eye is wide open, as he unequivocally responds to her commands. He tracks people with his eye too, opening and closing it on command. He lifts his chin from the

C-collar when asked by Rachel. This is the first time he has responded to a request by anyone; it is dramatic and undeniable. She's making this up as she goes along and it's working!

"Rachel, what did you do?" I excitedly ask.

She's in the zone so our mutual friend Kira answers, "She's channeling energy to Steve."

Yesterday was gloom and doom and today is flooded with milestones and generosity. I shift my focus to tending to Steve instead of his scans. I dip a stick with a sponge on the end of it into ice-cold water and rub his dry lips with it. By endearingly opening his mouth wide, he signals he knows what I'm doing. Steve expressing understanding is another huge step forward. Instead of trying to manage my husband's recovery by calling in outside experts, I am connecting to him through direct caring.

CHAPTER 8

Reflecting on Blessings

Day 34. I am reading Steve's racing blog again, slowly, holding myself back. What if it ends before I connect with him again? The way Steve handled the end of his Olympic pursuit speaks volumes about how he refocused his thoughts to reflect upon his blessings in life, instead of the losses. I will myself to do the same.

Posted by Steve...

VELOBISCUIT BLOG, MARCH 13, 2008

Maybe this is the end? That's what my mechanic friend, Mark, said after I finished the scratch race in Denmark running a fever. Mark's comment is a play on a previous quote, "Everything works out in the end. If it's not working out, you're not at the end." I asked, "Why can't I just catch a break?"

Mark replied, "Maybe being here is your break." He's right. This is the end of my professional cyclist lifestyle. This entire experience has been a break from reality. I've been living a dream. Emotionally, it's sad and frustrating that it's over and I didn't reach my goal, however improbable. I desperately want another shot at the goal. But, my rational mind creates a positive spin, and sees the silver lining.

I'm proud to have represented The Philippines against the best in the world. The competition was younger and faster than me and has been training and competing full time at the world class level for years. My expectations were unrealistic. My coach Vlad says I did great for a first timer and it's not possible to leap to the podium in the first year — unless you're a phenom like Taylor Phinney — a proof of genetics. I asked him why he didn't say this in the beginning? Vlad smiled. My coach is an Olympic gold medalist and World champion, who spent ten years of focused, relentless training to succeed at that level.

My friend Robin told me, "Life is lived forward and understood backwards." I can relate. I was so caught up with the training, travel and racing that I may not have enjoyed the moments as they happened. Retrospectively, I have fun memories of the places I've traveled and people I've met. Most of all, I'm proud to make a difference in the lives of impoverished children in the Philippines.

I pray to Steve on my blog: "Thank you, Velo Biscuit, for showing me what you have to get through this improbable recovery. No matter who you evolve into after this accident, I will love you for who you are. Just being alive is indeed your break this time, honey." But you know I won't stop there.

My earth angels teach me how to understand and support my children. I try my best to validate them but I cannot change who I am. I am hope; I am faith. I am trust in God. And now my warrior is emerging. I am building a dream team of doctors, healers and insurance experts to help our family recover from this nightmare. For the first time, I show Payton my warrior spirit. I say, "I've got this, Payton. You don't know who I am. I've never had to show you the fight in me, but hear this. Your Dad is going to make it.

He is going to get better and I will not stop until we get Dad back."

My children are upset that I regularly highlight the blessings of this tragedy. Today my friend Annie, a trauma therapist, is here with flowers, a gift for Payton, and a message. She explains that since I am carrying blessings and joy, Payton feels responsible for carrying anger, grief and sorrow on behalf of the family. I saw the movie *Inside Out.* How did I miss this? Can I carry anger, grief and sorrow too?

This morning I open my laptop and find a handwritten note: "Mom. Wake me up at 6:45. — Payton." Today is the eve of Grandparents Day, Payton's biggest catering job. I thought he was making 800 desserts. The count is actually 1,200. It's also Payton's thirteenth birthday but no one will wish him Happy Birthday. There are no gifts. No cake. No candle. Nothing. For his birthday, Payton asked that we not acknowledge him, to honor his father.

I asked myself, "Is this what Payton *really* wants? Is this the *right* thing to do?" I believe it is, but there is still a smidgen of doubt. My friend Virgine, who is an EMDR trauma therapist, talked to Payton while driving him to Stanford. She told us to trust Payton, give him space and time to process his grief. He wants to prove that he knows himself, that he's becoming a man. Payton expressed concern for me when he asked, "Is my mom worrying about me? I don't want to add to her list of worries."

In preparation for the non-birthday, I emailed the school. I tucked his gifts away in the closet. I hid the birthday cards. I told our family, our pastor and our friends not to call. And when my son woke up this morning next to me in bed, getting up well before 6:45am without my help, I forgot it was his birthday.

I hear Payton's sweet voice in the kitchen, chatting with his grandma, Nanny Nancy, about their schedule, plans, dessert counts. Nanny is telling stories, each with a lesson. I hear the knives chopping chocolate and the spoons hitting the mixing bowls. We have not one but two mixers humming. Payton says, "I didn't realize how much I love having a big family." Alexa is playing classical music and the sugary, buttery, chocolatey smells are floating into the bedrooms. Maybe this is the best birthday celebration of all. Payton is doing what he loves with the devoted grandmother who passed her baking genes onto him. In this present moment, life is sweet.

A sensitive soul named Lucinda posts on the blog, "Payton. Thirteen AND SEEN. I see you, Payton, missing and loving your dad, bravely rising to honor him and standing in your truth. You rock. God bless you."

DAY 37. It's 9am! I can't recall the last time I slept into the nines. The Bowen therapy treatment yesterday from Meghan extended my sleep. But there is another reason. Steve is ready to be transferred to a long-term acute care hospital, Kentfield, which is fifteen minutes from our home.

As we head to Stanford I feel the ache of nostalgia. We have so many friends at Stanford. We have a routine and we know the nurses. I casually pass by surgeons who have operated on Steve. Flight nurse Becky regularly visits. And who can forget Karyn, making us feel cozy and at home in the hospital? We laugh about our visitation policy violations. We feel comfortable and confident here, in "our place" — the place where Steve made it. I walk by the old spots we used to sit and wait, sit and cry, sit and talk. I am reminded of how far we've come in thirty-seven days. We made it.

This is a lateral move. Steve isn't ready for rehab because he needs his lung secretions suctioned every hour and must be tied down for safety. He wiggles, squeezes both hands, tries to open that right eye. He tracks people and sometimes appears to react with emotion. What's hard is the disconnect between Steve's robust physical movements and his mind. In his slow awakening, he is like a person with special needs. It's heartbreaking to see my husband's light so dim.

And that makes me wonder — what will his mind be like in the future? This is terrifying because the possibilities are endless. Times like this when Steve is in transition pull me out of the present moment because I have to make decisions about the future, which means I have to imagine the future. The one thing that has saved me from the depths of despair is staying as far away from the future as possible.

After saying goodbye to Becky and eating dinner, we return to Steve's room to quietly disassemble it. We've been told it's the most decorated hospital room Stanford has ever seen. I think, *They've never seen someone like Steve either.* Everything is packed up and the room sounds hollow and echoey. I think of all those who saved my beloved — hundreds of medical professionals, the people in the pictures on the walls, the people who made the posters, the people who offered prayer cards, holy water and cycling memorabilia. Balloons, cards, and flowers cocooned his room. So many souls filled this room with love to call Steve back to life.

DAY 38. How many times have I said, "Thanks be to God?" Today, I feel what it means. I wake up to a damp sleeping mask; tears of joy came to me in my sleep. I feel God's love blanketing me and am bursting with the desire to share this gift of being smothered in God's grace with anyone who will listen. It feels amazing!

On the night of his non-birthday Payton said, "I don't believe in God. I asked him for one thing on my birthday and he didn't give it to me." I prodded him, believing I could convince Payton he was, in fact, going to receive it, but it might take a little longer to surface. My anguished son shut down and the conversation ended. I shared his impenetrable doubt with Pastor Kim who offered to him: "Our God is a loving God who doesn't give us what we can't handle. He helps us get through our pain and suffering. He doesn't outright take our pain and suffering away..."

That resonates with me because it's how I feel. God gives me what I need to get through this: blessings in the form of miracles, signs of hope and faith, courage to face the day with support from family, friends, and an unfathomable array of poignant strangers. These expressions of love help me handle my pain. Every day, I feel a Divine presence inside me, whether I am happy about a new milestone or in the depths of despair from a doctor's bleak prognosis. God is there all the same.

I can't get out of bed and it feels so good. What have I been doing the past thirty-seven days that I couldn't lie in bed like this, especially given how painfully tired I am? There's been a shift. Either that or I'm just tapped out. I'm too tired to go to the hospital after finishing my insurance phone calls, so I listen to my body and wait for it to tell me to drive to Steve.

It's much later in the day and we are finally at Stanford. Steve is floating in and out of consciousnesses — awake for ten minutes, out for thirty. Lola, the kids and I take turns watching Steve sleep. On my way to the lounge, I smile at a man in scrubs. He stops and asks, "Are you Stephen's wife?"

"Yes."

"How's he doing?"

"Steve opens his left eye, responds to some commands, is wiggly and we are hopeful. How do you know me?"

"My name is John. I'm a nurse practitioner from the neurology team and treated Stephen in the ICU. I saw your pictures on the wall of his room and recognized you." I tell him how thoughtful he is to reach out to me.

John says, "Not too long ago, we treated a girl who was in a bad car accident. Her brain injury was similar to Stephen's. She was unresponsive for a month and her parents painfully decided to remove her life support. That same day, she started responding to commands. She has since recovered. She's not the same but she's doing well, given the circumstances. Never give up! Stephen is young and healthy. Give him a year to get better. He won't be the same but he will be better." I share John's message with Lola. In fact, it's for her. She prayed today for a sign that it's okay for her to leave her son and resume her life back home.

At 7pm Lola texts me, "Steve is awake!" I bolt. As I skip into his room, I notice his left eye is wide open. For the first time, I speak to Steve like everything is normal. I brag about how I got into his PayPal account. I joke that he needs to get his secretions and flailing arms under control so we can get him to rehab. I laugh, "The cost of gas driving to Stanford is burning a hole in our credit card. Good thing I found your PayPal stash." I'm being myself and cracking jokes as if he were normal Steve. Since he looks at me with interest and sincerity, I test him.

"Steve, grab my hand." He reaches for my hand.

"Steve, move your left leg if you want Payton to massage you." He moves his left leg. Payton starts massaging him.

"Steve, blink twice if you want Payton to massage you harder." He blinks his eye twice. His mom and I place our hands next to each other, close to Steve's hand.

"Steve, whose hand to do you want to grab? Mine or your mom's?" He grabs my hand.

Then the ultimate question from Payton: "Dad, raise your eyebrows if you love me." Steve raises his eyebrows and we go wild!

Those responses feel so real, so intentional, so communicative. He understands what we are saying and is responding. We can hardly contain our joy. I grab my cell phone to video a repeat performance but Steve doesn't comply. He can't. I feel how much energy he expended to perform those five mundane tasks. He is tapped out.

I am grateful for so many things, but especially for having the sharp vision to see and appreciate tiny milestones. I am thankful for my gratitude, my patience, my clarity. But most of all, I am thankful to God.

CHAPTER 9

Goodbye to Stanford

DAY **39.** We thought Steve was leaving Stanford days ago but we are still waiting for the paperwork, enjoying a slow goodbye. Steve responds with double blinks for yes and zero blinks for no. He's dozing off, so the kids head to the lounge to watch a movie. I stay. I notice a curious opening the way his body is angled in bed. I spontaneously hop in to occupy the space. Steve made this opening for me!

It doesn't take long for me to nestle into Steve. He wraps his legs around mine and plays footsies, just like old times! I release the strap on his right hand and take it in mine. I grab a pillow for myself and just like that, we are spooning. When Nurse Nina, one of the loving nurses who regularly cares for Steve catches us, she says it's adorable and not a problem. I explain to her what my friend, Nurse Megan, said about twin babies at the children's hospital. When one twin is sick and they snuggle next to each other, the sick baby gets better. Nurse Nina drapes us with toasty flannel sheets. I close my eyes and imagine, for a moment, as if it all never happened...

When Payton and Aria waltz back in, they smile at their cuddly parents. Then like clockwork, they start arguing. Payton pretends to box near Aria, who screams and runs in circles. At this moment our family is whole. Seeing their parents together in this normal way allows the children to let their guard down to be regular kids again, instead of grieving, heartbroken ones.

We leave the hospital as the sun sets and the fog rolls over the hills of Interstate 280. Aria gazes out the window, mesmerized. "Mommy, I'm seeing what I thought I could never see — things in clouds. I see dogs, myself, even Daddy. It's amazing! I see a huge cloud shaped like a bird. It's gigantic and it's soaring over heaven. It's following us home, Mommy. I still see it." Aria writes me a letter and places it on my nightstand. She tells me the bird was God. She kept seeing the bird because the bird is always with us. God is always with us.

The kind souls we meet teach me about humanity. One of the many helpers Marc Benioff sent us includes Dr. Kim Norman, a renowned UCSF child psychiatrist who helps me with Payton. Dr. Norman not only sits with me at Stanford and takes my calls when I'm struggling, but came to our home in Mill Valley last Sunday! He told me a story about Marc that touches the core of my being.

Marc prioritizes hiring people with special needs. One of these employees was hospitalized and Marc asked Kim, "Could you please go to the hospital and sit with this man for a couple of hours?" Walking into the hospital room, Kim heard the rustling of papers in the adjacent nook. He peeked around the corner and was stunned to see he was there to relieve Marc himself. When I think of a person like Marc Benioff, I can easily imagine wishing I had his business acumen, wealth or influence. But what I *really* want is to be the kind soul who *feels called* to sit in the hospital room, loving on the man who works in my company.

This teaches me how powerful our connections are, even with so-called strangers. The blog has opened my heart to so many people I have never met, but feel like I know. Others feel similarly. Martin and Joyce from Canada post, "Jenna. We don't know each other. As well, Steve and I have never spoken. The strength, bravery, and inspiration you and Steve have are beyond words. God works miracles through all of us." Ellen warms my heart when she says, "Thank you for everything you've been sharing. I'm one of the 'strangers' you've never met in your loving community." The blog has over two thousand readers and many of them don't know us personally. I feel loved; the blog is *my life support.*

DAY 40. Payton and I are driving to Stanford. I confess that I haven't been honoring his wishes and acknowledging how well he knows himself. I ask him to list his grievances with me and one-by-one, I list and accept his requests for corrective action. In exchange, I ask him to approach me for help. We are both happy; and now my baby boy who is quickly growing up is sound asleep. Payton never falls asleep in the car. Letting Payton be Payton in this impossible situation allows him to let go.

Steve is tired. He looks me in the eye and offers his hand. He makes the same offer to Payton with his other hand. He doesn't respond to questions with blinks but asking for our hands is a first, and we take it.

As we head home, I feel like we are driving into a painting. The fog blurs the colorful sky, making the landscape moody and mysterious. I listen to the song *"Room on Fire"* by Stevie Nicks and I daydream about Steve.

For as long as I can remember, Steve has wanted a nice watch — the kind of watch other men notice. There have been times when he's earned the money for this watch, but even with my blessing, he's never pulled the trigger. Our trip to Maui, a week before the accident, was a substitute for his watch.

Living in San Francisco and now Marin County, we've always been aware of the affluence of this part of the world. Often we are taunted by the privilege and occasionally sickened by it. We regularly acknowledge living in a bubble and play with the idea of popping it — or do we? When choosing between the two currencies of life, time and money, we've always chosen time. For nearly ten years while Steve and Ray ran their business, they both had a great deal of time, each pursuing something different with their currency. Ray traveled the world and explored other business ventures. Steve chased an Olympic dream and spent a great deal of time with his growing family. As the old saying goes, "Money doesn't matter, as long as you have enough." We've always had enough but in the Bay Area, you can easily feel like there's *never* enough.

Before this accident, Steve approached me about his dream of transitioning out of his for-profit, good-paying, high-tech career to start a non-profit. I protested, "We need to pay for the kids' college and beef up our retirement accounts. Are you planning to work until you're ninety?"

Steve kept reassuring me. "Jenna, we have enough." He used to tell me that he's never going to stop working. He also used to tell me he was going to die young.

Lately, I daydream about pushing Steve in a wheelchair down the walking path in our neighborhood. I dream of having a huge homecoming party to celebrate his miraculous recovery. And sometimes I dream of giving my sweet husband the fancy watch he's always wanted. But I can't imagine him wanting that anymore.

Regardless of where we land a year from now or God willing, our old age, we know that this tragedy set us down on a path we wouldn't have chosen. I'm not stalking retirement calculators, nor am I worried about how we'll pay for college. I now know that the more we give, the more we receive. I think about what Steve used to say as an athlete: "Everything works out in the end. If it's not working out, you're not at the end." Sometimes, I have to repeat the phrase to believe it. "Everything works out in the end. If it's not working out, you're not at the end."

DAY 42. The C-collar is gone, and Steve is transferred to Kentfield. I arrive there to greet their new patient. Steve looks miserable. They don't cushion the gurney in the ambulance; bumps in the road agitated his broken back, neck and shoulder. The nurses give him pain medication, but he's wiped. So am I. I tell Steve I'll return tomorrow.

Taking the country road home, I spot a hawk soaring in front of the car carrying a dead, bloody squirrel, dropping it in front of me. Now, a turkey appears. I stop and beep my horn. The turkey casually looks at me and slowly meanders across the road. In my heightened state of awareness, I think of Steve. Seeing a hawk means to pay attention — a message is coming. When I think about the bloody squirrel on the road, I wonder if that's how Steve looked after the car hit him? Is the turkey a reminder that Steve can't quickly respond right now but he will eventually "cross the road?"

DAY 43. "This is our family's new normal"— one of the thoughts tonight. I'm trying to reduce my children's desperate desire for their Dad to get better *now*. "Daddy did the unthinkable! He survived a terrible accident! He's going to live! Let's celebrate that!"… Crickets.

Payton is the 'no' man. He doesn't want to celebrate his friends' birthdays; doesn't want to go to Santa Cruz with Todd; doesn't want to sleep at Brad's; doesn't want to go camping with Jared; doesn't want to go to Great America with Kelly; doesn't want to go to school. *No, no, no.* It's wearing on me. I want him to see the glass as half full but he sees the glass as shattered. My friend Tara says, "Most people see the glass as half empty or half full. Jenna looks at her glass and says, 'Hey guys, check out my glass! I've got one drop! Isn't that amazing?'" How do I meet my kids where they are at when I'm someplace dramatically different? I know my kids need to grieve; I know they will be sad for a long time. But I want them to see better days, at least a few. I carry their pain too and I'm feeling pretty full of my own sorrows right now.

After cleaning the house, fixing my computer and writing me a letter about why he doesn't want to go to school, Payton hops in the car to see his Dad. There's an upside-down baby's playpen over Steve's bed — a vail bed. My "baby" Steve wiggles so much so this fully contained bed gives him the freedom to safely move without restraints. I unzip it, climb in and massage Steve, while Payton cuts his Dad's fingernails. Steve starts swinging his legs, so I bolt.

No longer in emergency mode, it's time to wake up the brain. The progress is painstakingly slow but the feeling of danger looming is distant. Fearing the limit of Steve's recovery is not. I try not to go there. Just when I start sinking, I receive reassurance from my loved ones — a chat with Mary, a text from Rachel, a heartfelt conversation with my kids. And just like that, I'm back on the surface floating, surrounded by love.

DAY 44. I climb in bed with Steve and he wraps his legs around mine. He doesn't look me in the eyes but the spooning gesture overshadows that. I close my eyes and fall asleep, daydreaming about my childhood.

For as long as I can remember, I slept anxiously at night because our front door did not lock. Every evening, like clockwork, I tried desperately to get that lock to latch and every night, it failed. I went to sleep with anxiety that we were not safe. I recently discovered that my sisters had the same worrisome thoughts. No one mentioned this concern to our parents, nor each other.

Growing up in the country in the 80s and attending Catholic school, as a child I feared adults and everything in between. Even my performance measures were fear-driven. I was afraid of getting in trouble, afraid of breaking the rules, afraid of getting bad grades. I was afraid of the nuns, afraid of causing a stir, afraid of disobeying God. I was afraid of being afraid. I remember the time, place, and situation that drove me to utter my first curse word at age thirteen. The classmate I said it to knew exactly how fearful I felt saying it. He taunted me with it afterwards.

Until this tragedy, my deeply rooted childhood fears served as a baseline for many adult decisions. Steve helped me recognize that and begin to change, but deep-rooted fear remained a driving force in my life. Steve and I didn't want Payton and Aria to operate from the same platform of fear we did. We wanted them to stand their ground and speak their truth. As a result, we formed an unconscious contract with our kids. We gave them an adult license to free speech in exchange for using their voice to better themselves, know themselves and communicate what they need. The intention was promising, the execution flawed. An unanticipated outcome of that contract is backtalk.

During one of my Dad's visits, I was embarrassed by how much the kids were talking back. I asked, "Dad, why do you think my kids speak like this to me?"

He instantly replied, "You talk to your children like adults. Let them know that *you* are the adult and *they* are children and what you say goes. Period." That made sense. Fearing adults worked in my childhood. I need to reinforce that I'm the boss. But when Steve and I tried that approach it felt false. Only recently, through a new friend named Alice, a professional intuitive, did I learn why.

Payton was born an "old soul." As he enters young adulthood under the umbrella of trauma, his perspective runs even deeper. Aria has an "old heart." She feels her emotions with intensity and expresses them the same. She tells me God speaks to her; she sees statues move; she sees signs and images of God all around her. When channeling her heart, Aria speaks poetry. What's happening is both kids are growing an adult mindset at a young age. However, the physical puberty side is progressing at a normal rate, which triggers their emotions to run off the rails. The outcome is talking back. Since they cannot control their hormonal, emotional responses they get upset or frustrated when speaking to us. This shared reality of our family is creating a unique outcome that some people would understand but many would not. I know it's working when our kids clearly articulate their thoughts and feelings.

My neighbor, a therapist, says, "As long as you get it right eighty percent of the time, the twenty percent of the time you mess up teaches your kids coping skills." Sounds good to me!

DAY 45. I'm back at Bikram yoga for the first time. My body feels like jello, my arms feel like lead and my fatigue is constant. My radiant, loving teacher Anna cradles me during class, giving me space to unearth my shattered mind as I fall apart crying during camel pose. Afterwards she tells me her story of overcoming pain and loss. Like my new intuitive friends, I discover she's been a "seer" since childhood and a near-death experience as an adult validated what she's sensed her whole life. We are spirits in bodies.

Walking home, my inner focus fades and I'm anxious to see Steve.

The kids and I walk into Steve's room and meet Susan the Chaplain. She says, "There was nothing any of you could have done to stop this tragedy."

Looking into Payton and Aria's eyes I ask, "Could you please repeat that, Susan?"

Susan adds, "If only this. If only that. Had we done this. Had he done that. What happened on April 21st at that exact moment, in that exact place just *happened*. Positive things have come from this tragedy. One blessing is that your life has been paused. This pause is helping you find blessings."

That *pause* has given us space to find new meaning and new purpose, which can only be done in the absence of movement. As Susan sings, Steve's eyes flutter and open. My attention has been so focused on Steve that in this gentle moment I realize our entire family needs the same kind of softness and comfort Steve does.

Payton says, "The reason I feel worse now versus the beginning is because back then, there were only two possibilities. Dad would either live or die. Now, we have no idea what the possibilities are. Am I going to get my Dad back?" My heart breaks.

CHAPTER 10

A Non-linear Prescription for Traumatic Brain Injury

DAY 46. I walk into the hospital room and see Steve sitting in a wheelchair for the first time. I'm elated! He can't go anywhere but he's out of bed. Two nurse aides airlift Steve back to bed via a robust medical device that looks like a carnival ride. Eventually I tell Steve we have to leave, and he awkwardly squeezes my arm, pulling me toward him. I think of Ray who says, "Steve is inside there."

I stumble upon one of Steve's racing blog posts about dealing with nonlinear progress. It could be his own prescription for surviving traumatic brain injury.

Posted by Steve...

VELOBISCUIT BLOG, MARCH 31, 2008:
"The Regular Guy and Nonlinear Progress"

I'm a regular, highly competitive, emotionally driven guy. I realize extraordinary dreams progress nonlinearly. The road to the top is not straight. This is hard for us regular guys. Do you have the mental stamina to make it through ups-and-downs? How do you stay committed to impossible goals?

Why do most people give up before the rewards?

We struggle with nonlinearities because our brains prefer linear terms. For instance, if you train every day, you expect to ride faster, but that rarely happens. Often we train hard for weeks, months, and years, but only see incremental improvement. If you are not disheartened and persist, then you reach the tipping point — your payday.

Some handle nonlinearities better than others. There is a neural and success correlation. When failure presents itself, we get less doped. Our pleasure brain system is like the stock market. It monitors how we do, relative to expectations. If we don't meet "market expectations," then our brain produces less of the pleasure neurotransmitters and we feel down. It's even worse when you succeed early because the expectations become larger. The paradox of success is that it takes more success to fuel the brain.

You need small wins consistently, which is difficult when the path is nonlinear. I've read books on neuroscience, psychology, and philosophy to help with this. For example, I've learned "When the little guy doesn't know he's the little guy, he can do great things." I believe a regular guy can achieve great things if he has the right mental model to deal with nonlinearities.

I am filling the prescription Steve himself wrote — lots of small doses of happiness, positivity and belief that he will reach his goal, strength to hold on when it gets hard, and permission to falter. I pray on the blog, *"I hope you recognize your own prescription, my love. And by the way, you are anything but a 'regular guy.'"*

DAY 47. Steve and I are asleep in the vail bed. Payton's hunched over in his chair, wearing an airplane neck pillow, staring into space, holding his Dad's hand. We are beat. Steve wakes up to the respiratory therapist, Debbie, inserting a speaking valve into his trach so he can try to speak. Debbie coaches me on identifying distress signals if Steve can't breathe and how to read the machine, remove the valve and encourage him to talk. He doesn't. But when my sweetheart coughs, we hear his voice — a sound we haven't heard in 47 days. When it's time to leave, Steve pulls me into his armpit and squeezes me. I feel bad leaving. It's a bit of a Catch-22: I hope it's good he misses me because it means he's in there, but if he's in there what does he make of all this? He's lived alone in hospitals for nearly two months. He can barely move, can't speak, can't go to the bathroom. I leave him alone every night and often for hours during the day. What happens when I'm gone? How does he feel then?

Flowers, gifts, and books adorn our front porch daily. Cards, poems and prayers line our walls, reminding us we are loved by all. From heart-shaped rocks to prayer flags to holy artifacts, our entire home is an altar. Surprise bags of groceries, dinner deliveries and homemade treats mean no one goes hungry. We've received spontaneous acts of kindness, warm embraces and tech tune-ups. The gentle smiles, gardening hands and massaging hands lift us up. Mindfulness workshops, therapy talks and cleaning sessions help us sort ourselves out. Someone even takes out our trash! Never in my life have I been supported like this, nor could I have envisioned these endless gifts.

The other day while daydreaming about how we can use this tragedy to give back, my neighbor Matt, who showed up unannounced to tend our front garden, asks "I'm wondering if your back yard is providing you with a calm, relaxing space? I'll stop by to give your backyard a little love and attention." A short while later, Matt transformed it by weeding, repositioning and tilling. He even put a floral tablecloth on the plastic foldable table we use for al fresco dining. We have dined in the back yard every night since Matt "gave it some love."

Matt, someone I just met, does so much for our family and community that I rename him "Mayor Matt." He shares, "In all my years growing up and living in this neighborhood, the wonderful people have never held back their love and support when my family faced its darkest hours. One day, when the time is right, I'll share my story with you."

DAY 49. Steve looks sad. His doctor reinforces the importance of minimizing stimuli. One person speaks at a time, in a calm and soothing voice. Payton is sound asleep, sitting on a chair, with his head resting on his father's leg. He wakes up startled to find the pee tube smashed in his face. I laugh. Payton does not.

Steve's left arm is twitching as he manically pulls the fingers of his right hand, like he's trying to crack his knuckles. I just spoke to his doctor about the seizure meds and wonder if this is a seizure? It's not. Just when I feel secure about Steve's state, I am prompted to worry. I resist, reminding myself there's nowhere to go but the present. I too am rewiring my mind. Steve's eye is closed so I'm guessing he's asleep but when I stand up, he scratches my back.

Leaving the house this morning, I stumble upon a tray of plants and seeds on the front porch before heading to yoga. The note reads: *"Jenna — I'm a friend of Leslie's and therefore a friend of yours. I read your blog and wanted to drop some seeds for your planter box. — Love, Molly"* I grin ear-to-ear walking to yoga, feeling this thoughtful gesture will give me so much strength this morning. I share this touching gesture with the blog.

A blogger comments, "Witnessing how others care for your

family has taught me how to be a better human being." Our family is learning how to care for others because of the remarkable kindness we receive from our community.

DAY 51. Steve walked on his own! His therapists got him up from his wheelchair in the hallway. He held onto the handicap bar and took three steps. He won't be back home next week, but we are pumped. I'm trying *not* to expect a repeat performance because he turns it off as quickly as he turns it on. The doctor said we can wheel Steve outside and eat lunch in front of him. He can grab at his feed tube while we savor leftover salmon with spring vegetables and Chez Pay's sweet, buttery, banana bread. I'm sure Steve will love watching us eat in front of him and be thankful for his feed tube.

My life is filled with gut-wrenching days where my heart gets leveled, followed by miracles. We have no choice but to ride through the turbulence, feeling the rough days as deeply as the smooth ones. There's no escaping any of it. Change is our new constant. Pain is the prelude to possibility. When you come from the depths of darkness, the tiniest slivers of light feel like fireworks. That is the gift of pain.

Doctors are concerned that Steve's physical body is healing faster than his brain. It's been fifty days and Steve still does not consistently follow commands. If Steve can fully function physically but remains mentally childlike, he will become what doctors call the "walking wounded." The rehab hospital I have in mind won't take a walking wounded patient, and insurance issues go hand-in-hand. In recognizing physical progress, the insurance company could stop funding the cost of acute care, despite Steve's significant cognitive deficits. They could try and put Steve in a nursing home.

I'm aware of these issues but not fixating on them. One day at a time.

DAY 52. Steve is outside for the first time. We're on the deck playing music, Face-timing his family. Fabio and Katherine are enthusiastically expressing their love for Steve. Our favorite patient moves his lips just enough to tell us he understands the conversation but does not speak. It doesn't matter. The essence of Steve is here and that is enough. He has another new trick — massaging me!

Driving to and from the hospital on Camino Alto is a bitter irony; I pass at least forty cyclists. I think about their families, where they take their lines in the road, if they bike defensively. I can't help but wonder if they too will get hit someday. The road is steep and windy, with a narrow shoulder. I take my time, refusing the pressure from the tail behind me, only passing if it's safe. As a result, I drive slowly.

I use the time I spend slowing down *to slow down.* It's a pretty drive through trees, houses and peekaboo views of the water. It takes six minutes to drive up and over the hill. Today as we were driving to the hospital, a large truck heading in the opposite direction passed a cyclist on a blind turn. As the driver crossed over the yellow line, he was heading right for us. I thought, "How ironic for us to be in a head-on car collision because a car unsafely passes a cyclist." We squeeze by with less than twelve inches between us and the truck. Payton observes matter-of-factly, "If the shoulder in that section of roadway was twelve inches narrower, we would have been hit, Mom."

I thought, *Why are these drivers so desperate to gain thirty seconds that they almost kill a cyclist?* I wanted to scream, "There is a living, human being on that bike! Slow down and protect their life!"

Day 53. Today is our eighteenth wedding anniversary. I dash to the hospital with our wedding album and engagement diary. "Happy Anniversary, Steve! I love you. Raise your eyebrows if you love me too." He wiggles them up and down. I say, "Look, this is the Irish Claddagh Ring Victoria gave me." I demonstrate heart-in-hands, and he copies me.

I exclaim, "You're massaging my hand again? This is the best anniversary!" With anticipation, I finally show my sweetheart our wedding album. Steve earnestly looks at the photos while I slowly turn each page. Does he remember our wedding? Out of nowhere, his hands move over the buttons on my cardigan. Is my husband remembering what it feels like to undress me? When he tries to re-button it with a blank look on his face, I wonder if he's a curious child learning to button for the first time or someone just blankly moving his hands. I choose to believe that Steve is facilitating his own non-linear occupational therapy.

Day 54. Steve is tired but genuinely tries to respond to commands. He has another new trick: spontaneously nodding in agreement to any question from Payton. My loving friend Natasha, a fellow mom from Payton's school, encourages me to communicate using baby sign language but cautions me not to speak like a baby because he is a grown adult. We practice the peace sign for yes and one finger for no. I ask, "Are you in pain?" He holds two fingers and I call the nurse.

I visit Steve a second time tonight. Sitting quietly in the dark I whisper, "Although the kids and I are sad about what happened to you and miss you terribly, we are okay. You are with us always." I explain that we have loads of support.

I add, "The house is clean, Millie had nine puppies, Payton is baking." Steve stares at me in earnest.

Then I say, "And, I'm not working." He's frowning! I knew he would be worried about money, so I lay out the financial facts and describe the support we have received.

I try to reassure: "All you need to do is get better and you can take as long as you like. Thank you for coming back to us. I know you had a choice. All the pain and heartache you are experiencing is worth it. You are going to recover, you are going to come home and you are going to experience life again." I think he understands what I'm saying. I hope I'm saying the right things.

A Kentfield staff member approaches me and says, "Jenna, I'm Lynn — a nurse on Steve's wound team. We met the day you arrived." She tells me Steve's first responders, Otis and Alexis, came today and that she's friends with Alexis. Lynn says something that strikes a chord, "We're not just medical professionals taking care of Steve. Your *community* is taking care of him." Several people at Kentfield Hospital knew of Steve before he got there or know friends of his. It's deeply comforting living in a small town with a sense of belonging. Lynn reminds me we're all in this together, and every single person makes a difference.

My Dad flew in yesterday. He hasn't been here since the ICU days and is excited seeing Steve "looking like himself," seated in a wheelchair. Payton rolls his Dad to the deck, where we all four talk, almost like old times. At Stanford, my Dad's optimism stood out above all others. He predicted, "Steve is going to wake up sooner than you think. And, when he does that, he is going to give us a big thumbs up." Today, while sitting outside, my Dad asked his son-in-law for a thumbs up and got it.

CHAPTER 11

The Need for Sweetness

TODAY, Steve's brother Joe and family arrive. Joe last saw his *"kuya, Steve,"* a Filipino term of endearment for a beloved elder, on Day 7 in the ICU. Joe questions whether Steve's responses are meaningful.

I answer, "We don't know for sure, but we believe he understands. In a situation like this, all we have is our belief."

I ask Steve, "Are you in pain?" He nods no.

"Are you meditating?" He nods yes. I ask him other questions, but he looks at me blankly. Steve has been pulling zippers up and down, buttoning and unbuttoning. He wears boxing gloves because of his sporadic and dangerous flailing hands. His brain does not register when his actions inflict pain, even if the pain is obviously self-inflicted. Today, I remove his gloves and unstrap his wrist bands so he can freestyle under supervision.

When scratching his head, Steve picks at the scabbed-over hole where his brain drain was. Each time he picks at it he grimaces, but there is zero connection between his actions and the resulting pain. Next, he removes the top of his gown and sticks his hands underneath his chest band, poking at his feeding tube. He frowns in pain from that. Then he goes after his catheter and I have to use all my strength to pull his hand away. The final pang of anxiety hits me when Steve tries to remove the trach, pulling so hard I see the hole in his neck. That's the final straw. I re-strap him.

There are times I've been head-locked between Steve's legs. Other times, my chest has been a bench press for his feet. Before April 21st, such maneuvers would have done some serious damage, but now he is harmless. When chronically sedentary, three percent of the muscle tissue degrades daily. Nearly out of muscle, the old Steve must be going bonkers!

If I had to choose one word for what Steve desires most from me, it's sweetness. But that's not my strength. I'm nice and like helping people, but my dominant character trait is determination — I get shit done! As my friend Robin says, I "work my fingers to the bone." To have the strength and endurance to work as hard as I do, I lose some sugar along the way. I'm surprised I'm not tired and angry, as one might expect. I often feel tired and loving, tired and hopeful, if not tired and sweet. Before I can be naturally sweet on my own, I must train for it.

One of the challenges I face is the dark side of traumatic brain injury. I've read that the phases of traumatic brain injury recovery include: agitation, frustration, and irritability to the point of violent outbursts. I need sweetness to counter the negativity. Concerned, Payton says, "How will you handle Dad when he's raging, Mom? This is not your strong suit." In hearing Payton say this, I realize he is referring to me before the accident but I feel differently now. I believe I am already the person I need to be to handle whatever comes our way.

DAY 56. I am tucking in Steve. I gasp, "The trach is gone!" I see a wrinkled-up, bloody hole in Steve's neck. I know the nurses removed it and not Steve, yet I'm surprised there's no bandage. This means nothing is blocking Steve's vocal cords from speaking — except Steve's brain. I stare with deep curiosity and softly speak to him. I'm afraid to ask; I don't want to push him. I look into his eye and know he's not going to speak. It doesn't matter. Knowing the possibility of speech is there is enough. We are entering a new phase of possibilities.

Steve has given me the gift of patience. Rather than speaking, I want him to show me what he needs to feel supported and loved. Tucking Steve in I say, "You are doing a great job, honey. We are here for you. Take your time. Do you want to leave this place?" He gently nods yes.

I explain, "Okay. Stop pulling at the hole in your head, your tubes, and your bandages so you can get outta here." He signals *okay*. I feel like he understands me. Is that possible?

I play the Mozart CD, buckle his wrist restraints, put on his boxing gloves and sleeping mask and dim the lights. I tell Steve I love him and will see him tomorrow morning. I zip up the posey and leave. It's getting harder to leave him at night. I feel badly imagining him in the hospital all alone. The other night I was anxious and needed Steve. I turned to my blog for comfort. A blog reader posts, "I know this sounds crazy but I'm so happy for you." We both understand what that means without talking about it. Having endured profound trauma herself, this woman understands how grief can coexist with joy. It is soothing to be truly understood.

When Payton was four, I sensed he might be Jewish. He played dreidel non-stop, attended Shabbat dinners at friends' houses with deep curiosity and interest and did a few other things I wish I wrote down. Our family was attending an Episcopal Church, but I told Payton he may decide to be Jewish and to let me know if he needed my help.

One of my hidden heartaches is the loneliness I feel among my nuclear family. It's a strange sensation to physically see and touch Steve, Payton and Aria, but to feel void of the strong emotional and mental connection I had with each of them prior to the accident. Payton is distant; Aria needs to escape the family to break from the pain. There are signs Steve is "in there," but we don't know for sure. I miss him.

I feel closest to Aria but she turns on me like nuts in the oven. I am learning how to love her enough, as her father did. I channel Steve when we reach breaking points. The other night when Aria was inconsolable, I imagined what Steve would say and I said it. Her response confirmed my intuition. "Thank you, God."

For fifty-five days, Payton has expressed a constant undertone of irritation, frustration and disappointment with me. Any suggestion I make is bad and everything is a battle. Just when I feel the tension ease and I extend my reach, he snaps back and shuts down. I miss Payton. The perfect storm of becoming a teenager and losing his father is debilitating.

As devastating as this time is, it's as if there's a current of energy gently floating our family down a river. I whisper something in the wind and it shows up on my front porch. It's magical and mesmerizing to receive an abundance of surprise gifts that are exactly what I need when I need them. It's the essence of being known, and we are known by many.

Today's magic is a glimpse of Payton coming back to me and it's because of one person — our new friend Rachel. She is a fellow mom in our community who learned about the blog from a family we've known for years. Last week, when Payton fell sound asleep on her lap, I saw him physically releasing some of the pain and worry of his father. In doing so, he opened up to new possibilities. It's okay to feel happy and focus on fun things while Dad is in the hospital. I sense Payton felt he could have saved his Dad that fateful morning. Carrying that impossible charge is a weight no one can bear. Rachel gave Payton a new charge by saying, "I'm hiring you to bake cookies for the hospital staff." Payton shifted gears, going into catering mode.

My son delivered three hundred cookies to the hospital today. All afternoon, people stopped Payton in the hallway, thanking him for the treats. Before he could wipe the crumbs off the table, Rachel called with a business opportunity. The pitch lit a fire in Payton I haven't seen since the Food Network.

Rachel told Payton about the Jewish Family and Children's Services (JFCS). She said, "We have holidays when Jewish mothers have to bake cookies to give as gifts. Nobody likes to do this; they are incredibly difficult to make. There's an opportunity to help people, Payton." Just a few days later the kitchen is full of Hamantaschen cookies. My iPhone is blowing up with texts for the head baker from Rachel. (Payton has a business, but does not have a phone). The two of them are in cahoots, unstoppable. Says Payton, "Twenty years from now, when I'm ringing the New York Stock Exchange bell, taking Chez Pay public, I will say, 'I give special thanks to my mentor, Rachel.'" I can't make this stuff up! Rachel has truly made a difference in my son's life! Toda raba (הבר הדות),

Rachel and all the loving moms who supported Payton! More sweetness in our unpredictable new life.

DAY 57. I am profoundly thankful for the blog. As thoughts and ideas pour out of me, I feel like the blog is being written through me, not by me. Is God sprinkling our family's lives and the blog with Divine magic to open all our hearts? I see myself standing inside a snow globe, with my arms outstretched up to the heavens, smiling, feeling sparkles of magic envelop me. Yes, I am apparently trapped in a suffocating, no-way-out vessel of trauma, but at the same time it's snowing magic! I feel like screaming, *"Are you guys seeing this? This is the worst time in my life and the best! I am living heaven on earth in the midst of hell!"*

Steve is in the gym facing a set of makeshift stairs. His therapists want him to step up and down one stair, but this show-off is gunning for the entire stack. They stop Steve and demonstrate the objective. I am amazed he understands what they are asking.

Steve's ability to comprehend commands is exhilarating. His physical milestones are coming fast and furious; his conscious awakening is not. No one offers me a picture of the future. There are no percentages to shoot for and no statistics to point to. Steve has defied clinical expectations anyway. He has several new tricks that demonstrate he is "in there." When we sang *Happy Birthday* to Steve, he lip-synced the words. Payton tosses an airplane neck pillow to Steve, which he catches without skipping a beat. Then, he places it around his neck and buttons it. While Steve is looking at my iPhone, it falls and Steve quickly grabs it. His reflexes are impressive. My Dad asks Steve what kind of watch he wants, but Steve doesn't answer. Then Dad shows Steve his Rolex and asks,

"Do you want this watch?" Steve lunges for Dad's watch and tries to grab it!

I say to Steve, "Hey honey, you're so skinny now. I wonder if you have a six-pack?" He quickly rips open his hospital gown and shows me his chest! These responses give me so much hope that he is totally in there.

While driving home, I tell my Dad that so many people have approached me about how Steve helped them before the accident. I say, "Steve doesn't realize the positive impact he's had on others."

My Dad replies, "That's because it's all just another day's work for Steve."

We arrive home to find my friend Jenny dropping off bagels and cookies for the Kentfield staff and sampling Payton's Hamantaschens. Ray, Megan and their daughter Bella arrive to cook a delicious Mediterranean dinner to enjoy in our backyard. Several neighbors happily join the feast after returning from taking all the kids to the pool. We sit outside telling stories.

My sister-in-law Krista wears her Kentfield visitor's sticker all day since we go twice a day. A woman approached her at Target and said, "Hi there. Who did you visit today at Kentfield?"

Krista says, "Steve —"

Before she can finish, the woman announces Steve's last name.

Then she says, "Hi. I'm Alexis. I —"

Krista interrupts, "I know who you are!" Krista thanks Alexis for saving Steve's life. Sweet Alexis tells Krista she's bringing us dinner this weekend and that she'll pack heavy. The kind hearts of our community never tire. Alexis has done more than enough for our family, yet her soaring spirit continues to give. We should be making Alexis dinner.

Lost in conversation, I almost forget to tuck-in Steve. I arrive late, sneaking in the side entrance. I discover Steve lacking wrist harnesses and boxing gloves, having soiled his bed, with his gown completely removed, grabbing his healing trach hole with no bandage. I tell the nurse Steve is not ready for this level of freedom. I hand Steve a baby blanket. He places it over his head, completely covering his face — so endearing! I give Steve his eye mask and he places that over his head upside down and crooked. I initiate his bedtime routine and say goodnight.

What a good day and good night it's been.

CHAPTER 12

A Kiss, A Blessing, and Third Eye Opening

DAY 58. I have little expectations for Steve's day-to-day recovery, thanks to letting go of any long-term plan. I live in the present by necessity. This beats having expectations, assuming I have control over my life, and trying to regulate everything from a basis of fear. With zero input about what will come my way each day, Steve steals my heart with a cascade of tiny, precious moments. If I were standing around waiting for the "big wake-up," I would miss the little gifts my sweetheart doles out each day.

Speaking of precious moments, Steve kissed me for the first time! Prior to today, I would kiss him all over his face and he would lie still. Today, when I reached for him, he kissed me back. It was love's first kiss.

Steve is in his wheelchair in the gym, nodding that he's tired, but we want him to exercise his brain when he's out and rest his brain when he's in bed. The other day, a friend named Jeff handed Steve a pen and paper. Steve wrote the words "Yes" and "434" repeatedly. I looked up what "434" means. "Angel Number 434 is a message that your prayers have been heard and are being responded to in Divine right time. Expect miracles to happen." We copy Jeff, asking Steve to write a slew of names. He does so. Now he is spontaneously writing my name. We are screaming with excitement! We initiate a game of tic-tac-toe. Steve has no problem picking Xs or Os, winning often. Aria is playing with him now, but Steve is letting her win. We are spellbound.

We give Steve a container of small objects that Rachel put together. When he pulls out the small plastic "S" we ask who's name starts with "S," and he points to himself! We clap for joy. We show Steve a picture collage and ask him to locate people on it. We select hard people to recall, like Payton's preschool classmates and he does. We are blown away and reminded NOT to talk to Steve like a baby. Anything feels possible right now. We are in the moment, soaking in these small victories.

Last night, Steve's racing buddy Brian explained how athletes get "in the zone." He said, "Your brain doesn't know the difference between what you visualize and what you experience, so athletes for decades have been picturing their games in their minds before competing." Steve used this same technique as an athlete. In fact, I know being in the zone is getting him through this and he thoughtfully left a trail for me to follow his path into the zone.

Posted by Steve...

VELOBISCUIT BLOG, MAY 21, 2009:
"There Are No Ordinary Moments"

"Yesterday is but a dream, tomorrow is but a vision. But today well lived makes every yesterday a dream of happiness, and every tomorrow a vision of hope. Look well, therefore, to this day." – Sanskrit Proverb.

Watching videos of my children as babies reminds me how quickly time flies and to be more attentive in the times I spend with them. Every moment is precious. The things that matter most in our lives are not materialistic or grand. They are moments when we are in the moment—present in the most attentive or caring way. I recall the poignant experiences of my life: when I asked Jenna to marry me and she said yes, when Jenna took my breath away walking down the aisle, when I gave my best man speeches at my brothers' weddings, when my Pay Pay and my Princess were born, when I first held my children and made a promise to always be there no matter what, when I took my Grandma to Italy while she was battling cancer. When we bring full attention to our acts, the quality of the moment grows in us. It permeates more deeply in our hearts and minds.

Oh, how I wish I could live these Zen moments always. How can I be more aware, more peaceful, happier? How do I get in the zone? The most magnificent moment in sport is arguably the 1998 Game Six Finals between the Chicago Bulls and Utah Jazz. The last-minute of that game I was so nervous, I ate a bucket of wings and drank a 40 during the commercial break before the final possession. The Bulls were down by one point with sixteen seconds left. Jordan said, "I was in the moment. Everything moved in slow motion." There was no panic. He wasn't thinking of the outcome. He was simply letting the game flow. He nailed the sweetest jay from the top of the key, holding his shooting form long enough for us to never forget the greatest player ever.

Similarly, the moments I enjoy most in cycling are when I am in the zone. Whether it's climbing Mt. Tam above the fog bank or descending Panoramic to the Pacific Coast, my mind is not wandering. In the races I've performed well, I have a heightened sense of awareness and am really calm. The race is in slow motion. I feel my heart pounding, but my breath is relaxed.

In the stress of our daily lives, we forget our deepest intentions. But when someone we know dies, we remind ourselves that we should 'live now'— meaning be present to what's happening now. The quality of each moment depends not on what we get from it, but on what we give to it — bringing more of ourselves to each moment every day. Life is a series of moments. In each, you are either awake or asleep—fully alive or relatively dead. Let's not treat any moment as ordinary, no matter how mundane or routine it appears. "The Greeks didn't write obituaries. They only asked one question after a man died— did he have passion?" Let's be passionate, simply by being present. All we have is now. Give us this day, our daily bread…"

Day 59. I say to the blog, "Hot off the presses! Steve wrote again with his friend Jeff this morning: 'Amber. DO YOUR THING!!!' 'First comes the hard work.' 'Help me get better. PLEASE.' 'Twice as long.' 'Be better.' Does anyone know who Amber is?" I'm searching Facebook, asking Steve's closest friends and colleagues if anyone knows Amber. I hope she surfaces.

Today Mary says, "My friend Khenpo Thinley is visiting from a monastery in India. He is a precious human being — the highest master of meditation in his cluster of monks. He looks twenty, but is in his forties. I am bringing him straight from the airport to the hospital to give Steve a blessing."

Thinley is his first name and "Khenpo" is the term signifying a degree for higher Tibetan Buddhist studies. Mary explains that when we refer to Thinley as "Khenpo" we are showing deep reverence for his mastery in Buddhism. I am so excited. I invite my new intuitive friend Alice in addition to our family. We are buzzing around in anticipation.

Khenpo is exactly my height, 5'7". He wears thin black wire-rim glasses and his black hair has a buzz cut. His skin is soft and smooth, reminding me of Steve's skin before the accident. He is wearing a bright yellow, sleeveless button-down shirt with a dark maroon skirt, camel-colored moccasins, a thin red necklace made from thread, and a light brown prayer bead bracelet. Khenpo kindly offers Steve a bouquet of vibrant orange and yellow flowers that match his clothing. The color yellow represents hope.

Khenpo carries himself gently, speaking softly. He exudes an air of simplicity and Divinity that I instinctively want to mirror. Standing next to him puts me at ease; my voice softens and I say only what's needed. We lift up the netting around Steve's vail bed and surround him. Payton's best friend, Mia, is here. I am happy to see her. Payton has avoided all his friends since the accident. Khenpo is wholly focused on Steve, holding his hands and silently praying. Steve peers into Khenpo's eyes, conveying deep gratitude. When finished praying, Khenpo looks up and says, "Steve is very strong. He will recover. He needs peace and quiet."

After Khenpo gives Steve his blessing, we gather in the hallway to thank him. Mary makes several inspiring remarks about the incredible medical and spiritual journey Steve is on. She is in a state of wonder thinking about Steve's brain "creating a new manual." Mary is an ancient soul. I find great comfort in her wisdom. Khenpo, Mary, and Mia leave and we gather bedside again for another knock at Steve's spirit. Alice is ready to read Steve in a conscious state for the first time.

Friends and family gather around the vail bed while I lie next to my beloved. We are so curious about what is going to happen. When reading Steve last month, Alice said he was "swimming in the soup." Having progressed so much since then, she's uncertain whom she will encounter in this reading — spirit guides, relatives who passed, or Steve himself? Alice says, "I feel Steve wanting to communicate so I'm going to close my eyes to see images. I also hear and feel things. I'm getting that Steve wants to speak. Is that true, Steve?" He nods his head yes. This is what Steve, who cannot speak, says through Alice:

"I am screaming at the top of my lungs — desperate to speak! I want you to know that I'm coming back!" Alice looks directly at Steve and asks him if that statement is true and he nods yes again.

Alice continues talking as Steve's conduit: "Everyone knows I love my family and all the people who have visited and everyone who is close to my heart. This is why I make every effort to come back to you all."

I tell Steve, "We thank God and we thank you."

Alice continues: "The work takes everything I have but nothing makes me happier. Nothing will stop me. I know what it's going to be like when I'm back. It's just a matter of getting from here to there. I want a big party! This is worth celebrating! I want you all to know there is nothing to worry about. The path is clear. I'm doing it and we'll all celebrate together.

"Before this accident, there was so much going on at once. My mind was in a million different places, thinking about all the possibilities. Now I know the most important thing is where I am right now. The people in front of me are the most important people and every minute is precious. Don't worry that I'm struggling and in pain. All I see is a grassy field with all of you on it. I'm doing what it takes to get there."

I am holding Steve's hand, and he's squeezing it so tightly right now. His voice is finally being heard, and I am crying tears of joy.

Alice continues: "Jenna, every single word you say, every

single thing you do lights me up. We have so much to look forward to. When I think about how I'm going to be with you, I would never have gotten there without this."

Crying, I look at Steve and explain, "I feel everything you are feeling and I'm here."

Alice relates, "Our future is beautiful. It's inevitable. Don't worry. It's just a matter of time. I want to send a message to Aria. She's a star in my sky who shines so bright. I don't want to dim her brightness. I don't want it to change. I want to embrace it. I want her to shine as much as she wants to. I want to hug her and know that she is being held to shine.

"I want Payton to know that he is a strong boy and he doesn't need to do anything other than what he's doing. When I come back we'll have long talks. We'll both learn a lot from this."

Alice concludes the communication in her own words. "Steve wants you all to know there is much to talk about. He wants deep, quality time with each person to connect. He's glad he got to send these messages. He wants you to know he's connected to the future he just spoke about and everything he does is for the joy of it. It's like someone who decides they are going to run a marathon; he likes the training. When he finishes this marathon he wants to sit on the grass and have long conversations. He wants to be with people in a way he wasn't before. He's tired now, but is happy and peaceful. When I started, he was standing and wanting to scream. Now I see him floating."

While Steve's words thrill me, I am not surprised by what he says. The accident has heightened my connection with Steve at a depth I did not know was possible. I can feel my third eye opening. Also called the "eye of insight," the third eye is our ability to see potentials. Yoga or meditation can trigger its activation, but in my case it was trauma. Hunches, for example, provide evidence of your third eye, but that's only the beginning. We can develop the third eye to be as refined and accurate as any of our five senses. This "sixth sense" accesses deep wisdom and insights. Before this tragedy, I marveled at Steve's insight, but I was blocked. I couldn't find my third eye, never mind see through it. Through this incredibly painful, physically numbing and mind-blowing tragedy, I have finally found my third eye and my vision has never been clearer.

CHAPTER 13

Whisperers

DAY 60. It's 91 degrees outside, so our Father's Day picnic is inside. Steve is in his wheelchair facing the fan. The kids and cousins are fanning him with paper plates, laughing. I suddenly scream, "Steve just spoke! He said, 'Great!'" No one believes me. I lean in close to Steve and say, "You are doing a great job, Steve." I shush everyone.

Steve whispers, "You are doing a great job." The room goes bonkers!

I ask a flurry of questions, "Can you say Aria? How about Payton? Who's that? What's my name? What's her name?" Steve gets most of the questions correct, answering in a faint whisper. He spontaneously says "Jenna" without me asking, but the real winner today is Steve calling out "Dad" to my father. Each whisper feels like a winning lottery ticket. When I pick up my phone to start videoing Steve's first words, I see a text from Leslie: "My Mala beads broke. Once they break, it's because they are no longer needed. Can't wait to hear what happens today!"

We decide today is Steve's Re-birthday — June 18th. After pummeling him with questions, we ease up on the interrogation.

We perform several songs for Steve, ironically including "When You Say Nothing at All." After listening, Steve says, "Good job." Then he adds "Happy Father's Day!" followed by "Shhh…"

We ask him if we are too loud and he says, "Yes." This is the second time we have heard the request for peace and quiet in the past 24 hours. I ask Steve to rate his pain from a scale of 1 to 10 with 10 being severe pain and one being a mild headache. He answers, "Nine."

I ask, "Do you want to go to bed?"

"Yes." I wheel him to his room.

"Are you in pain all the time?"

"No."

"Do you remember the accident?"

"Yes."

"Do you know how much I love you?"

"Yes."

I'm not sure his answers are real, so I test him: "Do you own a Porsche?"

"No."

"Do you *want* a Porsche?"

"Yes."

It's official: Steve is inside Steve. Welcome back!

The nurse transfers Steve to bed. I climb in with him. My Dad sits next to us as we conk out for twenty minutes, and during that time Dad visits the cafeteria. When Steve and I awaken simultaneously, I'm suddenly next to Mr. Hyde! Steve decides to high-tail it out of the vail bed; his restraints are off. He throws both legs over the side of the bed and lunges his chest forward to escape. I wrap my arms around his chest from behind, my legs around his stomach, while frantically pressing the call button. (Steve's strength is rapidly returning!) No one is picking up and I scream, "Help!" A nurse half my size shows up, followed by my Dad, and after a fierce struggle, we lock Steve back up. Relieved, Dad and I sit down, catch our breath, and release the nurse. But then we are watching Mr. Hyde slowly dismantle his imprisonment.

I say, "Oh look. He's trying to hop…"

My dad chimes in, "He's using his feet to take off the mittens!"

Before we know it, Hyde performs another sensational escape as we speed dial the nurse.

Two nurses return to trap Steve but it takes the combined strength of all four of us to corral him. It is mentally and emotionally exhausting. We talk about administering a sedative. It's not ideal since it slumbers the brain, but Steve's agitation is a danger to himself and all others. While waiting for the medicine, I snap my fingers to nudge him to stop going wild in the pen. I'm overwhelmed by how to tame the beast.

My Dad, however, goes in a different direction, becoming a whisperer himself. He speaks to Steve with soothing, repetitive instructions, telling him to take deep breaths. It works; Steve calms down. Then my Dad tells Steve to kiss me, which he does. When he goes wild again, my Dad calmly brings him back. It's a cat and mouse game for a whole hour while waiting for Plan B, the meds.

I ask Steve, "Do you know where you are?"

"No."

"Do you remember the accident?"

"No."

I gently explain where he is and that he is safe. It's sad for me to see Steve like this, especially after today's milestone. Feeling depleted and depressed, I doubt whether today was his new birthday after all.

After receiving the medication Steve eventually drifts back to sleep. It's 5pm and I announce to my Dad, "I'm leaving and not coming back. We've been here six hours, three of which were exhausting. I need a break." The first half of the day was magical but I fear the next downturn. Joy and pain are never far apart.

DAY 62. Steve squeezes my upper arm. I laugh and ask, "Why are you squeezing my arm?" He doesn't answer but keeps squeezing. Back at home, I wake up next to a warm body, I realize it's not Steve and feel sad. Both children are sleeping with me. At that exact moment, while sound asleep, Payton reaches over Aria who is in between us and squeezes my upper arm twice.

I need to ask the blog if someone can trim Steve's hair and goatee at the hospital. I look at my phone only to be surprised by a text from a mom at our former school, Michele, a hairdresser. "Hi Jenna. I have been thinking of another way to help you. Does Steve need his hair cut? I would be glad to neaten his locks." I'm blissed out by the timing of this kind gesture. Is this how my life is going to work from now on?

Steve's medication protocols are complex. He receives medicine to wake up his brain, which causes agitation. When the agitation gets out of control he needs a sedative, but that inhibits brain recovery. It's an unfruitful cycle. Steve is out of it today; my Dad asks if he is frustrated and he nods yes, without whispering. The speech therapist says his vocal cords have atrophied like the rest of him and must relearn to activate. She reminds us that the brain injury itself inhibits speaking, which is painfully obvious.

Once the children learned their Dad survived his initial injuries, the next question was, "Who will Daddy be when his brain gets better?" Aria tells me she doesn't want to see the "hospital Dad." She wants to see "*her* Dad." We don't know who is emerging, but there are clues which give me hope.

When I chat with Steve, trying to up-sell running as a thrilling replacement for cycling, Velo Biscuit frowns; I guess he's still a cyclist. (Good luck without any bikes!) Steve's habit of rubbing his nose restarted five days ago and I sensed the hint of a giggle when I balked at it. In other words, we shared a moment from the *past*. Another old, re-engaged habit is smelling his fingers after he touches something. I can't express how much these tiny habits that used to irritate me now uplift me.

The kids and I are outside hanging with Steve's aunt, Tita, and my friend Ruthie, our former next door neighbor and remodel client. Steve stares at me intensely, pulls me toward him for a kiss and leans back. He does it a second time and a third. When the fourth pull comes, instead of giving me another kiss, he grabs my shirt with great excitement. Ruthie and Tita are on the floor laughing. So am I. He's all in there!

We are back in Steve's room chatting when he mutters, "*Annoyed!*"

Payton asks, "At who?"

"YOU!" One of Steve's personality traits is being easily annoyed, so now we can celebrate another sign of recovery.

Payton asks, "Do you want us to leave, Dad?" He nods yes.

"Do you want us to come back?" He nods yes.

"Okay. We'll be back in twenty minutes, Dad."

Steve, who looks like a pirate with his one eye, facial scars, and rough goatee, grits his teeth and replies in an angry, slow, salty voice, "TENNN..." We cannot stop laughing.

I'm curious about which of Steve's characteristics will return. What if some of his bad habits fall away and some new amazing ones emerge? Like loving to clean or cooking something for dinner besides tacos and curry-in-a-hurry?! There can never be enough silver linings.

DAY 62. We move into the sunshine on the hospital deck with Steve. Michele is here at "Salon Kentfield" giving my beloved a haircut and shave. Steve's aunt, Tita, Aria and I are giving Steve a mani-pedi, including a complimentary leg massage. It's his first spa day. Steve cooperates with getting his nails cut, appropriately re-positioning each finger as needed. It's endearing to care for him in this way, and for him to acknowledge the care with his gentle expressions.

I wonder why I receive so many blessings and signs day after day. Have they always been there but I didn't notice? Could I lose them? Can I help others receive them too? Many mixed emotions arise while dealing with traumatic brain injury. I feel dramatically low on the same day I feel blissfully high. I live with whatever emotion is presenting itself at the time, without attachment. Like the wind, the course of events can change without notice. A gust can blow me to the ground or give me a tailwind to launch me into a heavenly, effortless ascent. I can fight the wind, but it will wear me down. Instead, I have to lean into it and let it take me where it takes me. Then life can flow.

My neighbor Ross and his wife Erin stop by, handing me the *Brain Injury Information Handbook.* Ross is a nurse, our neighbor and friend of Steve's who was on the Chicken Ride. They know the woman who wrote this handbook, Beth. Ross explains, "Beth has three decades of experience in traumatic brain injury and works at CMPC Davies Rehab Hospital. She lives down the street." This center rings a bell. Recommended by my friend Megan, who's also a nurse, it has an entire floor dedicated to brain injury with specific, targeted TBI therapies. I am excited to speak with Beth and ask Ross, "Which neighborhood does Beth live in?"

He replies, "Jenna, she's four houses down from you." Hello, flow!

I don't waste a minute. It's a few hours later and Beth is in my living room. I describe Steve's progress and his agitation struggles. She exclaims, "Steve is ready for rehab!"

I say, "What? I'm confused. The facility I've been eyeing says Steve isn't eligible because of his restraints."

Beth says, "CMPC uses 'shadows.' These are certified nursing assistants (CNAs) who sit bedside 24/7 to help patients through agitation. If the patient tries to get up, the CNA calmly works through the issues by speaking to the patient." She describes how awful restraints are. I didn't know there is another method of dealing with the "walking wounded" besides medication and restraints. I am both excited and frustrated by this news. It's a full-time job to research the best care for Steve, and I've developed a long list of recommendations for the healthcare industry. I wonder if our family is going through this so I can advocate for sweeping healthcare reform — in my spare time? Back to reality, Beth is coming to Kentfield tomorrow to evaluate Steve. I can't wait.

Day 64. It's 6:45am and my Dad is driving me to the scene of the accident. This is a business trip; my emotions are at home. We go early to replicate the sunlight on April 21st. I want to know how this tragedy happened, imagining myself as the driver. I examine the long stretch of dead flat roadway where the brightly clad cyclists were riding toward her. I stare into the beaming sun rays without sunglasses. I want to be blinded, but I see it all. How the hell did she turn? I turn to my Dad and say, "There are no answers here. Only questions. Let's go."

Up until now I haven't pondered the crash much because I've been busy advocating for Steve's recovery, managing our household, and raising our kids. With Steve improving, my mind frees up space to dwell on the accident. Today I took a picture of the crash site in my mind. No matter how many times I visualize this image, there will never be an explanation for why this happened. I need to release the memory, purge my mind of the *why*, and focus on the *how*. How are we going to move forward with our new life? How are we going to turn this nightmare into something positive?

Steve ate solids for the first time in sixty-four days today — mashed potatoes and a mashed vegetable. Thanksgiving came early!

I tell Steve that when his voice comes back to communicate, I can give him exactly what he needs. He whispers, "Thank you." Grimacing in pain, he pulls himself up to a seated position in bed with his knees in front of his chest. He rips off his hospital gown, grabbing the chest band, which protects his feeding tube. I ask, "What hurts?"

Steve replies, "Eye." It's his right eye, which is locked shut. The nurse places a cool washcloth on his eyes, which seems to soothe him.

I ask, "What else can I do to help ease your pain?"

"You are here." My heart floods.

I mention the impact his recovery has on others, including his mom. I say, "She's returning in Au—."

"August," he finishes.

I ask, "How long is your mom staying?"

"Christmas." This is a thrilling short-term memory moment! I ask Steve who else has been affected by his accident, and he replies his brothers. This question is conceptual. We wonder how deep Steve's mind goes. It seems to go pretty far.

It's getting harder to leave my beloved at night. I receive advice from Jill, the founder of *One Hit Away*, which provides resources and support for navigating traumatic brain injury. Jill was introduced to me by my friend's sister, a regular reader of my blog. It's amazing how many resources have come my way through sharing our story online. Jill told me one of the functional medicine prescriptions for TBI is oxytocin hormone therapy. It assists with PTSD and depression, common side effects of TBI. Friends say the feeling they get with Steve is like holding a baby; Steve stimulates everyone's natural oxytocin.

CHAPTER 14

"Bullshit!"

DAY 65. Steve is lethargic, with debilitating diarrhea. His body did not tolerate yesterday's first meal. He looks awful and cannot speak. To convey what it feels like to have a severe traumatic brain injury, Beth said: "You have the flu. You have a migraine headache. Someone is knocking on your door. Your phone is ringing. The kitchen sink is overflowing. The radio is blaring. The oven timer is buzzing. There is a child tugging on your shirt. It's all happening at once, and you can't stop any of it." So this is how Steve feels. Bless his heart.

Begrudgingly I leave Steve all alone today to tour Beth's rehab hospital. I return home exhausted, but I can't get Steve's lethargy out of my mind. I harness a second wind after eating the fresh meal dropped off for dinner. Payton hops in the car too. Nurse Molly summons me from her station. She knows why I'm back and fills me in. I am grateful for the personal attention we receive from the Kentfield staff. They moved Steve to another room because his roommate has C-DIFF and he needs more space to accommodate a sitter — in other words, a shadow. When I mentioned the shadow at CMPC, Kentfield followed suit. I hadn't known this was an option.

I speak softly to Steve to soothe his manic mind. I whisper, "You are a living miracle." I mention our friend Kimberley, who has kept her neurosurgeon friend up-to-date. This doctor said, "Steve is the *one* miracle who survives this level of brain injury." My miracle nods in agreement. I thank my selfless husband for choosing to come back. As I continue my praise for his hard work, Steve does something new and spectacular. He sits up in bed, pulls me toward him and gives me a hug. I'm in heaven.

Being so close to the death of my husband has brought me closer to life than ever. I feel an enormous sense of gratitude and joy for being alive. That feeling washes away the burdens that normally cloud life. When all that matters is living, you see the essence of life clearly. When you see the essence of life, you receive all the beauty and love from God that comes with it. As my dear friend and God-translator Sara says, "God's love doesn't fix everything. It makes the fact that everything has always been fixed more obvious."

The liberating truth that everything is already fixed can be overwhelming. *What am I supposed to do with my life now?* When the food stops being dropped off on my porch, when the cards stop coming in the mail, when people stop reading my blog… will our life slowly slip back to where it was before? What will Steve say when he truly wakes up? Before this tragedy, Steve was light years ahead of me in his wakefulness, deepening his presence even more. I cannot fathom how far down the rabbit hole he has gone now. I hope I can meet him there.

After going to the scene of the accident and facing the obvious truth — *there is no explanation for the crash* — it reinforces what I believe. The crash itself was impossible. Such an impossible tragedy must be answered with an impossible response — unconditional happiness. Our family is going through this gut-wrenching trauma so we can help others.

I say to the blog: "There is definitely something happening here. I feel it in my bones and I clench it in my heart everywhere I go. Something is happening here and we are all a part of it. I know you feel it because you cry when you see me. You send me handwritten letters about the encounters you had with my sweetheart twenty-five years ago. You suddenly hop in cars and fly on airplanes to tell Steve you love him. You read poetry to Steve, having met him once. You knit quilts and decorate dinners. You paint on canvas, paper and wood. You pour your hearts out in songs, letters and cards. Do you feel it? There is definitely something happening here and we are being called to share it.— God Bless and Godspeed, Jenna"

DAY 66. Today Steve is wildly agitated — frantically moving body parts, his wheelchair seat belt, strings and buttons on the hospital gown. Small objects go right in the mouth. He's in the "confused and agitated" phase. When we hand him a paper and pen to write, he scribbles maniacally. He's literally gone "mad." I'm sad seeing him this way but I tell myself repeatedly, "This is a phase of TBI recovery and is normal." It's harder to leave Steve now because I imagine him being painfully bored. Between the agony of a broken mind and the inability to control or manipulate the environment, I would go mad myself.

Before going to the hospital, my Dad and I attended a support group for caretakers of people with a brain injury at the Schurig Center for Brain Injury Recovery in Larkspur. I was seeking feedback on which rehab hospital to choose, CPMC in San Francisco or Care Meridian in Fairfax. After hearing from two caregivers with experiences at each, I conclude my instincts were right: CPMC. To double-check I asked Steve himself. "There are two rehab facilities I am considering. One is easy; the other is hard. Which one do you want?"

Steve replied, "Hard." This guy never takes the easy route. In fact, I'm counting on it.

DAY 67. Walking into the hospital room, I am thrilled to see our neighbor, Mayor Matt. I notice something strange about Steve. It's his eyes — plural — the right eye is open! Just this morning I told the blog that day ninety is the marker for whether or not we know if the third nerve was stunned or obliterated. The right eye opening is a sign that it's repairing itself.

Although Steve's right pupil hangs off to the side, I believe he can see out of it. During my "eye exam" last week, he cleverly peeled open the right eye, as he willingly closed the left eye using his other hand. Today, Steve is way too fidgety for an eye exam. He's masticating, which is concerning. His mouth makes fast, repetitive, awkward movements, like he is smiling and un-smiling rapidly as he keeps flashing his teeth. My Dad thinks Steve is practicing how to flex his previously dormant facial muscles. It makes sense from a physiological standpoint but emotionally it's difficult to witness.

Matt explains Steve has been biting his hands so he's wearing mittens again. Despite his agitated state, I initiate a conversation. Slowly and quietly I say, "Hello. How are you, Steve?" I smile and wait.

No acknowledgment, so I add "It's nice to see you." I pause

before asking, "May I speak to you?"

Once I receive the nonverbal okay to speak, I say, "I have a question for you." I wait again and ask, "Do you feel okay when I leave you each day?"

Finally he responds aloud. "Yes."

"Are you upset when I go home?"

"No."

Then, slowly I tell him what I do when I'm home, pausing between statements. "I think about you when I'm not here… I email your doctors… I take care of the kids… I research things you need… I speak to friends and family… I work on preparing the house for your homecoming… I always think of you." He seems okay with all of it — a huge relief.

The *Traumatic Brain Injury Handbook* explains that when a patient is in an agitated state, you should walk away where the patient can't see you. Maybe that's why Steve is okay when we leave; he gets a break from stimuli. That said, we think Steve likes the diverse and creative energy of friends and neighbors who stop by less frequently than family. I receive incredible reports about Steve's performance from others.

Today, he played *Connect Four* and *Scrabble* with his friend Soren. Steve motioned he wanted to get in his wheelchair and Soren made it happen. This kind heart noticed my beloved's mouth was bloody and got a nurse to brush his teeth. Then, our patient said he wanted water so Soren got the nurse to sponge his lips.

I think about my own accident twenty years ago. The cards and visits from people I barely knew or didn't know elevated my recovery. So many people cared. And isn't that one of the greatest desires of life — to be cared for? Care is an expression of love. One of the readings at church today spoke to me: "…Whoever does not love, does not know God, for God is love…" I didn't get that before, but I get it now. God and love are inseparable. When I feel and experience acts of love, I feel and experience God. God is everywhere.

DAY 68. It's lunchtime at Kentfield. A nurse says, "Steve is tired and hungry from his drive to Stanford."

Confused, I ask, "Why did he go there and how come no one told me about it?" A couple of weeks ago Stanford informed me about automatic follow-up appointments scheduled for Steve. After doing research, I deemed them unnecessary and canceled.

You can imagine my shock and irritation upon hearing Steve traveled two hours one-way via ambulance to Stanford, only to find out his appointment had been canceled a week prior! By the time Steve returned to Kentfield, he was bonking — famished and somewhat delirious, shaking, and weak. Normally this occurs during or after intense exercise without proper nutrition. Steve missed his morning feed since they spontaneously hurried him onto the ambulance to make the 8am appointment sixty miles away. Since Steve had to endure a four-hour bumpy round-trip ambulance ride, that was considered exercise! When I first saw Steve at twelve noon today, he told us he was hungry, which we temporarily dismissed, not knowing what happened. I feel horrible about that.

While waiting for lunch, we have a big surprise for Steve. We wheel him outside to see someone very special, someone he hasn't seen in two months. We can hardly wait for this magical reunion. Steve is seeing our labradoodle, Millie, for the first time. But there is a problem we never could have anticipated: Millie does not recognize Steve.

This exchange is a bitter reminder of why I need to have zero expectations. I confidently assumed this exchange would be transformative for them both. Millie would leap into Steve's arms, lick him all over — reunited at last! She would wash away his pain and he'd respond to her with healing emotion. Instead, Steve instantly realizes that Millie doesn't recognize him, and his response is heartbreaking. He looks sadder than I have seen him look the past 68 days.

Millie's dog breeder Shanti explains that Steve's face, hair, body and clothes look different; he's also in a wheelchair and smells different. There is nothing Millie can latch onto to recognize her favorite person in the world. This is one of the most disappointing moments of the recovery for me and the kids.

Steve whispers he is hungry, so we wheel him to his room, while Aria and Shanti stay with Millie. We work with Steve's speech therapist to feed him. Steve savors his first banana, sweet potato puree, water, and juice. Once I get organized, juice will be eliminated from his diet, unless it's fresh and unsweetened. We start with baby food consistency, following instructions plastered on the wall. Each chew and swallow is carefully witnessed.

Nurse Jay is setting up Steve's tube feed as we simultaneously mouth feed him. Despite this concerted effort to satisfy his hunger, Steve looks visibly irritated. He even grabs the fork to feed himself, and complains, "This guy's fucking slow!" It takes us a moment to process his comment before we all start laughing. This is the first time Steve has said a swear word but it's a pivotal comment because he sounded like himself.

After dinner, we return to Steve's room and find our friends

Ron, Cherie, and Mark bedside. Ron and Cherie are some of our oldest San Francisco friends, while Mark is our former neighbor and Salesforce colleague of Steve's. Ron, once a cyclist and now an ultra-marathon runner, responds to my playful request to "sell" Steve on the joys of running. Cherie, Ron's wife, shares a touching moment: when they were praising Steve for his incredible recovery, he contemplatively replied, "You have been part of it."

The room gets loud and Steve pleads, "You all leave. Mark can stay." I was half expecting Steve to unlock the mystery of life. Instead, what he unlocks is power over his environment. He's self-sourcing solutions for his recovery. While enjoying more un-expected milestones today, Beth from CPMC calls to say Steve is approved for rehab.

DAY 69. Payton and I are with Steve having our first back-and-forth conversation with him in sixty-nine days. I am proud of us both; this is not easy. I can see Payton as a psychiatrist. He may already be Steve's.

I say, "I'm sorry I missed lunch and you ate hospital food."

Steve replies, "That's bullshit that you're late."

Payton and I commiserate about Steve's misery stemming from lack of sleep, loud noises, bright lights, and pain. He's in a triple room with two other loud roommates. It looks like an orphanage and sounds like a roller rink.

"Do you feel anything good, Dad?" Payton asks.

Steve barks, "No."

Payton reaches: "Do you feel like you're getting better?"

"No."

I say, "You were at Stanford for forty-one days. You have

come so far. It's because you're a winner and you're a miracle!"

Payton follows my lead. "What are you, Dad?"

"I'm bullshit."

Payton responds, "*That's* bullshit, but *you* are not. Tell me who you are, Dad."

Steve plays along. "I'm a winner."

Payton says, "Yes! Are you a fighter?"

"I'm a fighter."

I suggest to Steve, "Say 'I'm a miracle.'"

Steve obeys: "I'm a miracle."

I offer, "You really are all those things, Steve. You are amazing and don't you forget it. You've come this far. You've done the hard work. And it's going to get harder. But that's what you're made for — hard work. Did you get to the World Cup by sitting on your ass?"

Steve interrupts with a raging fire in his eyes. "It's bullshit! THIS is bullshit!"

I admit, "Yes, all of this is bullshit. It's not fair that you have to sit here and suffer. But I'm here and Payton's here —"

He snaps, "*You're* bullshit!"

"Yes. I'm bullshit because I'm sitting here and I'm not in pain. We're all bullshit. But we're going to help you. We're going to take care of you."

Payton says, "We're going to do everything we can. Okay? You're going to fight—"

Steve interrupts Payton and says to his face, "You too. You are bullshit."

Payton doesn't flinch. "Dad, we're doing everything we can. We're going to get you out of here. Say, 'I'm going to be okay.'"

"I'm going to be okay."

Payton elaborates. "It's not negotiable. You're going to come back here when you're all better and you're going to thank everyone. You know that, right? Even though it's bullshit."

"Yes."

I ask, "Do you know what happened to you?"

"Yes. Bullshit."

"That's right. Bullshit happened to you and we're going to get bullshit. And, bullshit is going to pay. Okay?"

Steve fires off, "Bullshit!" then looks at his son and mutters, "Just shoot me." Payton's face falls.

Nurse Danny comes in and asks, "How is your pain, Steve?"

Steve angrily responds, "It's bullshit. It sucks." Danny asks if Steve wants Tylenol; I tell Danny that Tylenol is not going to cut it. We ask Steve if he wants something strong that will put him to sleep. He nods yes, but his eyebrows furrow as he clenches his jaw. He starts kicking Payton who says, "Dad, you're going to be okay." I plead with Steve to not hurt his son.

Steve angrily replies, "Show me! Prove it to me!"

I say, "We're all proving it to you. You are right here, living and breathing. When they found you on the road, do you know who kept you alive? Your cycling friends and medical professionals, Otis and Alexis. And when the ambulance arrived, they took you to Marin General and they saved your life again. They had to resuscitate you all day long. You have other peoples' blood running through your veins."

In reply Steve grimaces and starts kicking his poor son again. I shout, begging Steve not to hurt our boy, but Payton is unfazed and refuses to move away from his Dad. Steve screams, "I'm annoyed with you. Fuck you. Show me! Show me! Show me! Help me! Help me!"

Payton responds heatedly. "Show you that you're going to be okay? That's up to you! Do you care about us, Dad? Do you care about me? Do you care about mom?"

Steve whispers, "I care about you."

Payton snaps back: "Then you're going to do the hard work and you're going to get better, because you're going to help yourself, Dad."

"Show me," Steve begs.

Payton zeroes in: "All these other people — they're bullshit, right? This is up to you, right? Tell me, Dad!"

"This is up to me," Steve professes.

Payton begs, "Yeah. It's up to you. You're going to help yourself get better. I know you're pissed. Use that to help yourself. Will you try?"

Steve nods in agreement.

I chime in, "Steve, your anger is normal. Getting angry is part of your recovery, but Payton is saying use your anger to heal yourself, okay? Are you meditating? When you feel the anger, close your eyes and take a deep breath."

In the most endearing way imaginable, Steve tries to meditate. He grits his teeth, raises his eyebrows, crinkles his nose, and breathes deeply while snorting. He looks like a child trying to smile for the camera. For a moment he relaxes, looking peaceful, and then explodes like the Incredible Hulk. His face actually turns greenish and he yells in his raspy whisper, "You guys are annoying me. Fuck yeah!"

I ask, "Do you mean you want us to leave?"

"Yeah."

"Okay. We're leaving." It was a thirty-minute visit, a new speed record. The Bullshit Wife and Son are out.

Personally I don't feel too bothered by this afternoon's bullshit session, but it pains me to see Steve hurt Payton. Sadly, we'll have to get guidance on angry TBI outbursts and how to protect ourselves. I never could have imagined my life this way.

After meeting with Steve's doctor, I get him transferred to his fourth room at Kentfield. Pastor Kim is here. When I tell her about this afternoon's outburst, she bravely cuts to the chase. "You're mad at God, aren't you, Steve?" This leads to the ultimate show of anger. Steve F-bombs God himself. Who could blame him? Pastor Kim dives straight into Steve's fears, heartbreak and anger. He asks her, "What's it all for?"

She answers, "We don't know. This is your journey."

After Pastor Kim leaves, Steve happily whispers, "This is awesome." I'm stunned. This is the same, desperate, angry man who told his young son to "just shoot me." Will our family be on a permanent roller coaster the rest of our lives?

My friend Kelly is here to whisk Aria away with her daughter Lucy, one of Aria's closest friends. We met after their family bought one of the houses I remodeled. Kelly is that dear friend who stayed by my side at both Marin General and Stanford Hospitals, even sleeping next to me that first fateful night. We talk about how I have a greater appreciation for people with mental challenges. Kelly talks about her sister Jayme, who has an adult child with special needs. Kelly reflects, "Jayme has the richest heart because it's always softened. Her heart is always breaking. People like my niece, who are pure, teach us that we are all one, big, imperfect, human family."

As soon as Kelly walks out the door I see an email from Robin, the woman who recounted a turning point in her life through a chance encounter with Steve, twenty-five years ago. Robin and Kelly, two women who've never met, express the same idea to me at the same time. Plus, Robin's email contains the "proof" Steve begged us to show him during his earlier outburst at the hospital.

Dearest Jenna,   *June 27, 2017*

I experienced something today that reminded me of the incredible and undeniable connection of our human family, and the ways in which we are joined at times we need it most.

My family is vacationing in Bar Harbor, Maine, an entire country's journey from you and yours. Today, my family made a spur of the moment decision to go to a beach a few miles away from where we are staying. The kids chose a specific area on this stretch of shore to look for flat, smooth rocks to take home. This area contained thousands of such stones.

We walked and picked up various rocks for several minutes. Suddenly, my 6-year-old daughter Allie exclaimed, "Look, mama! This rock has something written on it!" What I saw took my breath away. Written on this rock, nestled among thousands of other rocks, was "Jenna. CA." I couldn't deny what my heart told me- that this was a sign, a reminder that although you are there and I am here, so many thousands of miles apart, you are in my heart.

I talked to my daughter about Steve and what a force Steve is. She asked a million questions and offered the most innocent and powerful statement: "Mommy, if Mr. Steve is that strong, he will get better."

Better. A relative term. Something that means different things in different

circumstances. But still, better. And better still. Keep the faith. My continued love to you and yours, Jenna.
  Robin

And there is your proof, my darling Steve. All you have to do is ask.

CHAPTER 15

Knockin' On Heaven's Door

D**AY 70.** I tell the blog, "I found Amber. Steve repeatedly talks about Amber telling him how to come back to life. After days of searching, I deduce she is Steve's guardian angel!"

Steve is irritated, speaking in Tagalog to his aunt, Tita. He says, "This place sucks." Since he's scheduled to leave tomorrow, we reply, "Okay. No problem. We'll leave tomorrow." He nods in agreement. Cockily I reply, "See, Steve, we are taking care of you."

Steve is partially eating on his own, feeding himself the food I prepared — scrambled eggs, pureed veggies and Payton's berry compote sans sugar, of course. He's drinking Can-Can juices and mashed sweet potato. When asked which food he likes best he whispers, "Teresa"— the name of our former next-door neighbor and the owner of Can-Can.

For weeks after the accident, my stomach was in knots and I couldn't eat. My friend Teresa saved me with her Can-Can juices. When researching traumatic brain injury, I happened to discover that Teresa's "Brain Juice," which is essentially beet juice, an incredibly healing vegetable for the brain, is recommended for TBI patients. I will be her biggest client when Steve can start drinking!

Food can be medicinal for healing and I can't wait to learn about the best food for Steve's healing brain.

I'm building my earth-side team, which includes TBI nutritionist Carol McDonnell to help with recipes and supplementation. I allow Steve to eat chicken and mashed potatoes from the hospital during lunch but that's it. I was livid about the sugar they were trying to feed him — three fruit juices made from concentrate, processed fruit with preservatives and sugar, and ice cream! And if that's not enough, Steve's feed tube at Stanford was full of corn syrup.

I tell Steve the story of his accident again. He forgets it every day. Since becoming conscious, I have been curious to ask Steve about the afterlife but have needed to take my time because of how easily he gets overstimulated. Carefully I ask, "Steve, did you go to heaven?"

He responds, "Yes."

"What did God say to you?"

Steve replies, "Wake up."

"Did you talk to Amber?"

"Yes."

I wonder: "What did she say to you?"

"Jenna needs you."

"Did you speak to Papa Jerry?"

"Yes."

"What did your grandfather say to you?"

"Jenna could use the help."

While taking notes on our conversation about people Steve met on the other side, I asked Tita to spell Papa Jerry and guess who answered the question?

DAY 71. Steve rolls into CPMC's North Tower from Kentfield. He asks, "Why is this place the best?"

I reply, "You will soon find out. But check out the stylish hotel vibe." It feels spa-like, peaceful and tranquil with a modern design. There is a huge mirror for Steve to look at himself and say, "I look good! You'd never know I've been in the hospital for seventy days!" Spending the night here would feel like a date night. It's like the Four Seasons.

Settling Steve in, I serve homemade lentil soup and berry compote. My friend Kelly arrives with two delicious brain salads — sweet potato and kale, and watermelon, kale and coconut. Having dropped down to 146 pounds from 180, I am thankful Steve eats all his food.

Caring for Steve is joyful. He's a sweet soul, regardless of the bullshit that arises as his brain is trying to reconnect. That's why feeding him whole, nutritious, organic food is important. No sugar. No gluten. Nothing processed. For twelve weeks, no nuts and grains, while I detoxify the feed tube crap. I am rebuilding his gut and sending powerhouse vitamins and minerals to his brain. I don't want anything inflaming his brain or gut. We need every ounce of healing energy we can send him. His baseline is shockingly low. There is no room for error.

He receives breakfast, lunch and dinner menus that I select. I circle fresh fruit, salmon, vegetable soup, veggies. I doubt that it's organic, which is important for brain healing. I will be sup-plementing and substituting until his nutrition is dialed in. I'm waiting for the TBI nutritionist's "food prescription."

I say, "Let's pretend we're on vacation, Steve." He agrees. The physical space impacts his mental outlook, especially as his awareness increases. He complained a lot about the noise at Kentfield and the crowded feeling of roommates. This place is quiet.

Steve's speech therapist John introduces himself just as I am breaking the eating rules. After watching Steve eat a peach, John removes the mushy food restrictions on Steve's diet protocol. Just like that, Steve is crushing milestones!

When John asks Steve where he is, he responds, "In my kind of place." We chuckle.

I say, "Yes, Steve — especially when you hit the gym!" I forgot to bring Steve's street clothes. It dawns on me that Steve wears glasses.

John asks Steve if he has any religious preferences. Steve nods, "I'm Jewish." I laugh. Over the years Steve has been Catholic, Episcopalian and recently Methodist. Between my Jewish baker son and my now-Jewish husband, I feel a calling.

Speaking of religion, we have received blessings from a wide range of faiths. Rachel placed our written prayers in the cracks of the Western Wall in Jerusalem. Mary had a hundred candles lit at a nunnery in Tibet and brought his highest holiness llama to bless Steve. The Filipinos have the Catholics covered. The Christians, in general, have represented. Of course, we have direct access to the Methodists.

As I'm leaving, a Rabbi enters. I ask, "Are you here to see Steve?"

He replies, "Yes, I'm the chaplain." Of course!

Day 71. I am handed a hard dose of reality by the hospital staff — Steve is over-stimulated. No visitors until further notice. The kids and I are highly restricted too. We are allowed fifteen minutes on;

thirty minutes off. Soft, quiet, simple voices. I remove everything from the walls except one photo collage for low stim mode.

I learned that if a loving couple has a problem in their relationship, it's because one or both of them hasn't "done the work." The "work" is confronting issues of your past, including your childhood, that you carry into your present life. Any unresolved negative energy is manifested through pain, anger, fear, sadness. You unconsciously inflict this negative energy onto others. Typically, this negative energy emerges at the wrong time with your significant other. When this happens, the energy can balloon into a tirade of insults, empty promises, threats, and put-downs. We've all been there.

Steve has spent his adult life "doing the work," and occasionally asked me why I wasn't doing mine. My stock response: "I'm too busy to read 'self-help' books. It must be nice to have time to work on yourself."

Well, I'm doing my work now. Before the accident, I was not focused on my purpose. Now, I have an overwhelming sense of purpose to help people. I don't know what I am going to do but I'm working on it. Right now, I have a powerful impulse to write. Reminded that our family visitation is restricted, I realize that I can write during the day instead of at night. At the exact moment I crave more writing time, God delivers.

I answer a phone call from Leslie in Steve's room, which I learn is inappropriate, but today I had to.

Steve lovingly asks Leslie, "What can I do to help you?"

She replies, "There is nothing to do, Steve. You're already helping."

I ask Steve if he saw God in heaven.

He says, "Yes."

I ask, "What did God say?"

Steve says, "God told me I am going to get better."

I inquire, "What did Amber say?"

Steve explains, "She's helping me get better."

I ask Steve, "Do you remember talking to Meghan?" (Meghan is the Bowen therapist whom Steve's spirit talked to on the first few nights at Stanford and his spirit continues to talk with her to this day).

Steve says, "Yes. Meghan told me that I need to be there for Jenna and the kids."

I add: "Do you remember returning to your body? There was a rope you climbed down?"

He says, "Yes."

I ask, "What did you do with the rope, Steve?"

"I climbed down the rope and went into my body."

"Which way did you go into your body?"

"I went with my head down."

"Then what did you do?"

"I turned around."

"Why did you go face-down into your body, Steve?"

"I wanted to see her?"

"See whom?"

"I wanted to see Meghan."

"Why did you turn around again?"

"I wanted to see everybody in the room."

I already know from Meghan that Steve's soul still talks to her but he confirmed that too. Meghan hasn't physically seen Steve since day two at Stanford when he was in a coma. They talk to each other in the spirit world only.

The vision Meghan saw of Steve climbing back into his body occurred on Saturday, April 22, 2017 — the day after the accident. Meghan said, "Steve has continued to talk to us. Steve says this is hard, not like he was giving up, but just stating the facts. Saturday night, if you imagine facing his hospital bed, on the left there was a rope with knots every couple of feet. The rope was hanging from the sky and Steve climbed down. He entered his body, but he insisted on entering it face first, even though he is lying face up in the hospital bed. It was as if he hugged his whole body once inside and then he flipped over so he matched the presentation. I asked him why he did that and he repeated the motion."

DAY 73. To help Steve feel confident in his healing, we identify five things to focus on so he feels in control: Sleep. Work hard during therapy. Eat healthily. Focus the mind (that was Steve's, of course). Breathe when scared.

For dinner, he has sweet potato and ginger soup and zucchini basil soup, along with almond milk and mixed berry compote. For "dessert" Steve eats chia seeds and blueberries with banana. Time to fatten him up without sugar. While feeding Steve beet juice, I alert his sitter that his bowel movements will be pink tomorrow, so don't freak out.

I ask Steve, "What was heaven like?"

Steve smiles. "It was full of good food."

"What did you say to God?"

"Protect my kids."

"What did God say?"

"God said, 'You bet.'"

Curious, I ask, "What did Amber say?"

"You have the wind with you."

I wonder, "What did Meghan want you to do?"

Steve replies, "Let people know."

This jogs a memory of my own. This morning, I spoke to Meghan about her past conversations with Steve's soul. One of the days Meghan performed remote Bowen Therapy she urged Steve "to let people know you are in there!" Those were her exact words to me this morning, long before I saw Steve today. And, four hours after that remote treatment back in June, I texted Meghan, "Steve spoke!" I can't make this up! I wonder how much of Steve's healing is happening on the spirit plane and how much is happening here on Earth? Or is it integrated?

I leave the room to get more food. While gone, the sitter says she's going to start eating healthy too, asking Steve about his food. I return, and eagerly ask Steve, "What is God like?"

"God is forgiving. He is peaceful."

"What does God look like?"

"He looks like cousin Mark."

"Do you love God?"

Steve tenderly says, "Yes. I love every bit of God. I want to record every moment with God."

"What did you tell God?"

"I told him he's doing a great job."

"What else did you tell God?"

"I told him not to lose interest in us."

Something occurs to me that must be said. "Steve, I know you could have stayed with God. Thank you for coming back."

"Thanks for having me."

"I know it's hard. Everything is hard, isn't it? It's worth it because you are getting better. You were badly hurt. You were in a coma. It's not like the movies when you wake up and say, 'Where am I?' It's a slow awakening. Are you happy to be back?"

"Yeah. I love my family."

"We love you more than anything. And we'll do whatever it takes because we are so happy to have you."

"Payton and Aria?"

"Absolutely. When you got hurt, they were devastated. They cried and cried. Payton dropped out of school, stopped talking to his friends. They were so sad. Does your eye hurt?"

"I can't see."

"We'll get it looked at. What city are we in now?"

"Palo Alto."

"No, we are in San Francisco. You are an awesome eater, Steve! Let's finish the beet juice. I hope you're full."

"I am. I am full of pink poo."

CHAPTER 16

Low Stim

DAY 74. I read something powerful on the blog the other day: "I feel sorry for people who don't receive the gift of pain." My gift came on April 21, 2017. Before Steve's accident, I had a pain-free life. When hit by a bus years ago, I was more grateful than hurt. When I used to imagine Steve getting catastrophically hurt cycling, I thought my reaction and reality would be far worse than it has been. I pictured myself overflowing with anger, spiraling into the coulda-woulda-shoulda's, unable to get out of bed, feeling isolated and alone. My reality has been just the opposite.

Rachel insists, "Without losing everything, we appreciate nothing." Certainly losing everything evokes gut-wrenching pain. She too knows the contrast between the good life and pain. My wise friend Kerry, a poet and writer, says, "We need to suffer to break through life." She paraphrases St. Francis of Assisi: "If we knew the gifts of pain, we would beg for it."

I used to think that the "hard work" of rehab was all physical effort. I pictured the body being pushed to sweat in the gym, walking with the aid of pulleys hanging from the ceiling. I didn't contemplate the mental anguish. As Steve's mind awakens, so do his tender emotions. The emotional ups-and-downs are difficult for everyone. Referring to the restricted visitation, Payton says, "Just when we felt like we got Dad back, we can't get to him anymore."

Sitting in the hospital lounge, I hear a faint whimper in the room next door. A reassuring voice is followed by more soft weeping. Payton and I both make sad faces. I want to hug the woman crying. I overhear her saying, "I can't do it anymore."

It's been a half-hour, and I am walking back to Steve. I see the crying woman in her wheelchair leaving. As I start to connect with her, I see a faint smile emerge. I comment, "You're doing a great job. This is not easy. Look at your smile."

She grins wider and says, "Thank you."

Steve lets me snuggle with him, repeatedly asking how we know he's getting better. I reassure him, "Just breathe."

Then he says, "I wish I died." My heart dissolves onto the floor. I want to sink into the earth and for all of this to disappear. It's too much but I have to be strong for Steve.

"Why do you wish you died, Steve?"

"Because it's easier. This is so hard…"

I acknowledge that it's hard now, but every day he's improving.

He frowns, "How do you know?" Full circle again. It's time to reduce the stimulation, but difficult leaving on that bitter comment. Steve repeats the challenge and I feel sunken. Even as I type this, my fingers feel numb and weak. Just yesterday, Steve said he loves us and is glad he survived. I know this is the cycle of TBI but it's hard for me too. Steve asks several times, "Do they know how hard this is?"

I question, "Does who know?"

"Everyone."

"Yes, everyone knows. It's why they bring us food, donate to our family, help with the kids and the house. We are so blessed." But I wonder if I actually know how hard this is for Steve?

An image Meghan saw of Steve before doctors told us he survived flashes in my mind. Steve was lying on his bed completely healed, repeatedly flip-flopping his body, back and forth. Meghan didn't know what to make of it but I did. Steve couldn't make up his mind. He was a classic flip-flopper on Earth. He carried that character trait to the afterlife.

Although my friends say that pain is life and life is not really lived without it, I could use a little less pain right now as I'm driving home. I text my friend Sara, who's visiting from Minnesota, about Steve wishing he died and she responds, "Oh Jenna. Heartbreaking. Don't come tonight. Let's catch up later." I hit traffic feeling sorry for myself and then something hits me — where is Steve's cell phone?

His phone contains pictures and videos of the past seventy-two days and although those images are supposedly in the cloud, I do not know this for sure. I tear into Payton, who was gaming on the phone. The bad mom in me is raging. There's one more exit before the bridge, we're crawling in traffic and Payton cannot remember the last place he saw the phone. I shout, "Call CPMC! Now!"

We screech back to the hospital. Payton bolts out of the car. I gun it to park. As I'm walking toward the building, my cell phone rings. Phew — it's Steve's number. I answer and hear something I haven't heard in over two months: Steve speaking on the phone. How clever of Payton. He knows exactly what to do to bring me out of my spin.

I enter the hospital room. Payton has a huge smile on his face. We get one more tender moment with Steve, who looks wiped but content. In those few moments of a second goodbye, I am reassured and the weight of those words an hour ago lifts. Suddenly I am no longer tired and the traffic lightens for our second drive home. I call Sara, "I'm coming, thanks to yet another miracle in my life."

I pick up Aria and ask, "Do you want to go to the fair?"

Aria smiles, "Yes! But I don't have anyone to go on the rides with." I tell her I am meeting two old friends who both have eleven-year-old daughters. And, just like that, I'm back on track.

My friend Sara is visiting with her new husband Greg and their three children. She meets up with our old friends JJ and Kerry and their two kids. It is great to see them all and give Aria a dose of good old-fashioned summer fun. I meet Greg for the first time. Thank goodness he reminds me of his profession. How could I forget? Greg is a skilled rehab psychologist for TBI patients.

Greg confirms what Sara said — that he can cut to the chase with me like we've known each other for years. Then he tells me what I need to hear. "Low stim, low stim, low stim." That's what Steve needs. Then we process what I need, and I realize I've been selfish. I've been needing my husband but that's not in his best interest. Steve's therapists repeatedly say he does better when I'm around. So I can be around him, but I should hardly speak! I'm going to try just breathing around my beloved, and save the voices for my head. Greg asks, "Is there another way to get your Steve fix?" Maybe I can talk to him like Bowen Meghan does — in the clouds?

Kerry relates that she has a friend who works with TBI

pa-tients. Her facility puts brain-injured patients in a dark room with no noise and no visitors. After Kerry gets that off her chest, she talks to me about me. She is so wise about all I am experiencing. And she speaks about the last time she and JJ saw Steve — a month before the accident.

Kerry says Steve revealed so much to them in the brief encounter they had at the mall. It was related to his searching. We really are called to the moments in our lives. Everything is always as it should be — even horrible events like this. When you remove the barriers to opening up your heart, the essence of life becomes clear. I speak to Kerry about my experiences with this, starting day one of this tragedy.

God Translator Sara takes her turn, paraphrasing a theologian who said, "If you put the world between yourself and God, you see pain and suffering — a big mess. If you put God between yourself and the world, you see beauty." Tonight these friends are showing me how to see beauty again.

Aria appreciates the gift of one more "real" summer night from the county fair, adding it to her thin collection of summer 2017 memories. She says, "I liked meeting your friends' kids tonight. They were all nice and I really got along with Naomi. At first, when I meet people, I'm kind of shy. When we get to know each other, and I have a friend, it's actually pretty easy."

After eating cotton kale, and slipping down the coconut oil slide which ruins my pants but makes my skin feel silky smooth, Aria and I hop in our electric convertible. We drive home barefoot, singing about our connections to people, as a balmy breeze blows our stiff, coconut-oiled hair. We slurp the last bit of chia seed kombucha from our compost cup. Life is good.

CHAPTER 17

The Voice That Doesn't Use Words

THE FOURTH OF JULY was full of mystical moments, as my blissed-out running streak continues. Each morning, I awaken to a blessing and every evening I retire with one, with countless gifts from God in between. Quite often, these blessings are jaw-dropping blowouts. This may sound crazy, but it feels like my new normal.

When I'm confused by why we have received so many blessings during this horrific time, I remember the boomerang effect that yoga teacher Anna taught me. By sending love into the Universe, instead of anger, we receive joy in return — it boomerangs back to us. I experience the boomerang effect because I don't have negativity in my heart. I am amazed that for the past two months I have not encountered a single negative person or witnessed an unsettling act.

The same effect seems to apply to Steve. He is receiving attentive care at CPMC. I am sure they treat every single person the same, but I see how the nurses look into Steve's eyes and react when he says *Salamat* ("thank you" in Tagalog) for the hundredth time. Steve always expresses the deepest and sincerest gratitude for his caretakers. I brought this up with the attending Dr. Rome and his crew of therapists and nurses. Dr. Rome replied, "Maybe Steve's a good guy and this is the inside coming out?" That we know is true. The good guy, Steve, is boomeranging goodness all around.

DAY 75. Besides the return of Steve's kindness, he's walking better each day — with assistance, of course. And, for the first time in 74 days he showered, using a shower wheelchair. That's why he has wild, fluffy hair.

Steve falls asleep right after lunch; the shower exhausted him. As soon as he wakes up, he has therapy and after that, it's time to go. I give Steve beet juice with fish oil, say a few words and pack up. I say, "I have to leave to take Payton to CrossFit."

Steve asks, "What's he doing in CrossFit?" I look at Payton, shrugging my shoulders.

Steve answers his own question: "He's manning up."

The phase we are in now is "sitting quietly," bringing the gift of listening and communicating from inside. Bowen Meghan reminds me of this when she sends me a powerful quote from Rumi, Steve's favorite poet: "There is a voice that doesn't use words. Listen."

DAY 77. I place my hand on Steve's leg but he brushes it off. I get it. I thank him for showing me it's too much. It's like he's in a coma again. He's right there in front of me but I can't reach him. I spend twenty minutes with Steve today so he can sleep. As he becomes more verbal, he says things that are difficult to hear — mostly about wishing he had died. Since I can no longer sleep off those painful words by snuggling with him, it's harder for them to melt away.

After 18 years living in San Francisco, in February 2016 Steve tricked me into moving to Mill Valley. I was kicking and screaming, "It's snobby…. People in the suburbs are boring…. I'll lose my city edge." Who was I kidding? What "city edge"?

Steve loves Mill Valley. He has hundreds of pictures of bike rides on Mt. Tam, his holy land. There are even images of Steve riding with business partners during his infamous *"Salesforce Executive Summit Ride"* in October 2016. Somehow, Steve merged cycling with work. His video advertisement for this business event brings me to tears. There are only a few words sprinkled in the ad, but the statements at the end reflect the essence of Steve: "Life is about the people you meet. Feel like a kid again."

Mill Valley quickly grew on me as the fears in my head un-raveled themselves one-by-one. In fact, our family is surviving this tragedy because we moved to Mill Valley. It produced a world of healers and lifelong friends I never would have met otherwise. Out-of-town family members are in awe of how well we are cared for by our locals. They name our hometown Wonderland.

DAY 78. During therapy, I suggest Steve do the "half tortoise" yoga pose — the greatest anti-anxiety asana. Too bad it requires two fully functioning arms, which Steve does not have. As soon as I demo the pose, I feel terrible suggesting it. Naturally, Steve scoffs at me, but in diehard athletic form, does not quit. Devoid of arm support to brace his fall, Steve collapses into the pose, plopping his head smack onto the mat.

When I look at Steve, I see more of him than I used to, which surprises me. Witnessing this rebirth shows how many nuanced layers there are to a person. Recognizing daily, subtle changes requires patience with the slow process, rather than dwelling on disappointments. When that process seems dark or negative, I tie it to the positive. "The darkest hour is just before dawn" is one of Steve's favorite quotes. Reducing stimuli has produced results. The therapists see progress, but my determined husband is hard on himself, thinking the improvements are small.

I am in a habitual state of wonder and curiosity about the gifts I receive while being simultaneously drenched in pain. Most importantly, I remind myself to take everything as nothing more than the present, whether it's good or bad. As I told my friend Kerry, I've never been happier and sadder in my whole life. While suffering, the Light continues to flow alongside the darkness.

Aria asks who her dad will be when the dust settles. I tell her the truth: he will be different. Upset, she wants the dad she knows and loves. I explain that all of us are changing, and we are falling in love with each other all over again, especially with Steve. Payton remarks, "Dad is the cutest special needs person ever." Even still, change is hard and I actively dig deep to find the good buried in the rubble.

Kerry shares, "When the heart cracks open, God squeezes in." When my heart shattered in a million pieces on April 21, 2017, that wasn't easy and it certainly wasn't the change I was looking for in my life. But it was my lot and I accepted it. Look who squeezed right in.

Day 79. Aria and I arrive at the North Tower as the last EMT leaves. Steve's sitter Ivonne tells me Steve was the "perfect patient," after making sure I approved his surgery, which was down the street.

The Greenfield filter, inserted at Stanford in response to a blood clot in Steve's leg, was removed today. Steve's blood thinners are doing the job the filter did.

Steve is starving. We give him Kristine's leftover pork loin with brussel sprouts, sweet potato, and pancetta; loads of mixed veggies; tomato with avocado salad; chia seeds with Ron's mixed berries and a date-cocoa paste mixed in; plus, carrot and ginger soup. Aria feeds Steve while I chop, mix and dice other items out of sight. I'm the wizard behind the curtain concocting Steve's brain food. Each time he eats, Steve sets his intention: "I want to be sure I am eating the right food. Will this make me better?" He reminds me to think about every morsel of food I provide. I focus on animal fats (meat), fish, healthy fats (avocado, olive, and coconut oils), vegetables and fruits, and eggs. I don't give him fillers like rice. I offer sweet potato over russet. I am learning as I go.

Steve says, "I'll eat whatever Aria gives me. She is a love." Aria melts. He adds, "I love you, Aria. Come lay down with me." Steve opens his arm for Aria to nestle her head.

She beams, "It's just like old times, Daddy. This is how you snuggled with me before the accident."

Payton and I are arguing about CrossFit. He wants to work out six days a week. I tell my friend Sara, who is visiting from Minnesota, that I can't meet up today because I have to take Payton to "Stations of the CrossFit." Sara laughs as hard as I do at that Catholic joke. Thankfully, Pastor Norma Jean kindly gives Payton a ride instead. Payton complains, "Why do you go to yoga every day but I can't go to CrossFit every day?" This is the age-old argument Steve and I had when the kids were little. It's yoga versus biking reborn and another reminder Payton is now subbing for Steve.

Sara faced her darkest hour when her two-year-old son was diagnosed with cancer. He is a fully recovered teenager now. When Sara wore her "Fuck Cancer" T-shirt, I imagine people felt squeamish. Now I get it. By swearing at God, we dig deep and scream out loud that suffering hurts, bearing the ultimate question — "why me?" When we look at *why* square in the eyes, we find the answer. It's linked to our purpose. The answer reveals itself when we surrender to the pain and trust the path to peace.

At first, much of my sadness stemmed from watching my children in agony. Since I've learned pain is connected to joy, which creates a meaningful and purposeful life, I can better handle their suffering. Unfortunately, I can't explain this to my kids; they're too young. Hopefully, they witness my core beliefs through my actions and will evolve along their own path becoming rock solid adults.

Am I turning into one of those "God people" who won't shut up? When Steve comes back home and life simmers down, am I going to be that person you avoid at parties or at the grocery store? I can't answer that but I know this. I haven't found God; God found me. He was inside me the entire time, just waiting to be known.

I receive my first voicemail message from Steve eighty days post-accident. "Jenna. It's… it's… it's your husband, Steve. I want to check that we are bringing the right food for me. I'm hungry for fresh vegetables. You talked to *Ate* about this yesterday and that's what I want." The Filipino term *Ate* (pronounced "ah-teh") refers to an older female relative or respected friend, especially one's own sister. Steve refers to all his female nurses as his *ates* and all the men as his *kuyas* — the same meaning for males. He does this regardless of their age. To him, everyone caring for him is a respected elder. It's so sweet and helps me feel better about leaving him each day. He's with caregivers he feels are his family.

We arrive at the North Tower with bags of fresh food. Steve greets us in rare form, telling tall tales. He is convincing and beaming with personality, so we enjoy the lies. He's so animated, I contemplate if some of this is true? Steve describes eating green beets with his brother at a baseball game. "Is the game in Texas?" I ask.

Steve replies, "No. It was in Austin." He says the green beets were prepared by his aunt, and tasted nasty! Steve goes on and on, erupting into fits of laughter. This is the first time I've seen Steve laugh since the accident! After talking for forty-five minutes, Steve yawns. Time to roll out. We draw the blinds and thank him for the entertainment. Steve says, "The best part about this injury is all the time I get to spend with my kids."

DAY 81. I went to the grocery store for the first time in eighty days. That's how well cared for we've been. We arrive at the hospital late; I'm worried that Steve ate two meals without my intervention. Nurse Daisy says, "He ate his entire container of beets! He also ate his zucchini soup, salmon, and a smoothie." I had days' worth of beets in that container. I am happy to pick up my week's supply of beet juice later from Teresa. Roasting and chopping beets is time consuming and something always gets stained! I am thrilled Daisy took the initiative to serve my homemade food. This is a sign I don't have to do it all.

Steve still draws blanks about what happened to him, where he is, what year and month it is, where he lives. He confuses dreams with reality. On the other hand, his intuition is fierce. Steve reads

Payton's facial expressions for "the truth." When Payton tasted my carrot ginger soup yesterday, Steve instantly knew he didn't like it, even though it wasn't obvious to me.

We show Steve photos, asking him to name people. He eventually gets them all. We mention our dog Millie. Steve says, "I'm going through a dog-ship right now. It's hard. I'm told what to do, where to be and what to wear. It's hard, this dog-ship." What an interesting concept — a "dog-ship!" It makes sense that he feels like a dog. When he was emerging from the coma, he reminded me of our dog, Millie. Although he couldn't communicate, I sensed he understood what we were saying and loved us. Now Steve compares his state of being to a dog.

Steve elaborates: "I'm a baby right now. Ask me anything. I'm like a kid with time." He says things aren't quite right with the kids and compares that to being a child. How introspective — just like old times. A nurse comes in and asks Steve how he is feeling on the pain scale. He says, "Ten."

The nurse replies, "You'd be screaming if you were a ten." Steve clears his throat, preparing to scream. The nurse reacts, "Don't scream! I'll get you some medicine."

Steve muses, "It's hard for you to know what I'm going through. It doesn't seem normal. I need you to know it's hard. I'm not sure I'm going to make it."

I offer, "You've already made it. It's normal to feel uncertain because you were so badly hurt." I explain the accident again and I ask if he still likes biking.

His heart beams across the room. "I love biking."

"The doctors say you cannot hit your head again."

"I promise, I will never smash my head into the window of a

car again when riding my bike."

After hearing this sweet and innocent expression, it strikes me that we are experiencing the best and highest version of Steve. He is loving, kind, thoughtful, thankful, hard-working, sincere, witty, devoid of ego and God-loving. His deficits are not in character traits, rather in intellect and memory. We can live without him knowing the year, remembering his accident or what his house looks like. All Steve's soulful attributes are intact, and that motivates us to call forth the best and highest versions of ourselves.

CHAPTER 18

Innocence

DAY 83. I feel like I'm doing something special, leaving Aria and Steve alone to nap together. I draw the curtains, tuck Aria in and announce my intentions, as the therapists taught me. After I leave the room, Steve bombards Aria with questions that cascade into BS bombs. Poor Aria holds center stage solo.

Steve shouts, "Where is mom?"

Confused, Aria responds, "Uh, she's somewhere..."

"What do you mean somewhere?" Steve explodes. "It's not okay. Are you safe?"

Aria nods her head.

Steve panics. "No, you're not safe with me! I have an injury. I'm not myself right now. Go find mom!" Aria springs out of bed to hunt me down, not knowing I've gone to a lounge farther from Steve's room. I wondered if that would be a problem if someone needed me. When Aria returns without me, Steve is fuming.

Steve yells, "Dial Mom's number!" Aria does so, handing over the phone.

"Where the fuck are you?" Steve scolds as a greeting. "Why is Aria here with me without you?"

I beeline for Steve's room, straight into my punishment. As soon as I enter Steve stares me down and says, "I am not happy with what's going on."

Aria laughs, and Steve's head jerks toward her. "Why are you laughing? This isn't funny! Your laughing is bullshit!"

I apologize for myself and Aria and announce we are leaving. When high stim rolls in, we roll out. Today marks our first co-parenting mishap.

Steve is like a four-year-old truth-seeking old soul who's on drugs. He might say something inappropriate because he's four, but since he's a truth seeker, you forgive him. His old soul emerges and you think the philosophical Steve is back, and then he says something so left field, you remember, *Oh yeah, this guy's on drugs.*

DAY 84. Today, Steve is Catholic. He hasn't been Catholic since the early 2000s. He was Jewish for nearly two weeks, meeting with the rabbi chaplain daily. Steve's tall tales continue. There is an animal theme now. Yesterday, Steve talked about donkeys in our backyard. Today, he mentions penguins. Steve claims, "Something happened to my face. I got shot with a, with a, with a…"

I fill in, "BB gun?"

Steve agrees. "Yes, a BB gun. Payton had it." Thankfully, he immediately changes the subject. "I'm tired. I want to make sure I do the work. I feel responsible for getting better. What do I need to do?"

Aria cleverly replies, "The responsibilities come after you are healed, Dad." Another empty future date on the calendar of our ever-present life.

Steve feels down so I say, "You are a treasure trove of presents.

Every day we come to see you, we open your treasure chest, and find a new gift from you." He softens.

Aria lights up. "That was so pretty, Mommy. Write that down!"

I whisper to Steve, "You are my everything."

My husband responds, "I want to say the same thing but I'm trying to figure out what that means." We laugh.

He says, "I think it means I'm an angel who has responsibilities."

Steve's internal medicine doctor, Dr. Moser, enters the room. He's a robust guy in his late sixties, with a head of white, curly hair. He's of his era with an old school vibe — even wears a bow tie every day. Dr. Moser asks Steve for a pain rating. The patient states he's a seven, so Dr. Moser offers pain meds. Steve clarifies that he's not in physical pain, rather mental pain, so he isn't certain pain meds will help. The doctor asks if my husband needs anything. I volunteer that he obviously needs a psychiatrist.

I realize Steve is no longer whispering! He talks with a raspy voice. I show Steve pictures in the ICU, which shock him. He repeats that he didn't know how bad the accident was. I describe the machines, point out visible injuries, and name the people who visited him. He says, "I have to thank all these people." Expressing heartfelt gratitude and doing all that he can to recover are my husband's biggest concerns. Sadness blankets everything.

Steve cries looking at images of the ICU wall blanketed with pictures and cards and says, "Seeing family and friends, seeing Payton and Aria, that's what got me through this." When Steve was shackled to the thin line between life and death, doctors told me repeatedly that this wall would be the best medicine.

Cousin Dane, whom I nicknamed the new "Kuya of the West" is here. Aria and I announce we have to go. For the first time, Steve surprises me by adamantly saying, "I want you to stay!"

I offer, "We'll stay a little longer, but sleep is important, honey."

He responds, "I don't need fucking sleep. I am arguing with you!"

Aria soothes her Dad, helping him breathe. He is still redirectable.

Today Steve's friend Funke is at the house to collect Steve's remaining bikes to sell. As he loads up his Sprinter van, the neighborhood gang of dads and dogs rolls up too. The crew cannot take their eyes off Funke's ride and he cannot stop dishing out juicy details about it. My mind drifts. I imagine us driving a Sprinter van across the country. I wonder — could that be how we spend next summer? All we'd do is bicker in the Sprinter. And then we could say, "At least part of our new life is just like old times..."

DAY 85. The level of consciousness after brain injury is different, but it's generally classified as Severe: Glasgow 3-8. Moderate: Glasgow 9-12. Mild: Glasgow 13-15. Steve's Glasgow score was 3, and that seems generous. Steve was a perfect disaster. A couple months ago when Dr. Manley asked me for the score, I told him to check the file. I didn't want to know it. Dr. Rome says you can come back from Glasgow 3 and recover to lead a normal life. That's the theme of Steve's life — a story of comebacks. I pray the biggest one is yet to come.

"Hi, Bina." Steve references my nickname for the first time. Another neuron firing. Steve's shoulder is bothering him so he needs x-rays and another MRI. There may be a cyst to blame. I'm not a doctor, but maybe it's the fact that his shoulder was ripped off his chest? Steve is low energy, barely touching the Sinagong soup his aunt made. He asks, "Is there rice for the soup?"

I say, "No, Steve. I need you to eat brain food: fish, eggs and meat, vegetables and fruits, and good fats like avocado, coconut, and olive oils. Rice is not brain food." I offer Steve a bowl of quinoa, fruit, chia seeds, coconut cream, and spices. Steve takes one bite and says, "Meh." We've only spent fifteen minutes with him today. He's highly stimulated so we excuse ourselves. One of his therapists remarks about how much progress he made today. It must have exhausted him.

When we get home from the hospital, I see a missed call from CPMC. Steve says, "Hi honey. It's me. I need your help. I'm in the hospital right where CPMC is, and I'm just concerned about how the night goes and make sure I connect with you and the family. Can you help me and come here? It's Thursday, July 13th. I'm in the hospital, healing from the brain injury. I need your help. Thank you."

I call Steve back. He has completely forgotten we visited him an hour ago. When I tell him we just drove an hour in traffic to get home, he asks his nurse if he can borrow her car! I put my hands over my face and think, *This guy is coming home? God help us!* Payton takes the phone and redirects Steve. I go to yoga to meditate on this emotionally taxing phase of recovery.

As I imagine who Steve will become, I wonder if he will remain childlike? What precious gifts will we lose in the desperate quest to bring Steve back whole?

DAY 86. Payton carries a cooler of homemade Mediterranean food into the North Tower while I park. A kind soul named Jen cooked culinary prescriptions for our TBI patient in our kitchen this morning. Steve is sick of my one-hit-wonder vegetable soup. He's in for a surprise:

- Raw beet and carrot salad with fresh mint
- Roasted beets with kale, walnut oil, and feta
- Carrot, ginger, sweet potato and coconut soup
- Beet greens and Curried Fingerling potatoes
- Mediterranean lentils with cucumber, red pepper, feta cheese
- Kale quinoa avocado salad with spinach and pumpkin seeds
- Coconut yogurt with chia seeds and fruit

Steve's occupational therapist Holli, a pretty, petite brunette with compassionate eyes, stops me at the hospital entrance and says, "Follow me." When I round the corner I see Steve, Payton and Millie casually sitting outside on a bench, poised for a family photo. This is Steve's first time outside in a conscious state in nearly three months. I smile and give Steve a kiss. He whimpers, "I'm scared."

I acknowledge, "I would be too."

Steve continues describing his fears and exhaustion from "all the work." Cocooned by his three therapists, Steve carefully stands up and walks solo inside. His chest is hollowed out and his shoulders slump, reminding me of his granddad. He enters the building and immediately collapses into a lobby chair, wasted. Holli asks, "How did that feel?"

He answers, "It felt like you were running away." We laugh.

Steve blurts, "Help me. This is hard work. I just want to wake up. Is there a moment when I can say to my brothers, 'I'm awake?'"

Holli explains he's had several "waking up moments" and

that question itself is evidence of waking up. Watching Steve walk is both sad and joyful. What a miracle he can walk; how sad that he has the fragility of an old man. In asking "When am I going to wake up?" Steve washes away my sadness. I hone in on his progress and untapped potential. I stop calling my husband a "miracle." Instead, I call him a "phenom"— a nickname he gave pro cyclist Taylor Phinney in his cycling blog. When I call Steve *phenom*, he lights up.

We enjoy our first lunch date in the lounge. Steve wipes his Mediterranean plate clean. Payton and I eat off the hospital tray since I didn't pack for us; typical. Payton and his dad snuggle in bed. Steve's sitter Daisy says, "He's much calmer when you're here, Jenna." I sit by the window instead of going to the lounge.

After resting Steve blurts, "Holli is working me very hard."

I say, "That's because phenoms get the hardest treatment."

"Simple things are so hard. It would have been easier to die. So much for being a phenom," he laments.

I wonder, "Would you like me to read you a letter Fabio wrote?"

Steve raises his eyebrows and asks, "Piersanti?"

"The one and only," I say.

Steve responds, "Sure."

Dear Steve,   *July 13, 2017*

I was glad to sneak in a visit before the "ban." Every time I see you, I am amazed by the leaps and bounds your recovery has taken. It is difficult to reconcile what we saw those first days, compared to how you are today.

You have come a long way in less than three months. Medical reports, X-rays, CT scans, and blood analyses will never measure a person's spirit, desire and reasons to live, bravery, discipline, tenacity, competitive drive, and love/support from family and friends. You are the type of person who exceeds the norm in all these metrics. It is this X factor, unseen in any medical file, that makes the difference in your journey of a personal renaissance. Do not accept any limited expectations for your recovery! Do not give up! Fight through all the pain, the temporary setbacks, and the emotional downers.

In those hard times, as you contemplate the difficult task ahead, remember who you are, where you come from, and what awaits you back home. Imagine the beauty in your life that is yet to come. YOU CAN DO THIS!!! As they say, the cream always rises to the top, and you, my friend, will soar once again.

Your friend,

Fabio Piersanti

As I read this uplifting letter from one of Steve's oldest and dearest West coast friends, Steve closes his eyes and listens intently. Every few sentences, his eyes pop open and he asks, "Fabio wrote this?"

I say, "Yes."

He closes his eyes again and I read a bit more before he says, "Did you *tell* Fabio to write this?"

I answer, "No."

I continue reading and then he breaks in again, "Wow. I need to thank him."

I say, "When you're better you can tell him you love him too." He nods his head in agreement and softens his eyes. I read again.

He stops me. "I have a lot of people to thank."

"Your secretary is thanking everyone."

"You are?"

I confirm, "The one and only." The nurse is here to wheel Steve to the MRI. As usual, Divine timing. Hearing those sweet and inspirational words calm his nerves for the procedure.

CHAPTER 19

A Hurricane of Feelings

D**AY 87.** I'm yearning to hear Steve's "old" voice. I'm overwhelmed preparing his daily meals and getting the house ready for his homecoming. Am I giving Steve too many beets? They produce nitric acid, which helps increase blood flow throughout your body, including to your brain. Studies show that a high-nitrate diet including beet juice produces greater blood flow to the white matter of frontal lobes. I also read that athletes who drank beet juice mixed with apple juice before working out reported better endurance, and a lower resting blood pressure than those who did not. The performance boost is thought to be from the nitrates found in the root. They also found that a beet-apple juice mixture could make certain activities like walking less exhausting for seniors, or perhaps people like Steve, who *act* senior. On the negative side, I read that beets are high in oxalate, which can contribute to gout, a type of arthritis that develops when too much uric acid builds up in the body. I'm spinning on all the research. I am unqualified to make these decisions. I wish I had a professional helping me!

Steve's progressive awakening comes with questions I don't have answers to, along with sad reality checks about how hard recovery is for him. He struggles with the basics: eating, walking, going outside. Things we take for granted are so difficult for Steve that he perceives dying as easier. I'm taking that in.

Today, my yoga class is suffocatingly hot, and all I think about is my beloved. I feel badly that I perceive yoga as "suffering," given what Steve is going through. I am in awe of his resilience. Each day, I gently remind him of how strong he is, how thankful we are for his work, and how much I believe in him. But, it's not enough. Every day, he hears these words for the first time. The accident, people's love for him, and his return to life is all *new* news. Every day I start rebuilding his confidence from scratch.

DAY 88. I'm slithering down a slippery slope. Our friend Jeremy and his kids are visiting from Switzerland and I make an exception for them to see Steve. We were supposed to reunite in Basel; instead we're at the hospital. Jeremy and his wife Amy are old friends. We survived some crazy pre-kids cycling adventures with these two die-hards. Jeremy asks Steve if he recalls the seven flats Steve got on the Death Ride many moons ago. I remember the stupid Death Ride: fifteen thousand feet of climbing over 120 miles! Steve feels bashful about his physical therapy accolades with Jeremy present. I can't blame him.

A former college athlete, Amy is a triple threat: a force on the bike, in the pool and on foot. Steve says, "Amy would not be proud of what I'm doing here." Jeremy quickly dismisses that. "We're all so proud of you, Steve." It's hard for Steve to receive our praise. I joke around that he's doing "Death Ride Rehab" at CPMC and it's no joke — it's only for phenoms. Steve shyly laughs, points to me and says, "Yeah. This one calls me a phenom."

Thinking about his sitter Ivonne, Steve says, "I wonder what she's up to because I know she has plans for me and I'm scared of those plans." Steve lives in a constant state of fear and anxiety. His mind rattles anticipating what's next, how he's being scored and how he's going to manage. He has a perpetual, internal battle of never-ending questions and self-evaluations running circles inside his battered mind.

With six of us in the room I monitor Steve closely until his therapist Jennifer whisks him away. I send Jeremy to tag along, observing Death Ride Rehab in real time. He witnesses Steve walk on sand, mulch, and cobblestones. I recall seeing those textured surfaces three weeks ago, never imagining he'd be there now.

Jeremy and company leave and Steve passes out. After eating dinner, Steve says, "I'm thankful. There's a lot to live for. Do you know who came to visit me today? Jeremy Wolf and his kids. I really liked having him here."

I smile and say, "I was here."

I read my journal entry describing Aria and me crying, three nights after the accident. While listening, he cries himself and states, "That must have been so hard for you guys." He's so thoughtful to think of our pain. This is the first time Steve feels what I feel. I wondered if we would ever sync up emotionally on the pain of his accident. It feels surreal that it's happening now.

Steve says, "You know who came to visit me today? Jeremy Wolf and his kids."

I reiterate, "Yes. I was here." Steve looks confused. This is my second over-stimulation cue; it's time to leave. His ruminating mind washes away the emotional moment we just shared.

Steve says, "I really liked having Jeremy here." By now, he's said that half a dozen times. But now there's a twist: "Jeremy came down from heaven and he's really appreciated. Can you tell him it was really awesome to see Saint Jeremy? I didn't know Saint Jeremy was white. I hope I didn't do something to scare Jer off?"

I explain, "You're not actually allowed to have visitors, honey. Jer would have stayed all day if he could."

We are leaving but Steve protests: "No. Please stay." We cautiously do. I receive another text I can't refuse — our dear friends Kara and Jamie are in the hallway. As they enter the room, I smell California: a mix of sunscreen, sand and sunlight. Then something hits me. Our dear friends are witnessing the "Hollywood coma wake-up." The last time Kara and Jamie saw Steve he was present, but not talking. He's now speaking with facial expressions, hand gestures, and a handsome smile. These dear souls are crying.

Steve says, "Kara and Jamie, you smell like the beach. Thank you for coming." Kara notices that as Steve fidgets, appearing overwhelmed, I breathe deeply. Steve instantly mirrors me. Kara senses how grounded I am in what Steve needs and how responsive he is to my motions. Before I can say namaste, the charge nurse barks, "Step outside, Jenna."

Irritated, the nurse complains, "You have too many people in that room and you've got another friend standing at the front desk." I apologize and tell her I will immediately get the extras out and deal with the other violation — Meredith, serving dinner for four.

I warn everyone, "I'm in trouble for this. You have five minutes tops." They get more love from Steve and before I can say "salmon with pesto," Payton clutches Meredith's grocery bags and barrels down the hallway to lay out the spread in the lounge. When I join him, Payton says through his gritted teeth, "Meredith brought an amazing meal, Mom! Salmon, salad, ratatouille and watermelon!" I didn't feed Payton today. Do I ever feed my kids?

Kara and Jamie leave; Steve falls asleep; Meredith, Payton and I dine in the lounge. They know what they're doing at The North Tower, and I spoiled their good intentions. I have to be firmer about leaving Steve when he shows the slightest overstimulation. I need to have a confident, emotionally void attitude to walk away when asked to stay.

Earlier, when Steve's nurse asked him if he was overstimulated, he talked through his thought process and concluded he was. He has come a long way. It's amazing how an old friend can heal a struggling mind.

DAY 89. Steve and I are lying in the hospital bed, holding hands, listening to *Fix You* by ColdPlay. Steve's eyes are closed; I am mesmerized by how perfect his face looks. I remember the feeling I had for weeks looking at Steve's face in an unconscious state. I didn't know if he was going to live or die, speak again, remember the kids and me. Now Steve is talking. Choked up, he says, "I have so many people to thank. I know you have done so much, Jenna. Thank you."

I smile, "You're welcome, Steve. I hope you're not worried about me."

"Oh, I'm not worried about you, Jenna. This is exactly your kind of project. I'm your kind of project. If I were in your shoes, I would be a mess."

"If I were in your shoes, Steve, I would be dead."

"You look good," he counters. "You don't look like you should look under these conditions. You talk like you are okay."

I admit, "I'm okay because you're okay, and together we're going to keep it that way!"

I'm driving home and Steve calls to check in, make sure he's in the right place, that I'm bringing Aria tomorrow, and that there is, in fact, a tomorrow. This is the third time he's called with the same questions. Each morning when Steve wakes up he says, "I made it to today." And after dinner, he says, "Let's hurry up and finish this day, so I can survive it."

DAY 90. We don't get to choose our life. We get to choose our response to it. Today, three months post-accident, I thankfully witness Steve respond to his life in meaningful ways. He rejects the lunch bag in the lounge refrigerator. He responds with sadness and frustration that Aria is not here. He deals with his shoulder pain by listing the medications he is on and says "It feels like there's something stuck in it — like something is pushing down my shoulder. It feels like an open wound." The shoulder pain is treated with medication, but its operability falls in the wait-and-see category. The nerves repair themselves at the rate of one inch per month. If enough progress isn't made naturally, Steve will have micro-nerve transfer surgery.

Witnessing Steve return from darkness is curious. The one time I count on Steve not remembering something, he does. "Why isn't Aria here?" he complains. (She got a better offer?) "I miss Aria. I need to see her," Steve sadly states. Today is light in conversation. He's tired and overstimulated. His therapy has increased by forty-five minutes per day and he feels overworked by the head therapist whom he calls "Aunt Holli."

DAY 91. I'm sitting in a conference room with Dr. Rome and half a dozen therapists and nurses discussing Steve. It is crystal clear that Steve still needs low stimulation and the moment we sense he's struggling, we should leave. I've memorized that protocol. There's a new issue: multiple phone calls and voicemails from Steve. Do I hang up because he can't finish a conversation? Redirecting is not easy, and I get tugged hard emotionally. Since TBI patients forget conversations moments after they happen, my guilt gets a pass. If Steve doesn't remember, why should I?

Today feels like old times. Steve is present, funny, endearing—like his old self, just softer and slower. He sits in bed shaving his shadow with an electric razor. "Dad! Don't you need a mirror?" Payton worries.

The Phenom calmly states, "Nope."

As Aria brushes Steve's hair, he addresses his mom on FaceTime. "I hope everything is okay, mom, because life here is pretty great." Aria joins Steve on his therapy walk, proudly witnessing her Dad achieve his objectives locating a fire extinguisher, linen closet and microwave. Steve can walk slowly by himself, with one therapist spotting him. Only a week ago, he was surrounded by three.

Steve crushes his lunch — bone broth, tri-tip with Meredith's pesto, sauerkraut, Brussel sprouts, ratatouille, beet and apple salad, sweet potato with coconut milk fruit salad, and a banana-pineapple kefir shake. I cheerlead him to eat during the entire meal. He earns a spoonful of fudge. After the brain lunch, Steve fires a Dad neuron: "Aria, sit properly. With one eye, I can tell your shorts are too short!"

After our great day, the clock strikes CrossFit. We confidently leave the North Tower, reminding Steve to eat the leftover beef and accompaniments with his sitter, Chris. We feel satisfied and grateful. As we happily cruise home down Divisadero Street, we glance out the window. I smile, "Oh, look. Dad's old BBQ place. We'll have to ask him if he remembers it." Millie's head sticks out the window. Aria's falling asleep in the back seat with the sun shining on her face. Payton says, "I love you, Paws." (my nickname). We blissfully float onto the luminous Golden Gate Bridge.

DAY 92. Steve is listening to a sweet voicemail message from my almost 90-year-old grandma today in her Italian accent: "Jennifer, sweetheart. I was so happy to hear your voice last night. Jennifer, I love you so much. You won't believe how much I care about your lovely husband. I am so happy he is doing better. I knew all the time he was going to be okay. For some reason, I just knew it was going to be fine. God bless you. Give him a big hug and kiss from Grandma Rosa." This prompts Steve to call Grandma Rosa and leave a similar loving message for her. Then Steve makes a series of phone calls — to his extended family.

As I listen to Steve well up, sharing feelings of gratitude, love and fear, I wonder how I can soothe his wounded heart. He brings up painful memories of his childhood. It's like he's teetering between the physical and spiritual worlds — as if calling his loved ones from an airplane that's about to crash. After the phone calls, Steve tells me he feels like he's in a nightmare. "I feel like something bad could happen," he warns.

"What could happen, Steve?" I ask.

Petrified, he says, "Can I stop the bad car accident from happening? I want to be the one who is run over to protect our kids." Is that what Steve did? Got run over by a car to protect our kids?

I feel what Steve is doing in the messages, conversations and car crash images. It's as if the pain he is carrying from his accident is reflecting his relatives' pain. He says, "I want to be sure your family is okay, Rich. Are your kids okay? As long as I know you and your family are okay, that makes me living worth it." Steve's pain is connected to the people he loves most in the world. Is that because he is absorbing the true connections we have with one another, feeling them as his own?

Waking up from a coma is not what I would have predicted. I didn't think about Steve understanding the severity of what happened to him and connecting that to his past, present, and future under a heavy emotional cloud. He doesn't remember us getting engaged in Maui twenty years ago, but he remembers painful feelings he had as a ten-year-old boy. What makes the cut and what doesn't is a whirlwind unraveling of painful emotions. The only joy that comes through is love and humor. So far, I haven't heard him talk about any joyful memories of the past.

As I leave, I tell Steve I am getting a massage tonight so I won't be available by phone. Steve understands and is happy to hear I am taking care of myself. The memory sticks; he doesn't call. Towards the end of my massage, tears come and the release happens. My comforting massage therapist, Kathy, says what I need to hear. I tell her I don't understand why Steve has to recall painful memories of his childhood at a time like this, when he's already in pain. Kathy says his soul needs to release the suffering. I remember the Rumi quote: "The wound is the place where the Light enters you."

Today, our entire family was tossed by a hurricane of feelings. No one could get a footing. I return home crying; Aria goes to bed crying; Payton slams the bedroom door, angry. Steve's emotions were front and center of the storm, difficult to witness. Steve's suffering actually signals progress in his recovery but is painful to watch. We've got boatloads of authentic despair, smashed together with joy in the palm of our hands. I'm holding on tight.

CHAPTER 20

Free Braces

Dᴀʏ **93.** I announce, "Steve, Payton is getting braces!" Frowning, Steve responds, "Really? Under these conditions? I hope you're getting a discount." The finance neuron is firing.

Every day around noon the kids and I are in a race, trying not to step on each other's toes from the stress of the ticking clock. We are dicing and sautéing, boiling and stirring, boxing and packing. We are in a mad dash to get Steve's lunch and dinner prepped for service. If we arrive late, he eats chemical-laden boxed mashed potatoes, overcooked carrots and rubber chicken. We need to be there to plate our food and sell Steve on eating it. As time passes in his healing, he's getting pickier.

Today, we arrive with cold beet soup with crème fraîche and fresh dill; coconut-oiled sweet potato fries; a vegetable salad with bacon; cucumbers with cream cheese and smoked salmon; bone broth; and a pineapple coconut smoothie. We're too late. Lunch was already eaten. We force-feed Steve beet soup. The rest of our anxiety-driven lunch is shoved in the lounge refrigerator. We barely sit down before Steve is overstimulated. Time to go. As I'm packing up, Payton and Aria are running and screaming, with

Millie in tow. "Dad's swearing!" Mr. Tourettes' 'bullshit' has been replaced by bigger guns. There's a speed dial risk leaving so early, but doctor's orders.

Mr. Tourettes calls me at 5pm and again at 6pm, wondering where I am and whether I want to find him "in a body bag tomorrow." Awesome. I'm at my friends, Brent and Claire's, trying to escape for a minute. He says, "You need to pick up the phone when I call. I don't give a fuck what you are doing…" And then: "Who is the other guy?" This cracks me up but his tone isn't funny.

I hear my Dad's voice: "Everything is just a phase." I have been patient, living in the moment. But right now I am over the present moment. I'm looking forward to the closing of Steve's emotionally taxing gutter mouth. This is exhausting and depressing.

I listen to this message: "Hi Bina. It's me. *Ate* is next to me, so I'm being nice. I'm disappointed you haven't been around. A lot has happened. I wish you could come to the hospital. It would be great to see you. Bring the kids. Thank you. Bye."

Meanwhile, back in our home town, out of town family nickname "Wonderland"… Before the accident, both kids were on the braces track. After the accident, I hemmed and hawed about whether to continue treatment for financial reasons. I missed not having Steve help me decide. I finally mustered up the courage to resume treatment, thinking that if I moved in the direction of things working out financially, they would.

The practice, Parikh Carlson Orthodontics, did something I never dreamed of. They told me Payton's treatment would be complimentary! I was deeply moved by their generosity. So today Payton is getting braces. Meanwhile, Aria and I are surprised to learn she's ready for them too. I turn the page of the treatment plan to look at the cost, but I'm confused. The cost says $0. I tell the manager, Lynne, there's a mistake. Only Payton's treatment is complimentary. With tears in her eyes, Lynne says that Dr. Carlson and Dr. Parikh both insist on this even grander gesture for our family. Aria asks me why I am crying.

This is on the heels of a woman from Alaska named Cheryl, whom I've never met, emailing me: "Your blog is sad sometimes but happy in so many ways…" Cheryl's dad, brother, and husband recently went to the Kenai River for their annual fishing trip in Anchorage, Alaska. Upon returning home with their fresh haul Cheryl says, "I would be humbled and excited to send you a box of the most amazing salmon for your family. I want you to feel comfortable since I know you don't know us!"

Steve's accident has raised my consciousness, enabling me to write in a way that opens people's hearts. Our family's blog captures the attention of a woman who's never met us, who lives thousands of miles away, and feels called to mail food to our family. Who knew how powerful streaming consciousness could be?

There are hundreds of people who have helped our family, and they are magic. We are supported in ways I could never imagine. What I have learned is the divide between the spiritual world and the physical world is blurry. As Richard Rohr posts: "Heaven is first of all, here."

Why do we have to suffer to find enlightenment, to find love or meaning? Rohr elaborates: "God is to be found in all things, and most especially in the painful, tragic, and sinful things — exactly where we do not want to look for God."

DAY 95. The moment I arrive at the North Tower, Steve's sitter Daisy tells me about the food The Phenom ate from the refrigerator — *my* food. This is another sign! The nurse is subbing in for me, feeding Steve my food, so I don't have to rush to him.

It's been three months since the accident and Steve wonders what he did for a living. I describe his profession and recount how his old company FinancialForce and new one, Salesforce, have taken care of our family. Steve is overcome with gratitude from their generosity. He thanks the CEOs of both companies in separate videos. Towards the end of one clip, he says, "If there is anything I can do to help the company in my situation, please let me know. I'm meeting a lot of people." I laugh out loud. This is so Steve — networking in the hospital while he hangs by a thread. I'm not sure what Steve's friends on the hospital staff could do for his old tech company but one thing is certain: Steve is popular.

The therapists say Steve is waking up more and more, which conjures up a feeling of dying — how ironic. He is awakening to the mental and physical severity of his condition. I've had 96 days to process his condition. For Steve, it's day one every day. I show Steve a picture of himself in the ICU with his brother. I explain how all the tubes and machines kept him alive. Steve points to his brother and says, "That's what kept me alive."

Today my friend Natasha visits and says, "The heart sends more information to the brain than the brain to the heart. Since Steve's heart is strong, if he strengthens his heart coherence and heart rate variability, this might strengthen his heart-brain communication to heal his brain."

I say, "I don't know what that means, but it sounds fantastic! What do we do?" The answer is an app called Inner Balance. You clip a heart rhythm monitor onto your ear lobe, plug the cord into your phone, and click on the app to measure your heart rhythm patterns, reflecting your inner state. You can visually track your heart rhythm to shift into a state of coherence, which produces feelings of relaxation, balance, and focus.

DAY 97. I've been waiting all day for a repairman and nervously call Steve's nurse Glenn to check in. He states, "Steve's mood has been good today." I'm surprised, given last week's death threats. Glenn explains, "Steve was going through 'withdrawal' then."

"Withdrawal from what?"

Glenn says, "They took him off his mood stabilizer." I forgot. I wish I remembered this when I was trying to make sense of Steve's wildly unstable mood last week. Because Steve is in a good mood today, Glenn says I can come for dinner; this is the longest I've waited to see him. I hop in the car with Millie to see Steve around 5pm. I feel uneasy arriving so late and I'm sans kids.

Living in trauma means feeling like another crisis is constantly brewing. Walking around our sleepy neighborhood, I've felt genuinely afraid I would be hit by a car and killed. In my neurotic preoccupation, I couldn't decide if Steve should be told about my death in his comatose state. I worried he would wonder why I wasn't coming. I worried my death would keep him from living. This is the ruminating mind of trauma — a dark waste of time.

As I drive on the Golden Gate Bridge, a car suddenly pulls out of his traffic-stopped lane into mine. *Shit! I'm driving at full speed.* I slam the brakes to the floor and think, *This is it. I'm going down the same way Steve did — someone pulled out without looking.* It's taking forever for the car to stop and I'm sure it's going to crash. But

I don't. Instead of crashing, I have an *aha* moment. This was you-know-who saying **S l o w d o w n .** Everything is going to be okay; I need to slow down.

At the hospital my guy is sitting at his dinner table by the window. He casually says, "Hi Bina. It's good to see you. I was wondering when the family was coming." I greet Steve with a kiss, explain my tardiness and excitedly say, "You ate your rice! Was it good?" Steve's friend Tommy Mike made special, Jenna-approved rice. It's cauliflower flavored with chicken Adobo, disguised as fried rice. Tommy hoped this favorite Filipino flavor would hide the bait-and-switch. I state how happy I am to see Steve eating home-cooked food. Laughing, he responds, "Your bags of food in the refrigerator overwhelm the nurses. Maybe you should simplify." I agree but point out two banned items on his hospital tray — ice cream and white rice, for real. "How did you get that?"

He smiles, "I ask for them." I give my healthy food speech and let it go, eating the hospital food myself, save the rice and ice cream. I have to set an example.

Steve flashes a goofy grin and says, "Guess what? My nurse is Ivy WEED!" He giggles. Can you believe that?"

Dubious, I frown. "No, I cannot." Ivy walks in the room and I ask her to flip her badge. Sure enough, it reads Ivy Weed. Boy, does it feel good to laugh with Steve.

I mention the name Rich Landry and Steve's eyebrows perk up. I say, "You were supposed to work for Rich at Salesforce." Steve goes nuts! He is hearing this news for the first time.

Steve exclaims in a video to his new boss, "I can't wait, Rich. What are we going to do to make it awesome? I know I have big shoes to fill, working for you, but I can do it. I hope you don't mind this face hanging out with you. Don't worry. It will get better. We gotta fix it up."

"Plastic surgery," I suggest.

Steve adds, "And hats!"

After the video Steve says, "If Rich is my new boss, I'm healed. I'm ready to work tomorrow." Just the idea that Steve is feeling good enough to say something like this is magic. I haven't felt this optimistic since Steve's ICU doctor told us he would live, nearly three months ago. As we teeter on the edge of overstimulation, I feel inspired to harvest a trick my friend's sister taught me: tapping. Introduced in the 1990s by Gary Craig, a Stanford graduate and certified master practitioner of neurolinguistic programming, Emotional Freedom Technique (EFT), commonly referred to as "tapping," is a tool for managing emotions. In EFT, individuals tap on specific meridian points on their bodies, similar to acupuncture points. Tapping is believed to soothe the nervous system by reducing the physiological stress response and promoting relaxation. As I tap Steve's head, face, and chest, I ask him to say words that bring coherence to his heart. He says, "friends," "Payton," "Aria," "my wife," "family." The tapping works; watching Steve sink into a deep, restful state after is comforting.

Today is just what I needed. Life on the home front is unstable and I've called for help. I'm living in a construction zone, getting the house ready for The Phenom's homecoming and it's not just the walls that are crumbling. So are the kids. I need more energy to care for my children, and they need their mom. I haven't focused on them in 97 days. And the implications of that are screaming at me.

CHAPTER 21

Gandhi Was at the Accident

DAY **98**. My Dad is back in town and has been at the hospital for the last three hours, while I've been on my first ever lunch break — at a restaurant down the street with Daniel, Steve's old cycling buddy and a dear friend of mine. I feel like an alien out in the world. The last time Dad saw his son-in-law was a month ago when he was speaking in a faint whisper. Seeing Steve walk solo for eighteen minutes on the treadmill brings tears to my Dad's eyes. Steve says he is trying to impress Dad since he's "dating his daughter" and needs to "gain his approval."

Dad says, "You received my approval long ago. Hey, when I saw you walking, Steve, I noticed your legs are muscular again."

Steve replies, "I was raising my calves to impress you. Actually, this entire accident was to impress you." The laughing continues. Dad stirs up trouble, talking about me outlawing rice. Steve comments, "I'm Asian. Rice is a personal thing."

Dad points to a picture of Steve on the wall. In that photo, Steve has a goatee. Dad says, "Steve, when you had a goatee you looked like Fu Manchu. You looked like a badass."

"What are you saying, Dad?" Steve counters. "I don't look like a badass anymore?" And just like that, the "Dad and Steve Show" ends. Steve communicates that he needs rest. I do some tapping and encourage coherent thinking: "Negative thoughts are clouds in the sky. Notice the clouds and watch them pass by." Steve says tapping helps and thanks me for helping him.

I reply, "It's my pleasure." It really is.

Steve's energy is low for the rest of the day. He has painful pressure in his left ear and difficulty hearing. He also has a headache and slept only two and a half hours last night. My latest upset is finding ice cream on his tray. I told the kitchen no sugar, but I think they took that literally, so they don't give him packets of sugar.

Tonight, Steve and I dine in the lounge overlooking the San Francisco fog. Steve eats delicious chicken piccata and green beans that Lynn from church made. Steve also eats Tommy Mike's pretend cauliflower rice, Yu Mei's beets, and corn on the cob — a summertime treat from the controlling wife. When Steve reaches for the ice cream, I cringe and make a few can't-help-myself comments. Steve doesn't skip a beat. He elegantly drops a dollop of chocolate ice-cream into his coffee. "It's cream," he casually clarifies. I tense up; caffeinated coffee with sugar when he had little sleep last night? He takes one sip and that's it. Phew. I march right to the nurse's station after dinner to tattle on the kitchen. The research on sugar and the brain is crystal clear.

I receive a text from Dr. Geoff Manley, the world-renowned neurosurgeon sent to me by Marc Benioff when Steve was heading into week four. I expected a miracle cure from him; instead, I received a gut-wrenching dose of reality: Steve's outlook was "ominous." Two months later, Dr. Manley wants to know if I have time for a call. I know exactly what this is about.

Yesterday, Steve sent Marc Benioff a video, thanking him for helping our family by sending us "his people," among other things. Steve had a message for this philanthropic tech leader:

"Hi Marc. Thank you for your help with my family. I thought I'd share with you what I've seen on the other side. A lot of belief needs to happen. We need leadership like you to help with that. When I say a lot of stuff needs to happen, what I mean is people are not really there. People don't have the right mindset to experience what I've experienced. It would be awesome to have your backing to do that. So, that's my request to an awesome leader. Thank you, Marc… Mahalo."

I call Dr. Manley and say, "Marc sent you the video?"

He replies, "That video is incredible, Jenna." That statement makes my day! We talk about Steve's unprecedented recovery. We talk about his anticipated hospital release date, what happens when he returns home, and what I should keep doing to help him. Then Geoff talks about how we should work together to improve TBI care. "Not everyone has an advocate like you, Jenna. Three cyclists get hit by cars every day in San Francisco. When Steve gets further along, we need to sit down and write some goals down with some other folks like you who want to work on the TBI care problem."

The same day, I receive another affirmation of my husband's remarkable recovery. The Phenom asks his hospital physician Dr. Moser, "How am I doing, Doc?"

"You are doing better than I ever thought you would do," he replies.

Steve asks, "Do we have a third child?"

I say, "No."

Steve's face wrinkles. "What?" He's confused.

I ask, "Do you know anything about this third child? Is it a boy or a girl?"

"It's a boy."

"What's his name?"

"Molder?"

Choking with laughter, I ask, "What did you say?"

He repeats, "Molder."

With great excitement, I exclaim, "MOLDER! Oh my gosh! MOLDER!" Now I am laughing uncontrollably. "When I was pregnant with Payton, we had a nickname for him. We called him 'Molder' before he was born. We figured out he was conceived on the day I asked you to install molding in the bathroom."

Steve laughs, "I remember that! For me to remember something right now is hard. I mean it's emotionally challenging, like pouring my soul out. So, for me to remember 'Molder' just shows you how tight we are."

"Yes, we are tight. I think your heart got stronger in this accident and you are sending powerful messages from your heart to your brain. That's why your healing is magnificent."

We talk about my previous brain injury and how I recovered "naturally." I comment that I didn't have any beet juice. Steve responds, "Yeah and I had to deal with it."

"Yes, you've had to deal with me for twenty-five years."

Steve laughs, "I need to file insurance on *you*! I've had to deal with my wife and her brain problems for twenty-five years."

"You are *so* funny."

Steve says, "This entire situation is comical — the stuff that keeps coming up — whether it's the help —"

I question, "The help?"

"Uncle Mario... your Dad. Your Dad is so funny."

"Did he say anything funny today?"

"He recognizes his badass son." Then the tone shifts: "My life keeps getting better as I wake up. What's hard is believing how serious the problem is and knowing the support is out there. What happens when I wake up from this and go home?"

I tell Steve he has well over a month here at the hospital, and he won't leave until he's ready.

Steve agrees, "A month here is a lot of work. I feel like I'm failing. Seeing you makes me want to improve, to work hard. I want to show Payton and Aria what's possible because I'm showing off to my wife's Dad. I didn't ask for your Dad's approval to marry you but I hope he approves." Steve is crying.

"You did ask for my Dad's approval."

"I don't remember."

"My Dad said, 'Thank God someone is putting up with her.'"

"I told your Dad you get shit done."

Speaking of putting up with me, back in Wonderland after dinner as my Dad reaches his hand into the freezer, he says, "I assume I'm the only one who wants the toxic ice cream?" My Dad is getting the hang of how I roll at TBI Headquarters.

DAY 99. Today, I celebrate my 44th birthday with a small group of girlfriends — "44 and hardcore!" We laugh, we cry, we catch up on The Phenom — and The Phenom's Wife. We talk about bringing more people onto a spiritual path.

One benefit of our situation is that expectations are low. My friend Claire is shocked I am having a birthday party at my house in its messy construction condition. Who cares! Payton feigned disinterest in my gathering so he could surprise me by cleaning up, baking cupcakes and instructing Granddad to buy a host of items I forgot — all while I was at yoga. Payton gave me the gift I've dreamed of as a Mom: someone else to manage the household on my birthday. Had Aria been home, she would have chaired the decorating committee.

I am nervous visiting Steve since I arrive late and need to leave early, but I come bearing a Chez Pay processed sugar cupcake… no date paste! Steve gobbles it up. He is funny and happy today, admitting when he's sad, lonely, or depressed he thinks of JAPS. My Dad raises his eyebrows and asks, "Okay… What are JAPS?"

Steve coyly smiles and says, "Jenna, Aria, Payton, and Steve."

This is our life. It's excruciatingly sad and magically beautiful, illuminated by hope and squashed by fear. It's whispering joy and shouting pain, holding on tight and letting go. It's everything all at once: the ups, the downs and the in-betweens. After 99 days I am beginning to understand what my friend Nina said to me in the Stanford ICU, reflecting on her frightening journey to that same hospital floor years ago. Nina whispered in my ear and said, "I wouldn't change a thing."

DAY 100. Today Steve celebrates staying alive for one hundred days! To go from the edge of death to the beginning of a new life signals a revitalized state of being. "Why do you call me a phenom?" Steve asks. I recount the doctors' "ominous" prognosis.

Steve replies, "So this wasn't supposed to happen?" I get what he means. *This moment* was not expected to happen. Steve pries himself up from bed, puckers his lips, gives me a kiss and plops back down. Pure romance. My Dad says, "Do you want me to leave the room?"

Steve snaps back, "After I recover."

My Dad acknowledges, "Steve, you have these incredible comebacks and you're so quick!"

Steve points to the picture of himself on the wall. He asks my Dad, "What was it you said about me in that photo?"

My Dad replies, "I called you a 'badass.'"

"What were your exact words?" We can't tell if he remembers the conversation and is toying with us. Steve cannot get enough of the "badass" banter with my Dad. I recall cousin Melissa's birthday card: "Steve, you are a badass father, husband, friend, human! Happy 45th Birthday! Love, Cousin Melissa." Melissa knew a card that reads "Badass Mother… *ahem*" on the front was for Steve.

I notice Steve's iPhone spontaneously made a video of the past three months today, of all days. When people ask how I imagined Day 100, I have no answer. I never thought about it. Each day I am gifted an abundance of blessings, signs and love, so there's no room to project into the future. The gifts of today keep me dialed into the present. I recall the first time we heard Steve speak, Father's Day. Yet, it took me a whole week to register that miracle date!

Before the accident, I had no time for the present. I was too busy living in the future — planning and projecting days, weeks, months, years down the line. Now I realize how much I was missing. Osho expresses this truth: "When you are here and now, sitting totally, not jumping ahead, the miracle has happened. To be in the moment *is* the miracle."

My high school best friend, Beth, is visiting from the East coast. A striking blonde with ageless, milky white skin and a near-constant smile, Beth's inner beauty shines just as brightly as her outer beauty. I have long admired her compassion for others and relentless work ethic. Since she is a high-risk OBGYN and mother of four young children, I am humbled she is here.

What I didn't know was the *underlying* purpose of the trip she booked four months ago. At the time, she was sharing my blog with a neurosurgeon friend who gave her the unfiltered reality of Steve's recovery. Beth worried my outlook was too hopeful. She was coming to California to convince me to take Steve off life support. By the grace of God, Steve is alive and supporting himself, at the very least with his breath.

I share that Steve's internal medicine doctor advised me to pull the plug on day three! I hung up the phone. We talk about how Beth got her nickname "Dr. Death." During residency, she garnered the highest number of "Do Not Resuscitate" signatures from her elderly patients' families. It reminds me of the conversation I had with a Stanford ICU nurse, who asked for our Advanced Directive. I couldn't bring myself to give it to her. Dr. Death *did* knock on our door, but thankfully, she has a new message to deliver. It's the same message our friend Brian has: "Think you know your limits? Think again."

DAY 101. Discussing the accident for the umpteenth time, Steve asks about the driver. We tell him she was a teenage girl. He asks one question, "Is the girl okay?" Then, out of left field, Steve says, "He was there."

"Who was there?" I ask.

He answers, "Gandhi."

"Gandhi was where?"

"He was at the accident."

"What was Gandhi doing at the accident?"

"He was moving the tires."

"Your bike tires?

"No. The tires of the car."

"The car that hit you?"

"No. The other car."

There was another car behind the one that hit Steve. Upon hearing the impact of the crash, this car instinctively swerved to the right. In doing so, the driver narrowly avoided running over the downed cyclists. In fact, the miss was so close that another cyclist had a tire imprint on the side of his face. According to Steve, those were Gandhi's tires. I can't make this stuff up. This non-stop magic thins the line between the spirit world and our lives on earth.

I recall the Red Thread Circle my friend Jenny introduced at my birthday party. In this ritual, people gather in a circle passing around a ball of red yarn. When the red thread comes to you, you hold the thread in your hand, wrap a few lengths around your wrist, and speak your truth. At the end of the circle, each person cuts off their thread to form a bracelet. The ceremony invites people to share "common threads" of their stories.

At my party, each person took turns speaking about how we lift ourselves up. Jenny said the red thread bracelets remind us of our shared connections. When we need support, we tug at the string around our wrists, activating those connections. The circle of intention broadens our opportunities for connection, protection, and blessings.

I think about the girl who caused the accident. We will always be connected to her. "Is the girl okay?" For this, we pray. I wish for her to have protection and blessings and someday, when Steve asks and she is old enough, we can connect with her to share in our forgiveness and healing.

CHAPTER 22

The Wedding CD

DAY 103. Big changes are happening at the North Tower; Steve's team is letting him loose. He selects his food, therapy schedule and when to ride the stationary bike. Afterwards, Steve meanders around, introducing himself to people he doesn't know.

Pastor Kim is here. Recalling her experience with brain-injured patients, she calls Steve's recovery "unprecedented." Steve tells her, "I'm afraid I'm dying." We both explain (again) that he is no longer in danger of dying. Hopefully, as he transitions from "being alive" to "living," the feeling of dying fades.

The home construction is humming along. It's comforting to be close to something I connected with before the accident. The smell of remodeling is always the same — the smell of possibilities, new beginnings, progress. I enjoy seeing a room down to studs with third-eye vision for what it will become. It's more exciting than the finished product. I love the energy of the workers buzzing around, the sound of the circular saw, the vibration of the nail gun compressor. Progress is visible every day.

Most people see chaos in construction; I see beauty. Looking back at the horrific pictures of Steve in the ICU, I realize I didn't see what I'm seeing now. I focused my vision on what would help *me* survive it. Instead of worrying about the countless tubes, I looked for indicators of life. "He *grabbed* at his feeding tube!" Instead of feeling afraid of wild neurostorming, I learned what neurostorming is — the body's reaction to the devastation and the brain's reboot. I asked about the medications and machines to control the reboot, rather than replaying images of storming. Instead of being afraid during surgery, I let go and thought, "We are at a world-renowned medical center!" I *chose* what I was seeing, hearing and feeling — and that's what got me through it.

Steve calls me to say he's listening to our wedding CD. I've carried it from hospital to hospital for three months, playing it a handful of times. Before the accident, Steve was a sentimental, romantic guy. Now he's that guy times a hundred. He's crying on the phone listening to our favorite romantic songs. Steve doesn't remember our engagement or our wedding, but he knows the feeling of being in love and he is head over heels. Thankfully, I'm his girl.

Aria and I roll into Steve's room as my Dad and Payton are heading to CrossFit. The wedding CD is still playing, three hours later. My Dad says Steve replayed one song non-stop. I hook Steve up to his heart rhythm monitor, open the Inner Balance app, hand Aria the frankincense and start tapping. The music plays as Aria applies the oil. We listen to the song *And Now You're Mine Love* from The Postman soundtrack. It's a poem with music. Steve listens intently to the words when he suddenly says to Aria, "Mom is Amber." My ears perk up. "Amber?" Before Steve could talk, he wrote the name Amber repeatedly, as well as "Amber: Do your thing!" When Steve said Amber talked to him in heaven,

I deduced she's Steve's guardian angel. I am taken aback hearing him reference *me* as Amber. He said this the other day too. Am I his "earthly" Amber? He replays the song and I listen to the words: "And now, you are mine. Rest with your dream in my dream. Love and pain and work should all sleep now. The night turns on its invisible wheels and you are pure beside me, as a sleeping **amber**…"

With his eyes closed, Steve repeats nearly every line of the poem after hearing it. Overcome with emotion, he says, "You can't imagine how much I love you." I tell him I can because I love him the same. Steve tells Aria repeatedly that I am his number one love and she feels sad. At one point, she snaps at something I say and Steve fires at her, "Speak to your mom with respect. Mom is number one!" Aria shuts down.

I comfort Aria, the mood settles and I joke with Steve. "This could have gone in the opposite direction."

Steve asks, "What do you mean?"

I reply with a coy smile, "You could have gone to the other side and decided you and I were finished."

Steve replies, "Then I wouldn't be here."

Dr. Moser enters as Steve is eating his hospital lunch, including salmon, broccoli, pineapple, a salad, and white rice. Dr. Moser notices his Asian patients are happier when they eat rice. I ask if we can substitute rice for Steve's mood-altering drugs.

Aria and I are home and Steve calls. He wants Aria to know how much we love each other. He is concerned Aria doesn't feel special because he kept saying I'm number one. He wants Aria to know that this statement is about her. Steve says, "I want Aria to know that her parents love one another and it's powerful. But nothing is more powerful than loving her. I want you to tell her how much you love her."

"What did you say to Aria?" I ask.

"That we love each other. That she's learning what love is. She'll hear me once she hears that you love her. She'll understand and it will all come together. When I told her, I felt like she was hanging up the phone. Just tell her I love her. I want her to know that Mom is number one and I need the kids to listen to their mom. At the end of the day, I love Mom. Mom's my partner."

I pull Aria aside and explain that Dad is in a vulnerable position, relying on me to be the pack leader of our family, triggering this "number one" talk. As we smooth things over, she laughs, "Yeah Dad says your number one, then it's Payton, Granddad… oh yeah — I'm number eight!" Steve's erratic emotions are hard for the kids, and me. You don't know when he's going to snap, what he's going to say or how he's going to feel about an innocent comment.

I play our Catholic wedding ceremony video. Finally we are at the end, which I dread out of embarrassment. I grab my iPhone to clock our kiss — twenty-six seconds! Aria says, "Ewwww!" We were in another world on our wedding day.

Steve's friend Ron appears after the adult film viewing with his Wednesday organic berry delivery. Ron and his wife Cherie were eating organic long before grocery stores knew the term. Steve, the attentive host, offers Ron a date paste dessert, but he laughs and declines. I notice Steve sits taller in his chair as he nonchalantly brags about riding the stationary bike. Then the Phenom laces up his shoes to show his old racing buddy his moves. While Steve spins the bike, Ron spins old tales of when they met, bike racing and only-Steve stories. One is about Steve forgetting cycling shoes at a race. He competed in his loafers. Ron also confesses some "don't-tell-Jenna" stories.

I've heard lots of these stories lately, including the time Steve said to his buddy at a bike race, "If you talk to Jenna, tell her we went to Home Depot."

I jokingly say to Steve, "I'm still waiting for your girlfriend to show up."

Steve responds in a serious tone, "That kind of talk overwhelms me. You are my one and only." I laugh because this is another line from a song in our wedding CD.

Not long ago I never could have imagined this day: Steve listening with longing to our wedding CD and video; reciting poetry to me; telling Aria how much he loves me so she can witness true love; Steve riding his stationary bike.

The challenges we face as a family are enormous. But if we face the pain and struggles directly and honestly by talking things through, we will "channel them into strength." Those were Payton's words to his Dad on the "bullshit day." When I think about all the sweetness coming from my husband losing his mind, sometimes I look at an old photo of Steve and wonder — does he really want to find it again?

DAY 104. Payton's running occupational therapy, teaching his Dad to bake. This is the first time Steve has baked anything his entire life, much less with his son. The kids' former preschool teacher Olivia visits, and Steve hands her a chocolate chip cookie. Olivia, in turn, hands Steve some *real* goodies — kale salad, fruit, salmon and curry chicken. The bakers stroll the North Tower doling out warm cookies, thanking the staff. Seeing Steve together with his son this way is pure bliss.

Exhausted, Payton, Steve and I squish into bed together. I lie on the bottom, while Steve and Payton spoon. Aria sits in a chair. I think of the bed scene in the movie *Willy Wonka's Chocolate Factory*. We fall fast asleep. I dream the four of us are sailing on a raft, stuck at sea… not far from reality.

In general Steve appears drunk, zigzagging when he walks, slurring when he talks. A former neighbor, Heidi, drops off a colorful brain-boosting dinner — Siracha rainbow noodle salad with veggies and beet hummus. Between her dishes and Olivia's sides, there are fifteen vegetables and three proteins in Steve's dinner tonight. Just thinking about all these nutrients elevates my own brain function. Dr. Moser is greeting us in the lounge. After I brag about Steve's medicinal meal, the doctor ruins the moment, asking where the ice cream is. "Dr. Moser! Have you read the research on sugar and the brain?" He claims there's new research stating fruits themselves may be worse than processed sugar. I throw my hands up in the air.

My friend Robin and her daughter Sophia arrive, announcing their intentions: "We are here to hear The Phenom speak and whisk Aria away for a girls' night out." Robin last saw Steve at Kentfield. Steve asks, "Is this what you expected a phenom to look like? *Zoom, zoom.*" We laugh, understanding that The Phenom is playfully implying that he himself is now speeding around with energy and vitality.

It's good to have visitors back to lighten the air. Robin is a former fundraiser for the VA Hospital and has a wealth of information on PTSD. Exercise is key. I think of Vasper Systems, which is used specifically by the military for PTSD. Vasper is a revolutionary training regiment developed by a NASA scientist which combines compression, liquid cooling, and interval training to enable individuals dealing with injury, illness, or other conditions to experience the benefits of anaerobic exercise. My friend Kira told me about it, so it's been in the back of my mind as a rehabilitation tool for Steve. I'm on the right track.

While Robin takes Aria away, I wrap the evening up with my sentimental phenom. Our wedding CD plays again. This time we listen to the whole shebang. It's been ages since I've done so. When the poem from Il Postino comes on and Steve hears the word amber, he repeats, "You keep mentioning Amber to me, Jenna. *You* are Amber." I think, "So many dots are connecting for Steve to make this comment."

As I'm packing to leave, a surprising song plays — *Every Little Thing She Does is Magic*. I am crying; Steve looks at me with curiosity. I explain: "This reminds me of the day Dr. Manley told me how bad your brain injury was, why you weren't waking up and that you might never wake up. My heart was shattered. I thought Dr. Manley was going to 'magically' cure you. At the exact moment I was thinking this, *Everything Little Thing She Does is Magic* came on the radio. I knew God was playing that song, telling me I am the magic. Here we are, one hundred four days later, and you are telling me God was right. You came back for me and our kids."

I continue, "When I point to the machines and the tubes in photos, you say, 'That's not what kept me alive. It was family.' When I thank you for being here, you say, 'You're the reason I'm alive.' When I thank you for fighting, you say, 'I'm doing this for you and the kids.' The love our family shares is magic, and in one month and three days, you are coming home and if that's not magic,

I don't know what is!"

Now Steve is crying. The perfect ending to a perfect day.

CHAPTER 23

A Prescription for Intimacy

DAY 106. Today's talk is about Steve turning down God. Steve, his friend Funke and I are chatting in the lounge looking at the San Francisco skyline. Steve reminisces about turning down heaven: "The fact that I said no to God — I hope that makes you happy. I can't believe I said no."

When Steve first started talking, I asked him as many questions as I could about going to the other side because I was curious to hear what it's like and I sensed his spiritual state was fleeting. As Steve reboots his brain, grounding himself into the earth, those spiritual thoughts and feelings fade further away. Now, he talks about these memories from my recollection or viewpoint, not his own. One of the things he cannot get over is that he said God looked like his cousin Mark.

"Are you sure I said kuya Mark? Not Marc Benioff?"

"No, Steve," I laugh. "Marc Benioff is not God. What religion are you now?"

Steve snaps, "Salesforce." Laughing, Funke looks out the lounge window, points to the brand-new Salesforce tower and says, "There's your church. When are you going back?"

Day 107. Payton is cutting Steve's hair, giving him a funky Cristiano Ronaldo hairdo. It's buzz-cut short on the sides and all hair on top. Aria is biting her nails while the rest of us are egging him on. Hair grows back, and Steve looks ten years younger.

His right ear is numb, the first I've heard of that. Treating a comatose patient is like shooting in the dark. The doctors don't know what hurts or what's wrong beyond the obvious, because the patient offers nothing, other than what oozes out. Now that Steve is conscious, we are discovering what else is wrong. I notice Steve has significantly discolored fingernails but no one is concerned about it.

Steve himself is not too concerned. He says, "I want to be the one helping people. I don't want to take pity and well wishes. I want to help people with their problems." Nearly every time Steve sees someone, he asks, "What can I do for *you*?"

Steve's friend Phil is here. He too experienced a life-changing cycling crash and wants to help Steve navigate the mind shifts of recovery. He pulls out the cross he wears around his neck. Steve looks at it and matter-of-factly says, "Your cross looks like the ones God was giving away, except God's were green."

Steve worries in circles, mainly that he's dying. I told Steve prior to the accident that every time he left the house I worried about him coming home safely but I taught myself to stop. If something was meant to be, it was meant to be. Plus, if fear drives my thoughts, I focus on the wrong things, as I recently learned.

When I dreaded Steve getting hurt cycling, I imagined myself being angry at the driver, angry at cycling, even angry at Steve. I pictured myself feeling weak and lifeless. One of my worst nightmares came true but without the accompanying concerns. The overriding feeling I had when I faced the nightmare I pictured hundreds of times was LOVE, and it surprised me.

I leave picture albums of the kids when they were small. Sadly, Steve sees our children as babies for the first time. He calls exclaiming, "We make the cutest kids!" In fact, Steve calls all the time. It's like having a high school boyfriend, except my guy sounds like a grandpa, and sometimes like a monk.

According to the schedule, Steve comes home in thirty-three days. I have no idea if that date will stick, but I know this: We are blessed. We are loved. We are grateful. The rest is filler. We already have everything that matters. All we have to do is nurture it.

DAY 108. Again, I ask Steve what religion he is. He replies, "Buddhist." He mentions God passing out green Buddhas in heaven.

I say, "Hey! Yesterday you said God was giving out green crosses!" Steve's religious flip-flopping sparks interesting conversations among friends. I researched that green in Buddhism is the color of action. In Christianity, green represents the triumph of life over death. When your body is in the presence of the color green, your pituitary gland gets stimulated and your muscles relax. The color green is associated with renewal, growth, and hope.

A swarm of friends visits. Steve recalls none of the details of how they've helped our family but he feels their love and lights up seeing them. I witness the reunion with Jamie. Steve gets out of bed, walks toward his dear friend and embraces him. We decide to FaceTime Jamie's wife, Kara and her extended family who are back East. This entire family has been a huge support, and we are excited for Steve to say hello for the first time. Before dialing, Steve asks Jamie a curious question, "Jamie, how should I address your wife, Kara?"

Jamie asks, "What do you mean?"'

Steve clarifies, "Is there a nickname you give Kara? I can use it and reference you — to make you look good?"

Jamie nods, "Ah, I see. I call Kara 'Peanut.'"

When Kara answers the call, Steve says, "Your husband is telling me all about you, Peanut, and how great you are." The charm neuron is firing at triple strength, but we have a problem. My affectionate husband loves people. He always has and always will. For Steve in his easily overstimulated state, loved ones are like chocolate cake for a diabetic. He can have a couple of bites but cannot eat a whole slice. It's so easy to take a few more bites and then one thing leads to another, and *poof* — the slice is gone and Steve is destabilized.

After Jamie leaves Steve says, "That was hard. I'm overwhelmed." We both agree to a fifteen-minute visitation limit no matter what. I tell potential visitors via the blog, "Please stay strong and focused. It will seem like Steve is perfectly fine having you stay longer. You will think, 'He must be better today. I can stay.' But underneath the hipster hairdo is a brain on overdrive. Please set the timer on your phone for ten minutes and when it beeps, set it to five and start saying goodbye. Just like the visitation ban, this won't last forever. I promise these fifteen minutes will be the best of your week."

My husband's overall state of being radiates from the depths of his soul. His soul was never buried to begin with, but the difference is that now he speaks from deep within it, all the time and without hesitation. My beloved is unencumbered, loose and free and as the doctors say — and medicate him for — "uninhibited."

I post: "Steve's soul is found. It rests firmly in his hands, brimming with Light for us to capture. It's why you feel so good when you visit him. It's why you can't get enough of him. It's why you read this blog. It's the reason you've felt good deep down through this entire, harrowing experience — even when his body was ravaged with machines keeping him alive. While his body was beaten, his soul was thriving. And the soul, my dear ones, is what we all live for."

From Richard Rohr: "God gives us our soul — our deepest identity, our True Self, our unique blueprint — at our very conception. Our unique little bit of heaven is installed by the Manufacturer at its beginning! We are given a span of years to discover it, to choose it, and to live our own unique destiny to the full. The discovery of our own soul is frankly what we are here for. Your soul is who you are in God and who God is in you. We do not 'make' or 'create' our souls. We only awaken them, allow them and live out of their deepest messages."

Steve and I are awakening our souls. I am "remodeling our lives" so our souls shine at the forefront, protected from the forces that overwhelmed them. We've gained so much from Steve's life being saved, but it's not for our family alone. We want to multiply it. How many others can we reach? We've got soul — let's do something with it!

DAY 109. Steve didn't get much sleep last night, worrying about his trial excursion this morning. He and three therapists left hospital grounds and walked to the Duboce Park Cafe. Steve was terrified. He ordered and paid for breakfast "on his own," as he reported.

He's back at the North Tower and so am I. Curious, I ask,

"How was your outing?"

My childlike husband responds, "It was successful. It was hard. It was a lot of numbers. I was hoping my therapist would help pay." What he means is his therapist didn't help him count the money and hand it to the cashier.

Steve giggles and says, "Afterwards, they took me to the park and we looked for poo and needles in the grass, just like you asked, Bina." I laugh hysterically. Those were my exact words. Steve needs to ground himself to the earth, since he was comatose and on the other side for so long. I suggested he lie on the grass and reconnect to the heartbeat of Mother Earth. This is called *earthing*.

After his outing, Steve called his son and said, "Don't tell Mom. I did something bad."

Payton asked, "What did you do?"

Steve whispered triumphantly, "I ate French toast with a lot of syrup. I ate gluten *and* sugar!"

"Good for you, Dad."

DAY 110. It's 7:30am. I pick up the phone to hear "Hi. I'm your yoga instructor. Why aren't you in yoga?"

"Is this Steve?"

Steve laughs, "Yes."

"Are you joking?"

"Yes. What's the name of your yoga teacher?"

"Jeff. Why?"

"Usually when I call, you're at yoga. I was surprised you answered. Am I being funny? I was pretending to be your yoga teacher."

Payton and I both have back pain. Payton googles "lower back pain, right side, dying" and reports: "I need an MRI. Back pain can indicate you have a cancer tumor, Mom." I tell Payton he doesn't have a tumor; he has a CrossFit addiction. He needs to listen to his body and chiropractor. Feeling paranoid about dying is another outcome of Steve's tragedy. We easily schedule a double appointment that afternoon, meaning the Phenom isn't going to see his crew until after 4pm. Thankfully, Steve has a packed day to tide him over.

Approaching the hospital, we see a former colleague, Michelle, from Salesforce. She tells us Steve is upstairs with two of Steve's former racing buddies, one of whom is a sports psychology mental skills coach. Michelle said she was so enamored with the energy of these three men, she stayed longer than expected.

Michelle witnessed a powerful and emotional connection between Steve and Brian who says Steve can draw from his competitive spirit to move energy throughout his body to heal, visualizing white and gold light shining inside him. After this powerful connection with Steve, Brian said, "I'm going to channel Steve during my next race."

Steve cannot comprehend how he is inspiring people. I say, "All you have to do is be yourself." Instead, he feels pressure to help others. There is something missing inside Steve that keeps him from believing in himself. I am determined to find out what it is because I think it's the key to unlocking a full recovery.

There are so many details to an individual person — mannerisms, facial expressions, sounds, phrases, attitudes, opinions, dislikes, body movements, tendencies, habits, and idiosyncrasies. Until they disappear, you don't have a sense of what makes you *you* on a physical level. I am sensitive to the hundreds of details that make Steve *Steve*. What a blessing to physically see Steve slowly returning to us day-by-day.

Doctors at all four hospitals told me many of Steve's brain connections will never return. I'm not sure which parts of Steve we lost forever, but I'm focused on what's coming back. Aria says she doesn't feel like her old Daddy is back and with each passing day, she forgets the Dad she lost.

I notice how Steve looks at himself in the bathroom mirror. He has a routine. When washing his hands, he methodically turns his face side-to-side, checking out his scars and lazy eye. Then he wets and smoothes his hair back. While watching him primp, I ask, "Steve, what do you see when you look in the mirror?"

He replies, "A man with one eye, trying to look good for his wife."

DAY 111. Dr. Moser knocks on the door and with raised eyebrows, says "I'm glad it's just the two of you. We need to talk about something that came up with the staff." He pauses before continuing: "Do you know I am also a sex doctor?"

"Um, I did *not* know that. What's up?" I ask with curiosity.

Dr. Moser meanders on about my husband being dis-inhibited before letting the cat out of the bag. He says, "Steve, you told one of the female staff members she's hot."

Steve's face turns white and his eyes pop; he is mortified. Picture Forest Gump with Jenny in her dorm room. He questions, "I *did? Who?*"

The *who* isn't revealed but I could take a few guesses. Dr. Moser reassures Steve: "This happens all the time. We know you still love your wife and the staff member isn't mad, but we want to prevent it from happening again."

Steve asks, "Is there a pill for this?"

Dr. Moser replies, "I have something else in mind." Then he writes a prescription for something I did not know could be prescribed. "I'm going to let the staff know that for two hours the door to your room will be locked. No one will be able to come in and disturb you. You and Jenna can do whatever you want in those two hours. But I want to hear about it afterward."

What?! He wants a play-by-play? I call my friends Sara and Kerry. "I'm being locked in Steve's room for two hours so I can whip the manhood out of him! Two naked hours with The Phenom! Let's be real, two naked hours with Steve before the accident would have been too much."

In the afternoon I take the bull by the horns. Aria didn't come to the hospital today; Payton's at a meeting for children with brain-injured Dads. Steve's former co-worker, Glenn, has Millie. It's now or never! I ask Steve's nurse if we can use the studio practice apartment at the end of the hall. The nurses get the room ready and escort us to the makeshift brothel. Everyone knows what's happening — after all, this is a prescription. We're taking a clinical walk of shame, shuffling down the hospital hallway as the staff smiles and winks.

"Should we wave to everyone, Steve? You think they're placing bets on us?" Steve is terrified, incapable of joking.

I put Steve's mind at ease and say there are no expectations. "Let's just get naked and see what happens!" When I take off my clothes Steve's eyes bulge and his jaw drops, as if he's never seen me before. I realize what's happening: I am the first naked woman Steve has ever seen! He's a teenager and I'm a hot cougar.

"Oh my God!" Steve blurts. "You look so good!"

Dr. Moser said things might not work properly but that's another prediction of the medical establishment that fails. Steve is so sweet and tender. His busted arm and shoulder make things a bit awkward at times but we manage. It's better than I would have imagined. We connect again and it's effortless — muscle memory at its best. I hope he needs this prescription every day!

CHAPTER 24

The Key to Resilience

DAY **112.** Dreaming, I get off an airplane in a huge airport. I lost my travel companion while walking in a daze to baggage claim. I veer off track and am lost. What terminal did I land in? Which terminal am I in now? I don't recall what airline I flew or where I flew from or to. I have no ticket to reference. I'm searching for baggage claim but without knowing what airline I flew from, how can I find my bags? I can't check my email, because I realize I don't have my purse. Did I bring a purse? I feel overwhelmed, helpless and hopeless.

My dream ends when the phone rings at 3:41 am. "Good morning, Bina."

"Steve, it's three o'clock in the morning."

Plaintively, he asks, "What time am I supposed to wake up?"

"Seven."

"I'm sorry, Bina."

"Steve, go back to sleep. You're not supposed to have the phone."

"Okay, Bina."

I'm momentarily worried about how I will find my way out

of that crazy airport and back home when I realize it was a dream. At seven I'm awakened again, to my second call from The North Tower, when it hits me: my dream is a portrayal of Steve's life. This is what it feels like to be my poor husband.

When I walk into the hospital room in real life, Steve barely acknowledges me because he's reading a book — *Where is God When it Hurts?* Steve says it's tough reading. I ask, "Is it tough to read the words, or thinking about the meaning of the words?"

"The meaning. Where was God, Bina?"

I say, "God is right here with you. God saved you." No response.

My friend Kelly is visiting. She looks at Steve and says, "Your right eye is really opening."

Without fluttering, The Phenom delivers: "My eye opens because it wants to see you." He uses that line on everyone, but what's sweet is that he means it with everyone.

Kelly mentions her husband Kai, reminding us he works at Google. Steve announces, "I'm alive because of Google." When we prod about how Google saved his life, he says cryptically, "There's messaging involved." He mentions other outcomes Google is supposedly responsible for, like his new job. "I found out I got a new job at Salesforce." I think Steve is as excited about Salesforce as he is about surviving.

I do something my friend Kara taught me. "Honey, give me three words to describe how you are feeling now."

Steve replies: "Fatigued. Overwhelmed. Scared." I was rooting for *happy*. I'm adding this question to my daily rituals, which include applying essential oils, tapping, giving him a spoonful of coconut oil, taking his daily photo, and napping together in the small hospital bed.

Day 113. I shout to the blog today:

"Dear Ones,

I am LIVID! Within moments of reading a letter congratulating me that Steve's inpatient benefits were extended by two weeks, in a separate communication direct to the hospital, our health insurance company, AKA "wealth insurance company," denies Steve further stays at the hospital — effective yesterday! That's ZERO notice to get up and go! This is despite doctors' medical requests for Steve to stay and them accepting it…

We've had zero training on my husband's care, no conversation about the transition home, no outpatient therapies lined up. His mom isn't coming for a week, so I'm alone with the kids, caring for Steve 24X7, getting ready for school to start.

How can our insurance company release a patient overnight who has been hospitalized for 111 days? I tell our case manager, Mabel, I can't take him. She tells me they will file an appeal but her outlook is bleak.

I know we'll get through this, but this is not how I envision Steve's homecoming — stressful, unplanned, last minute. What does Steve think of all of this? He says, "Can you imagine a sick person like me, coming home to a dirty house?"

God Bless and Godspeed,

Jenna

"The only things strong enough to break open our hearts are things like pain, mistakes, unjust suffering, tragedy, failure, and the general absurdity of life. We must be led to an experience or situation we cannot fix, control, or understand. That's where faith begins." — Richard Rohr

I thought we nailed preparation. Like so many moments in this journey, I never could have predicted this. After facing this unimaginable roadblock, I have nowhere to turn but my faith. To see clearly, I ask myself, "What is my lesson in this setback?"

I re-examine the situation. They could have told me, "Steve must leave tomorrow because he's not progressing." During the Stanford days, acute rehab specialists said we needed special approvals for a "slow-track" rehab hospital because his condition was so severe. They feared he would not progress through their average-patient, pre-determined, cookie-cutter milestones and needed a program for "slow riders." They were also worried Steve's physical progress would outpace his cognitive improvements. That's been true, so our insurance company is punishing him for it?

Relying on faith I ask, "What am I not seeing?" The answer I hear is that we are blessed. Build your strength from that. We saddle up to face this next challenge. Driving home from the hospital, I point to Payton and say, "It's you and me tonight. Do you want to go to the hotel tomorrow? If so, we're pulling a late-nighter. I need all hands on deck and an ice cream cone. Are you in or are you out?"

Payton says, "I'm in for the late night. Hold the ice cream. I'll get yours." I circle the block at BiRite. Payton returns with the cone. I drip chocolate on my new jacket that reads, "A sunshine state of mind."

We aren't rushing to clean because Steve is coming home this minute. We are rushing because of the hotel room. I received an incredible invitation from a friend of Steve's, an angel, whom we'll call "Up Above": "Our family wants to give the Pelaez's a summer holiday! Can we send you, Aria and Payton to a posh San Francisco hotel for a little pampering? A place close to Steve but far away from the chaos? Think room service, swimming, spa, high tea!"

I would *never* do something like this at a time like this, which makes it the perfect gift. I am so practical, such a workhorse. My poor children have been with their task-executing-force-of-a-mother for over one hundred days straight. They've been on-deck, cleaning up, packing up. They've been asked to organize and re-organize, cook and clean. They have been starving ("You only cook for Dad!") and patiently waiting. The other day another kind friend sent professional cleaners to scrub our home. That evening Aria asked me, "What are we going to do tonight since we don't have to clean?"

We open the door to the pit we call home and size it up. It's Friday night. The appeal gives me three days to get the house in order. I call Leslie and tell her Steve got kicked out of rehab. Amy Winehouse rings in my ear: *"They tried to make me go to rehab. I said, no, no, no…"* I hang up the phone and run around in circles, chasing Payton and screaming. Before I can yell at Payton for firing up StarCraft, the doorbell rings. It's Leslie, Molly and several friends I don't recognize, ready to pitch in.

We spend fifteen minutes zig-zagging around the house, muttering out loud about what needs to happen but making little headway. I need to let stuff go and direct other people on my behalf. By 10pm a dozen boxes read "DONATE" or "KEEP," and the house feels "low-stim." We high-five each other, the visiting angels disperse, and Payton and I keep going until he collapses at midnight. Each time I want to call it a night, I motivate myself by muttering, "hotel room."

It's Saturday morning. Mayor Matt is out front with his trimmer, leaf blower and yet another earth angel — neighbor Kier, who takes the boxes sitting on the sidewalk, thanks to Payton, to GoodWill. Matt is supposed to be in Mexico but his dog got sick. Instead of sulking at home about missing a beach vacation, he is hard at work at my house.

The Phenom spends the entire day in bed, repeatedly calling to make sure he hasn't missed the dinner party I planned. By twelve noon Steve is showered and dressed. Fishing for approval he says, "I'm wearing the tight pants and Spiritual Gangster T-shirt. Is that right?" I laugh. I brought him some pants that were too tight before the accident. I figure, it's now or never for these Euro trousers.

We enjoy a dinner party at the hospital lounge with a dozen friends tonight, including Steve's best friend Ray. We have ambiance, a spectacular view and a reason to celebrate. We still cannot believe the miracle that is Steve. I see how both joyful and hard it is for Steve to dine with us. I feel sad seeing him depleted on the sidelines, out of the conversation as the evening draws on. He used to be the center of dinner table chatter. But, still, here he is, seated at the table. What a blessing that is. This is a magical night, one we all agree we couldn't picture 112 days ago. After we finish eating, Payton hands Steve his daily treat — a Chez Pay peanut butter cup, a chocolate bar made of date paste, oats, pine nuts, and cocoa sandwiched in-between peanut butter.

Ray mentions something peculiar. He says, "When I talk to Steve, he has no memory of bike riding, racing the World cups, competing — any of it. Steve told me, 'I know cycling because people tell me I was a cyclist.'"

This surprises me. I realize I haven't talked about cycling with

Steve; I'm avoiding it. I fantasize about Steve having no memory of or interest in cycling. Hearing Ray talk about Steve having no memory of cycling, while also hearing that Steve yearns to ride outside is telling. The essence of Steve is all there — his compassion, passion and life purpose — and the underlying emotions driving his interests and actions are there. The memory of those interests and actions is not. This explains how he can make a comment to his CEO that he's "meeting a lot of people at the hospital and if there's anything I can do to help you, please let me know." In the same breath, he asked his former co-worker Glenn, "What does FinancialForce do?"

When Steve was in a coma, the kids and I wondered if we would ever see him again. Will the Dad my children have known and love come back? They still tell me it's not really Dad. It's Steve in a pure form, which is confusing; we're experiencing his deepest inner self. It's the essence of Steve stripped of ego, social norms, ordinary distractions and the other distorted clutter that buries our souls. Steve doesn't remember what his job was, racing his bike, or Payton and Aria's childhoods. He draws blanks on his wedding day, his home, and countless past events. We don't know if those shelves are empty, or if they just need to be dusted off. Regardless, as I've said throughout this long recovery, "I'll take him as he is today." Being with Steve now is like having a view of his open heart. What else could you ever want or need from another person besides that?

For the children, it's a different story. Aria has a hard time connecting with the current version of her father. She says she knows it's him, but doesn't "feel him" and her memory is blocking who he was before the accident. When Aria was born, Steve had trouble bonding with her too. It took him a while to grow close with her but when he did, it was magic — Daddy's little princess and Aria's "Miss You," as she called him. Whenever Daddy was not around, even if he was merely at work, Aria missed him. Now the roles are reversed.

When I ask Steve for three words to describe how he's feeling today, he replies, "Sad. Empty. What's it all for?" Trauma doesn't own our family, but it sure is getting in the way. My friend Natasha points me to an interesting interview with a leading trauma researcher named Bessel Van Der Kolk, who talks about treating PTSD with yoga and EMDR (Eye Movement Desensitization and Reprocessing). EMDR was invented by Francine Shapiro, who discovered that when moving your eyes side to side while thinking about upsetting memories, the emotional charge from those memories weakens.

The interview offers a scientific explanation for what I've discovered naturally through our own trauma:

- Pain is the entry point to joy.
- Connections to people are vital for surviving trauma.
- Our bodies and minds are linked. Knowing this enables a self-awareness that produces resilience.
- Resilience is the antidote to trauma.

Dr. Van Der Kolk says some of the most spiritual people have gone through great trauma — the only way to truly appreciate joy. The key to resilience during trauma is to be self-aware, inhabiting your body, noticing what's happening to you rather than being hijacked by the painful situation. "The big issue for traumatized people is that they don't own themselves anymore. Any loud sound, anybody insulting them, hurting them, saying bad things, can hijack them away from themselves… What makes you resilient to trauma is to own yourself fully."

Steve will need help owning his body. His fears are front and center; I can relate. I was a nervous nelly for months after the accident. Although Steve's accident was 113 days ago, he's still processing the accident in days not weeks, due to the coma and his short-term memory loss. Steve's deepest fears are related to free time. When he's not in therapy, he cannot figure out what to do. He's anxious that he's not performing a task required to further his recovery. This leads to multiple phone calls, asking for clarity. I need training as a therapist! How am I expected to care for Steve all alone when he comes home? Maybe I could develop lesson plans over the weekend to help when therapy is skeletal.

CHAPTER 25

Being the Hub

DAY 117. It's Saturday and an old cycling friend of Steve's, Christopher, emails me along with his buddy Josh, about keeping Steve in the hospital. Christopher mentions Josh works for our health insurance company and is a cycling teammate of his. When I read Christopher's response, I fall off my chair. Josh is the Chief Operating Officer of our health insurer!

Josh says, "I am very sorry to hear about your husband's accident. I can't imagine what you and your family are going through. As soon as I received your email, I forwarded it to three key folks — both Chief Medical Officers and the Chief Clinical Officer. I asked them to urgently look into the situation. I will get back to you the minute I hear anything."

This email gives me the strength to make it through the weekend. I suddenly have the energy to spend eight hours straight organizing the house. I feel humbled and grateful that someone of Josh's caliber in this billion-dollar organization is trying to help. I am deeply grateful to Christopher. "All you have to do is ask," I tell my kids often. Christopher probably last saw Steve twenty-five years ago!

And we are still on track for the posh life at the St. Regis Hotel tonight. After our health insurance shock I almost nixed the hotel stay, but Josh's email ignites my hope.

When we check into our gorgeous corner suite Payton says, "This hotel room is nicer than the best room in our entire house. I'm going to find a way to stay in hotels like this when I'm older." I race my kids in the saltwater pool. We drink mocktails at the hotel lounge. We escape reality watching movies, eating out, ordering room service and shopping at the mall. We stay up late watching *Wonder Woman*. Aria orders a cheeseburger and ice cream at 10pm, I finish her burger at 11pm, then wake up at 3am with acid reflux.

In the morning, I enjoy a relaxing cranio-sacral massage. The therapist starts with one hand under my sacrum and the other on my belly. It seemed like her hands were perfectly still. I am deeply relaxed, in a light sleep, when I wake with a start, suddenly on the verge of hyperventilating! I think that's an odd thing to happen during a relaxing massage. The therapist moves her hands to three more locations and it happens three more times. Afterwards, she explains that I was releasing trauma. I guess four traumas came out of me today — I wonder how many more I have stored inside?

We're at the pool again. I've been detached from my phone and when I check it, I cannot believe what I see. Unbeknownst to me, the momentum of my appeal to our health insurance company has been building since my blog post. Apparently, a lot of our friends know a lot of people in this organization. The blog has been streaming words of camaraderie and encouragement. Tyson's sister Tory reaches out. Mitch from Salesforce emails me. Beth and Ray offer to mastermind my "Save Steve" pitch. The love, support and generous offers to reach out to movers-and-shakers give me the confidence and peace of mind to enjoy twenty-four hours with my kids in a swanky hotel while I let the flow of life continue without me. At a time when I should feel stressed, I feel blessed.

One month ago, a woman named Shannon knocked on my door. The wind blew her to our prayer flags. "Hi. My name is Shannon. We've never met... I read your blog..." She sat on my sofa and we instantly became friends. Since then, Shannon has texted me research and articles, dropped off more gifts. She is a sweetheart. After reading the healthcare blog post, Shannon texts me: "Jenna, my husband knows the CEO of your health insurance company. He'll read your pitch and call him tomorrow."

It's Monday and Shannon's kind husband Darren emails me: "The CEO, Chief Medical Officer, and the rest of the C suite have been informed. Simply put, senior leadership is now directly aware of Steve's case." I am driving to the hospital squealing in delight. Not five minutes after reading that email, my phone rings. It's Steve's case manager Mabel who says, "Steve's release date mandate has been rescinded. He can stay."

Regardless of which C-Level pulled through, this I know — it was Divine intervention. Thank you! My friend, Old Soul Mary, says today happened because I am "in the Divine zone and on my path 100%. That's what happens when you hang with your destiny. You could have run and hidden, letting others handle it for you. Instead, you stepped up and opened up and you will never close down again."

The anxiety of bringing Steve home to chaos has lifted. We meet with Steve's occupational therapist Holli to receive a therapy session, motivational speech, and planning meeting in one. We establish a clear direction for the Phenom's homecoming, which involves Steve and me living in a practice apartment for two days.

We will act like we're on our own but will be inside the safety of the hospital. It feels so good to process this transition slowly and with care.

Day 119. "I'm thankful God has kept me alive for four months. I'm thankful to the team who helped me but I'm also wondering, 'Why? Why God? Why would you do this to me? What did I do to deserve this pain?' The stuff I've been through — I don't wish it on anyone. I'm feeling thankful but also questioning, 'Why me?'" – Steve Pelaez, August 16, 2017

"These pains you feel are messengers. Listen to them." – Rumi

I tell Steve we've been given a job. It's not one we applied for, definitely not one we would choose. It's been thrown in our lap. Now what? "God only gives you what you can handle." I hear this phrase so much I'm leaning on it as truth.

Here are the details of our job. A mountain of heavy and seemingly immovable boulders are trying to bury us alive. Instead of collapsing under the weight, we slowly wade through the debris, climbing out of the rubble, holding onto each other. We need a smooth surface to rest our tired feet and are searching for water. It was two months before Steve took his first sip of water. We don't know if we will find what we are looking for but there is no question we will never stop searching. Freedom is somewhere in here.

Kira, one of those friends who has a resource, connection and answer for nearly everything, sent me a great New York Times article: "How to Build Resilience in Midlife." Here's what the article says you need to survive a job like ours:

Practice Optimism. My kids are frustrated with my positive outlook and all the blessings I see. Now, my vision is clear to receive them.

Rewrite Your Story. Before this tragedy, our family story was fun and happy, but we yearned for a meaningful purpose. Now, I feel our story is a positive one that will help others. Although we are in pain, we project positivity — that's our new story.

Don't Personalize It. I never felt like we brought this tragedy on or felt sorry for ourselves. I felt like we could handle it and create more good from it than the pain we've received from it.

Support Others. Supporting others is the purpose in our pain. Pain is the entry point to healing ourselves and others.

Take Stress Breaks. Sometimes I have lunch with friends, occasionally get a massage. I go to yoga. I could de-stress more. I'm working on this.

Go Out of Your Comfort Zone. I thrive in discomfort. It seems to be how I'm made.

"Sorrow sweeps everything out of your house so that new joy can find space to enter." – Rumi

Our house is empty. Joy enters our space in everyday moments.

DAY 120. For the first time in four months, I am spending forty-eight hours with my husband. It's like old times. We eat dinner, at which point he brings up "why me?" again. When I offer my opinion about all the good that has come out of this tragedy, Steve says, "Speak for yourself." He should commiserate with the kids. I am reminded that I have no idea what kind of pain he is in.

I am tired but sleep poorly because of the hospital lights. This morning when I nudge Steve at 7:30am, he tells me to wake him at eight. I am relieved that Steve slept soundly.

After breakfast in bed, it's speech therapy. He does a dry run of the PowerPoint presentation he will deliver on his last day. I hear the "old Steve" come through. The public speaking neuron is sparking, and just needs time to strengthen.

In preparing his presentation, Steve sees images of himself before the accident for the first time, conjuring up deep pangs of sadness. "People are telling me I'm so much better but I don't feel it." I show Steve videos of himself as a vegetable in a coma, in restraints with jello-like calf muscles, and being machine harnessed to and from bed. He sees his first time sitting in a wheelchair, first time walking, first time going up a single stair. He's shocked hearing "this was you" three months ago, two months ago, one month ago. He has no recollection of any of it.

Steve has therapy again and watches the trailer for *Crash Reel,* the documentary of snowboarder Kevin Pearce who suffered a traumatic brain injury training for the 2010 Olympics. Steve is intrigued by his story. Kevin says traumatic brain injury is like a fingerprint; no two TBIs are alike. It's hard hearing there is no single roadmap to recovery. You have to be your own advocate and listen intently to your individual body. Steve's recovery rate to date has been better than anyone could have predicted, but will it continue? No one knows.

Thinking about Steve coming home to continue recovering under my care is daunting. I'm a force in the hospital, but what am I going to be at home, when I am the attending physician? I ask his doctor for guidelines and a checklist. They're skeletal.

After *Crash Reel* reminds Steve of being an athlete, he says, "I don't want to compare my present to my past. I consider it to be a negative moment." His therapist says to move forward, Steve must accept this reality. I offer, "Honey, your reality is constantly shifting.

Just because you can't do something now, doesn't mean you can't do it in the future. Some things you have lost forever and you need to accept those, but others you will get back. With stamina, will, and a positive attitude, you will build a new life. Acceptance is simply accepting where you are at now and acknowledging it." I ask Steve to describe how he's feeling. He says, "I need a hug from you. I'm overwhelmed. I need to hear you love me." I instantly deliver.

Steve's mom Lola flew to town last night and stayed with the kids, while I spent the night in the hospital. Tonight is our last night in the practice apartment. During Dr. Moser's rounds, we talk about decreasing Steve's pain medications over the weekend. I suggest we do this now while Steve is under hospital care, in case he suddenly needs more pain medication in the middle of the night. How does that work when we are home?

During Steve's psychiatry session, I ask how he feels about moving home. He says he's not afraid. I prod him: "Really?

Steve says, "I have you." I'm not sure I share his confidence. Then he asks, "Bina, what has your role in all of this been?"

"What do you think?"

"The hub."

"That's a great way to see it."

"The wheel doesn't spin without you."

"You're amazing. You're a poet."

Steve reflects, "You are amazing. There's so much going on."

"You know that's where I thrive, in chaos. That's why I'm here and you're there. Each of us is sitting in the right seat of this speeding train. Together, we'll stop it."

Steve admits, "If you weren't the hub, things would fall apart. They would stop spinning. Just sitting here seeing you is awesome,

premonition. But I stood between the kitchen and the family room and repeated in the back of my mind, *I will be okay if I never connect with Steve again.*

Steve emailed his brothers: "…I'll be as compassionate as I can be when speaking with her. But she'll hear the truth. We have to get in touch more with our deeper feelings. There is power and growth in it. It helps us heal. The mind will play tricks but feelings speak the truth… I plan to share my feelings with her…In the long run, it'll be healthier for all of us." Delivered at 1am, those were Steve's last words to his brothers before the accident, which occurred seven hours later.

After sharing this with Alice I take a deep breath and say, "I can't get weighed down by the gravity of this message. I'm not going to worry about the implications if I fail." It's just another mountain to climb in a range that never ends. I don't overthink it. We've gotten through so many impossibilities already. This is just the next one — and probably not the last.

In spite of it all, I sleep for a sound six hours. I need to deliver the message this afternoon, before I drive two hours away. I will spend all weekend on a soccer field, trying my hardest to live in the present with and for my daughter, while not worrying about my tender husband standing on the edge of a precipitous cliff.

Here it goes; I am delivering the message to Steve. I cringe inside having to restate his painful past, but I keep it high-level, devoid of deep emotion. Before Alice's input, I thought one of the hidden benefits of Steve's amnesia was not having to dredge up his painful childhood. I thought we could skip the bad memories and reignite the good ones. But the accident has taught me that trauma stays locked inside your body until you release it.

Steve doesn't need to relive his childhood, rather acknowledge it, connect with his mom, forgive her and release the pain. Hopefully, he will recognize the gifts his mother has given him and find that 'reverence' — the most important piece. I look up *reverence* in the dictionary: deep respect for someone; high esteem; high admiration.

I start my conversation with Steve by asking one simple question: "Steve, how do you feel about your mom being here?"

He replies, "I don't know what kind of relationship I'm supposed to have with her."

"What kind of relationship do you want?"

"I want to fix the pain I've had since I was five. And, then fix the pain for my brothers. I'm sure they have pain too. If my mom and I can talk about it, it would be great."

I couldn't hope for a better response. I meet with Steve's mom privately to fill her in, suggesting what she and her son have been guided to accomplish. I'm not sure if she believes in these messages but it doesn't matter. What Steve says and does reflects them. Lola tells me she's ready to hear her son speak, and I'm thankful for her courage. I feel reassured this will happen, take a deep breath and head to the tournament.

My friend Jenny calls. Today she happened to read the blog and feels called to Steve. She says, "I can be at the hospital in ten minutes."

When Steve was in the ICU, I showed Jenny photos Steve took of the Haleakala Crater in Maui, a week before the accident. He was mesmerized by this majestic, spiritual crater, which looks like heaven. With all that's transpired, it has new meaning and I asked Jenny to paint Haleakala. Jenny started the painting but said she needed Steve to infuse his energy into the piece; my precious friend is visiting him at the hospital now to do just that while I'm driving to Aria's tournament. Jenny describes the spiritual significance behind the current solar eclipse, tying that to my conversation with Steve about his childhood. Serendipitously, she is elevating my message and helping me feel relaxed for the weekend. Divine timing!

Jenny tells Steve to imagine himself as a baby and describe what he needs. Steve says, "My baby needs to be picked up. He's scared and needs to feel safe."

Jenny asks, "If you put your baby down, can your baby still feel safe?"

Steve responds, "Yes." Jenny teaches Steve how to create a "bubble of protection" that he can place his baby in, controlling who has access. Jenny has Steve write words and draw pictures about this image. Steve starts with a circle. During this time, Steve's mom has one hand on the canvas and one on his back, as he holds the painting. He and his mom form an actual circle with this painting at the center.

Jenny interprets the meaning of 'Healthy' to be *Heal thy self.* She explains that healing comes when you are in an enlightened state. Anger, hatred, and other negative emotions pull you away from this state. Forgiveness is key. *Forgive = For give. What do you have for giving?* Jenny gives Steve a mixture of "forgiving" essential oils to use. She instructs him to put oil on his heart once a day and focus on forgiving.

I am astounded by the pure magic of Jenny's surprise visit. I could not have created a better scenario if I tried. A series of spontaneous events are set in motion to navigate Steve toward forgiveness and reverence to heal. Jenny's teachings give Steve power at a time when he lacks control, all of which ties to forgiveness — a choice he can make every day.

DAY 120. Surprisingly, Aria's tournament is a fun diversion. My first weekend away in four months is a success. Aria and I are back home and to my relief, Steve and his mom are thick as thieves. Lola says she will continue sleeping in the hospital until her son is released. Steve says, "Mom is helping me and keeping me safe. I don't want her to leave and I want her to do the same thing for my brothers that she's doing for me." I feel like my dreams have come true.

Steve and his mom are bonding over old memories and piecing new information together from his broken childhood. The numbness, potential indications of a seizure, has lessened. Steve says, "I am fighting to live, even though it's so painful because I don't want to leave my children. My mom left me but now I know why. She did it to make a better life for me and my brothers and I'm glad she did it. My children and my wife are my WHY. I don't want to leave my children like I was left."

Steve discovers Aria knows about his difficult childhood and is upset. When Steve's mom asks why this is bothering him, he explains, "I don't want Aria to carry around anger in her heart and treat people badly because of it."

Turns out, the soccer tournament I dreaded was the opening Steve's mom needed to mend her boy's broken heart. The veil over Steve's childhood and his relationship with his mom has lifted.

It's almost twelve noon. Aria and I rush to the hospital gym where Steve is on the treadmill, pumping his calf muscles, trying to ignore his shoulder pain. I shout, "Steve! We have fourteen minutes left to see the solar eclipse!" We gently lead him to the window, put on the protective glasses, and tell him where to focus. We ask him to release painful feelings and memories, sending them out with the eclipse. When the moon crosses over, good memories can erase the bad.

I receive a touching text from Steve's FinancialForce colleague Blake, who last visited Steve when he first checked into rehab. Today, Blake visits Steve at the end of his time here so he has a clear view of before and after rehab. Blake texts me: "Truly one of the best moments of my life. Blessed to have my friend and mentor back."

My friend Saba sends me this message: "If one person falls, the other can reach out and help. But someone who falls alone is in real trouble." Friends and neighbors, family and strangers are helping our family survive by connecting through the blog. Steve is investing in his relationship with his Mom and vice versa. She has taken a three-month leave of absence from work to care for her hurt son and his family. We say Steve was re-born on Father's Day 2017, the day he spoke his first words. His mother is rebirthing Steve as he learns to be a living human being again. I am grateful she is here.

CHAPTER 27

Coming Home

DAY 125. Although I was not in a horrific accident, I have spent the majority of my time in a hospital the past four months. With Steve's homecoming days away, what happens now? I'm at Aria's school orientation for parents. As I blend in with the parents asking questions about homework, sports and academics, I notice how normal everything is. I wonder if we will feel normal again someday? When you are living at the brink of death and daily life is a stream of magical blessings mingled with unexpected turns down frightening paths, how do you weave back into the daily grind?

We are at the North Tower laughing with Steve's old boss, Johnny. Having last seen Steve in a coma, Johnny says he could not imagine the Steve who welcomed him today. We laugh about all Steve's recent religions, of which he has no memory. He repeats that God was giving out green Buddhas in heaven and he said, "Not right now, God." As Johnny tells stories about Steve's ideas at work and his thirst for challenge, it's like we are speaking about someone else. I recount that Johnny's faith in God rubbed off on Steve. In fact, Johnny's the reason our family started going to church on Sundays. Now, Steve is rubbing off on Johnny when he says, "This accident happened so that I know God lives. I have faith. God is real; he cares about us and wants us to know *that we are not alone.* Everyone who has given to my recovery knows this truth."

When looking at all the hospital photos, Steve asks, "Did all these people really visit me?" Steve remembers people — his affection for them and feelings. He recalls concepts and ideas, but has hardly any memories of the past. It must be disorienting. Everything is news: people dying, getting married, having another child. I feel like I'm in a time traveling movie. I retell information to Steve, already knowing what his previous reaction was, curious if it will be the same. Sometimes, I try to escalate Steve working through a particularly difficult piece of news because we've already been here and resolved it.

DAY 126. Aria asks, "When is Dad coming back?"

I answer, "Friday."

Aria gives me a look and says, "You know what I mean, Mom. When is DAD coming back?" I need to prepare our home for the kids, not just Steve. I need to talk with the children about the next phase of our new life and how we are going to support each other — not just the new guy moving in.

I am seated in the hospital conference room with a group of therapists, nurses, friends and family. It was forty-nine days ago that I sat here with a similar group of people who spoke more about what they *didn't* know about Steve than what they *did* know. At that time, Steve was restrained in a posey bed, constantly talked about dying, and was not allowed to have visitors. The children and I could see Steve for ten or fifteen minutes max, one or two times per day.

Today, Steve sits in a chair flipping through a printout of his

PowerPoint while his therapist clicks through slides projected onto a screen. Steve is delivering a thirty-minute presentation called *The Road to Recovery: Steve Pelaez.* He is wearing salmon-colored pants with dress shoes, and a coordinated striped v-neck T-shirt. His hair is gelled and he smiles and laughs the entire time. He speaks about living, not dying, and all the people who helped him survive. Steve speaks from the heart, with humor and gratitude. I laugh more than I cry. Had I thought about the difference between Steve a month and a half ago and today, I would have drenched the room with tears, but he is so funny that I allow myself to simply enjoy him. I don't carry the weight of the situation into the room.

My friend Natasha was one of the last people to see Steve before the visitation ban. She recalls when Steve started whispering at Kentfield. At the time, Steve asked Natasha why this happened to him and what was it all for? Natasha offered, "There's a jewel in this dark cave and it's yours to find."

Steve responded, "I'm going to find it."

Natasha says to Steve, "When you were in a coma at Stanford, I held your hand. When I thanked you for introducing me to your friend Eddy when I traveled to Cuba, I felt a squeeze in my hand. I thought to myself, 'He is definitely in there.' With all the tubes and machines that kept you alive, you still came through. When you weren't mobile, you wanted to strengthen yourself physically, so you stretched your legs and moved them around in your veil bed like you were working out. Where you've come from and where you are today, Steve, think, 'I can make the next step.'"

Tomorrow, August 25, 2017, Steve makes the next step, and it's all the way home. After 126 days living in hospitals — one-third of 2017— Steve comes back to us. Thank you, God.

DAY 127. I wake up feeling nervous about bringing Steve home and managing his medical care. Millie feels uneasy too — going ballistic, barking at a neighbor and her dog, walking by. I apologize, "I am so sorry about my dog."

She replies, "That's okay. I'm Tawnya." Tawnya tells me when she first found out about the accident, she wanted to reach out but felt shy. She says, "I'm a neurocritical care nurse at UCSF." Of course, the day I am feeling scared and vulnerable about bringing Steve home from the safety and security of a hospital, I find out one of my neighbors is a neurocritical care nurse! I feel like God is hosting Steve's homecoming. With deep pangs of gratitude, I breathe easier into the big day.

Planning Steve's arrival is exciting and overwhelming. Millie has fleas and an infection; Payton calls home sick from school; the filthy car needs to be washed; the laundry is piling up. I have to pick up all ten of Steve's medications from the pharmacist and make sure I know what to do with them. To top it all off Steve is calling, wondering if I "changed my mind and decided to bail." Seriously? Despite the chaos, it feels like my wedding day. I calmly roll up to the North Tower for the last time as an inpatient's wife.

I greet Steve and his mom, who are ready to go but not before The Phenom bids farewell. My sweetheart is on a float in a parade, waving goodbye to his hospital family. He glides down the hallways for one final sweep of the only place he will remember from his four-month hospitalization. Steve is teary-eyed and scared to death.

We gently place Steve in the front seat of the car and take him out into the world. I drive like I'm carrying my first newborn baby and even that's not gentle enough. The car ride is painful. Steve's mom asks, "How do you feel being in a car?"

Steve responds, "Scared."

Aria calls us on the phone and asks the same question. He responds, "Great!"

As we drive through the city, Steve recognizes Crissy Field. "I used to ride my bike there," he says.

We cross the Golden Gate Bridge, and he reflects, "I used to ride my bike on the bridge. If I did that now, I would run all those people over."

Steve recognizes the Marin Headlands and says, "I used to ride to the top in eight minutes. It would take me a lot longer now."

Aria says, "There's this boy at school…"

Before she can finish, Steve snaps back, "Big Daddy's coming home. I've got one giant eye and it's reserved for Aria!" The entire car erupts into laughter, Big Daddy included.

Bringing Steve home is surreal. We take a family photo in front of the life-size welcome home sign with a picture of Steve hanging on the chimney. Aria and I unload the car and settle in, while Steve explores his home — a place he's never been. I eagerly point out the Peloton stationary bike. "Shanti organized a fundraiser and bought you this. The screen plays a realistic video of the road you are riding on the stationary bike. You can ride Mt Tam, Tahoe, and even the French Alps from our family room." Steve nods his head, finds his way to the bedroom and crashes.

An hour later I say, "Hi Steve. I hope you had a nice nap. Say three words to describe how you feel."

Steve answers, "Tired. Thankful. Hungry. I'll see what's in the fridge…"

He finds his way to the kitchen but soon I'm screaming, "Steve!

Put that donut down! Who bought donuts? They are toxic to a healing brain! No sugar! No processed food! Here, can I make you a banana peanut butter milkshake?"

Steve and Payton sit on the front porch on the rocking chairs while I heat some brain soup. I make my way to the porch too, enjoying the warm sun and a visit from our neighbor. Our friend Katie is here with a delicious dinner and before we know it, we are seated at the kitchen table with a dozen family members and friends. What a blessing — except that Steve is struggling.

Our dog Millie overwhelms The Phenom. Although many people saw this coming, I did not. Steve says he cannot handle our puppy's barking, erratic moves — her very being. He urgently needs her OUT. Before I can say doodle, Millie's breeder, Shanti, takes her away indefinitely; Shanti was ready for this.

The kids are devastated and blame me. Aria storms into her room, slams the door. Alice is here to do a reading for Steve but I quickly realize she is here for Aria. Alice nails Aria's habits and ways of expressing herself, unlocks her hidden worries, explains the root of her concerns and suggests how Aria can take a different approach to lead a calmer and happier life. Aria is blown away and says, "Now I understand why Amelia and I fight, Mommy. My proverbial trash can was full and I was exploding at the tiniest little pieces of paper being thrown in it. Now I get it." Three hours later, long after Alice thought she was heading home, she reaches deep inside Aria's soul to burn away many of her heartaches. It's an incredible sight to watch Alice unravel Aria.

I ask Steve how he feels being at home. He says, "I miss the safety of the hospital, all the people helping me. It's scary here. I can't believe I'm counting on you to manage my medications."

I reassure him and say, "Of course you can count on me."

Steve relaxes and says, "I know what it's like to be married to an awesome woman." I pray to God I deliver on my assurances.

DAY 129. It's good to have my boyfriend back, even though he's the jealous type. He wants to know where I am at all times and, if I am leaving, he wants to clutch the landline in his hot little hands to dial my number. Today, I tell my boyfriend I am running to the pharmacy. Before I grab the car keys he's ringing me. "Steve, I haven't left. Why are you calling me?"

"I want to make sure I can reach you."

I patiently respond, "Remember, you're never alone. You are with me or your mom at all times."

"I know, but when I want to find you, my mom doesn't help."

"That's because I'm not always reachable. Where am I when you can't see me?"

He softens, "You're in my heart." It's sweet to be needed, but I do wonder — how will I get back to yoga? I know this won't last, but it's hard. It's like having a demanding baby who talks.

The dying talk is back. Steve's therapists told me his recovery will digress upon returning home, but this may be something else reflecting much deeper and profound layers in Steve. Steve says if he gets too close to God and visits the afterlife again, he is afraid he won't come back to earth. To find his true calling and purpose, he needs to connect to God, but he can't because he's scared of him right now. We think Alice is the perfect person to help Steve find his purpose, but he needs to morph a bit more before meeting with her. Alice has only read Steve while he was in a coma and minimally conscious. We know the awakened reading will be profound; we are not certain Steve's ready for it.

Steve hands the kids and me heartfelt letters he wrote each of us at the hospital with the help of his therapist. Payton can't stop talking about his letter and how sweet his Dad is. Payton, like me, calls Steve a poet. Steve asks me multiple times, "How can I be a good husband, Bina?"

I say, "Well, Steve, good husbands, hmm... they make their wives breakfast every morning, empty the dishwasher, sweep the floor constantly AND wipe surfaces, take out the trash from all cans (not just the kitchen), give evening foot rubs and spontaneous head rubs, cook gourmet dinners, keep fresh flowers in the house, schedule surprise date nights..." I go on and on, laughing, but Steve doesn't get the joke.

The kids are moping about Millie and I don't blame them. It's lonely without her. Steve wants to figure out how to bring her back, but right now his brain cannot handle her and no one knows if it ever will. The fact that this accident cost us our family dog nearly pushed me over the edge yesterday. As a coping mechanism, I don't think much about how hard this entire situation has been. When I dive in deep, it's impossible to bear so I jump back in my bubble and cling to the positive.

The Phenom has been home for two days. Tomorrow we plan to walk into our church as a family for the first time in four months. When this idea was presented to Steve he froze, unsure he could do it. Tonight he asks me for the tenth time what time we have to leave for church tomorrow. I am curious about what he will wear. Tonight he walks into the kitchen for dinner wearing basketball shorts, dress socks, a work T-shirt and a fancy blazer with a pin and handkerchief. I ask, "Why are you dressed like that?"

He replies, "Don't I have a meeting? I put on a blazer for my meeting."

DAY 130. Making it to the church by 9:30am is an ordeal. Steve wakes up at 7 to shower. He needs help lifting his legs over our extra tall tub. He doesn't know how to operate the shower or set a comfortable water temperature. And he showers wearing bright yellow, slip-resistant hospital socks — one of many memorized safety tricks. He says, "These towels are so heavy, Bina." There's a whole routine around putting on socks and underwear. My sweet husband needs all kinds of little things I know nothing about. I tell him I am impressed with his workarounds.

Steve picks out a Friday night cocktail outfit for church. I show him my colorful dress, which I optimistically earmarked early on as the celebration dress for this event. I am in tears looking at this dress; after four months, I finally get to wear it. I think his pink blazer coordinates best with my dress, so Steve and Aria select a coordinating dress shirt to match. Steve independently picks the vest and socks. He looks fabulous, but ruins the smooth look by tucking his vest into his pants. Part of me wants to pull the vest out, but my better self vetoes the notion. There is something so appealing about this endearing new version of Steve who just "is" without any concern for pretense or others' judgment. He's not wearing a thread of ego.

The walk to church is easier than I predict. Upon arrival, he effortlessly responds to the loving souls who greet him. Pastor Kim untucks his vest! When the service starts, Steve speaks the words to the songs instead of singing. It takes him a while to get the rhythm of the songs he speaks. Everything seems fine. He seems happy. I keep turning my head to look at his light-filled face. *Is this real? Are we really here?* I can't tell you how many times I've questioned whether the life I am living is a dream.

Today's sermon is about compassion but Steve looks sullen after hearing it. I ask him if he's okay and he replies, "I'm overwhelmed." I take him to the church office, where he lies down on a comfy sofa with his head in my lap like a pillow. I do some tapping and have him state his mantra: *I am safe. I am healthy. I am happy. I am loved.*

"Pastor Kim talked about compassion," he grumbles. "Where is God's compassion for me?"

I remind him that God saved his life. "You've received so many blessings, Steve." He slowly relaxes as I take note of the stillness inside the church office. The room reminds me of my grandparents' house, growing up — faint sounds of cars streaming by, birds chirping and the meditative ticking of an old-fashioned clock. It's soothing to connect with sounds from my childhood. Is it because, as children, we are closer to God?

Payton and I are arguing again, or maybe we never stopped. He's been home sick, living at his computer 24/7. I nudge him to take breaks with little response. I finally hit a wall and ask Steve if he can deal with Payton and let me know the outcome. To my relief, Steve agrees.

Devoid of emotion, Steve approaches Payton and says, "You're a test for your mom. She is eventually going to get frustrated with me and my recovery but is going to need to be nice to me, instead of getting upset and frustrated like she is with you. You need to help your mom learn how to do this."

Steve FaceTimes his brother and his nephews answer shouting: "Uncle Steve! Why are you a pirate?" We forget how funny Steve's eye patch is to a child. The patch eases the discomfort of double vision. Steve is the cutest pirate I've ever seen.

Reminded of the importance of Vitamin D, I send Steve and cousin Dane to the front porch where the sun is blazing. As friends drop off dinner, they smile at Steve and Dane who migrated to the front lawn. They are lying bare-chested with their hands behind their heads. I daydream about joining them, playing reggae music, sipping virgin Pina Coladas.

Our family skipped summer. I initiated a few classic summer diversions with Aria but we mostly missed the best season of the year. At first, I didn't care because of the alternative, but since we are upon happier times now, I feel the pangs of missing summer. I'm in the mood for a good ole-fashioned BBQ. I remember that fall feels like summer in Mill Valley so all is not lost. I thought about how we used to spontaneously bring our dinners to the picnic tables at the bayfront. On one of those days, Trauma Ambassador Gillian was riding by on her bike with her basket of flowers, and happily stopped to say, "Great idea! I'll join next time!" This was our life in Mill Valley before April 21, 2017. Could it possibly come back to us?

CHAPTER 28

No Longer Seeing Double

DAY 131. The Phenom greets me after his morning Peloton ride wearing his eye patch, rosary as a necklace, and Aria's tween sunglasses. Steve can pull off almost any look, but this one is a stretch.

I chirp, "How was your Peloton ride, Steve?"

He scoffs, "It was tough."

"Where did you ride?"

"The beach," he moans. "It was my third scenic ride that felt like forever." I cannot stop laughing, as Steve trudges away with slumped shoulders. My husband doesn't know who he was prior, as an athlete or even as a person. If that memory kicks in, I wonder how he's going to cope with his new body and training regimen.

I learn why Steve was so dedicated to cycling. He says, "Cycling was my escape."

"What were you escaping from?"

"My childhood. Cycling gave me something else to focus on. It gave me passion." Now that cycling has been taken from him, it's an opportunity to heal from what drove him to it. A big part of healing is forgiveness. Richard Rohr states, "Grace re-creates all things. Nothing new happens without forgiveness. [Otherwise], we keep repeating the same old patterns, illusions, and half-truths."

Steve has a Bowen Therapy appointment with Meghan Marks today. Meghan is the earth angel who energetically worked on him at Stanford on day two, helping him restore his Life Force. She has worked on Steve remotely for the past four months. Steve's soul has visited Meghan dozens of times during his recovery, including several weeks ago. He has no mental recollection of Meghan or these visits. Today, Steve and Meghan work together, consciously, for the first time on the physical plane.

According to *www.bowen-training.com*, The Bowen technique is "an alternative type of physical manipulation named after Australian Thomas Ambrose Bowen (1916–1982). Recipients are fully clothed. Each session involves gentle rolling motions along with the muscles, tendons, and fascia. The therapy's distinctive features are the minimal nature of the physical intervention and pauses incorporated in the treatment. Proponents claim these pauses allow the body to 'reset' itself…"

Meghan's practice is in downtown Mill Valley. Steve and I discuss when we will leave to meet her, how we will get there, and what we will do prior. Steve has a slew of questions about downtown Wonderland. I suggest we spend some time there before the appointment. I say, "Let's go to your favorite coffee shop, Steve — Equator Coffee."

"Can I get a cronut, Bina?" You can imagine my response.

As we inch toward the car, parked across the street, I question whether Steve looked both ways. Driving off, he mumbles, "I guess I should put my seat belt on."

Cruising the mile and a half downtown, Steve and I both point out landmarks. We park the car and Steve says, "There's Equator

Coffee. There's a burrito place around here I love."

I quiz, "What's unique about it?"

Steve answers, "It's Indian." Jackpot! We fist bump.

After ordering at Equator we sit outside where it's quiet waiting for the barista to yell, "Steve!" What a privilege this has become! Just as we are hoping to see Helen, the owner of Equator, she whizzes by. When we tap her on the shoulder, she nearly loses her coffee beans. We take several photos, chat about miracles and life, and how she is donating coffee for an upcoming fundraiser concert for Steve.

It's time for Bowen therapy. I reassure Steve that he can trust Meghan. I explain that his soul visited here during my first Bowen treatment when he was still in the hospital. Steve giggles about his soul escapades. I settle him in and ask for three words to describe his feelings. He offers: "Excited. Happy. Safe…" My cue to exit.

I check out the Clear Center of Health Integrative Medical Clinic. Several friends see a naturopathic doctor there named Dr. Kate Tenney, a mom from school. I want to see her about strengthening my health to continue my ridiculous pace. I see a flyer describing the health benefits of forgiveness and think of what Alice said a couple weekends ago, plus Richard Rohr's devotion this morning. Forgiveness keeps surfacing.

When I return to Bowen for Steve he is swaddled in a blanket, snoring peacefully on the massage table. We wake him up and Meghan says, "Look at his eye." I'm confused.

I confess, "It's not obvious which eye is damaged."

Steve awakens and says, "I only see one of you, Bina."

I hug Meghan and start crying. "Steve! You no longer see double? Do you need your patch?" His answers are no and no.

I ask, 'What else do you feel?"

"The numbness and pain on my right side are gone. When I swallow, my throat doesn't hurt anymore. I can sit up without pain in my back. Mentally I feel okay. When I fell asleep I felt no worries. And when I woke up, you were there."

Thrilled, I say, "Steve, give me three words to describe your feelings."

"Amazing. I can see. I can sleep."

Afterward Steve passes out, but I wake him to see Dr. Moser. A potential infection brings us back, as well as numbness. Steve receives antibiotics that will hopefully clear the infection. When I mention how Meghan fixed Steve's numbness with Bowen Therapy, the doctor looks at me as if I'm delusional. If I didn't witness the healing myself, I might not believe it either. By the time we get home, Steve is wiped. After dinner, he hits the pillow but he calls from the bedroom, "Bina, you were going to make my dessert?"

I laugh. "Thanks for the reminder, Steve." I brainstorm something healthy. I'm told peanut butter is inflammatory but he craves it. I blend organic rice crispies with cocoa, coconut oil, butter, honey from Mary's backyard beehive and an egg to make a crust, which I bake. I spread the peanut crispy crunch on the chocolate "wafer" and drizzle melted chocolate on top to seal it. I struggle with Steve's sweet tooth but want to honor it in the healthiest way possible.

Besides sweets, Steve craves a routine. Unable to reproduce the predictability of the hospital, I try to establish a home therapy schedule. Like everything, it takes time. Time is the one thing I don't feel anymore; I have no sense of time.

DAY 132. I ask, "Steve, can you still see single vision?"

"Yes."

Curious, I inquire, "Why are you wearing an eye patch?"

"It makes what I see less busy."

I wonder if freeing his physical pain allows The Phenom to dive headfirst into the emotional pain? I take Steve to a psychiatrist, Dr. Saal, whom we saw before the accident for parenting advice. He greets us with exuberance. Dr. Saal is a blog reader and in awe of Steve's survival. The Phenom has no interest in his miracles and sharply shifts the tone, becoming a puddle on the floor. "What's it all for?" he complains. "Why did this happen to me? Dying would be easier." We leave the session early; it's too much.

I tell the blog, "I see God everywhere. Those who read my blog see God too. If you've seen Steve, you've seen God. God pours out of Steve, washing all over those who surround him. But poor Steve, the one who's awakened us all, can't find God himself; and he desperately searches for him day-in and day-out."

I suggest, "You need to pray to God, Steve, and ask for answers to your questions." Steve says he's afraid to talk to God in his dreams because he's desperate for sleep. He's still scared that if he keeps going back to heaven, he won't come back to earth.

Steve laments about the pressure he is putting on himself to be a good husband and father, and to thank all those who have helped our family. He says, "I feel like I'm drafting off Jenna and I want to pull. She needs a break." Steve keeps prodding Payton about biking to school so I don't have to drive. He doesn't understand that biking is heartbreaking for his son. No matter how much I try to reassure Steve, I can't break him free of his emotional pain. I remind myself this is Steve's journey and he's not mine to fix.

Payton is watching a battle movie. Steve says, "That's scary, Pay. Turn it off." Steve takes one look at Martha Stewart's *Grandin Road Halloween* issue and tells me that's scary too. I pick up the harmless *San Francisco Magazine,* and he thinks the models are people we know. When we drive around town, every stranger on the street is someone he knows. What exactly does Steve see?

We love surprise knocks on the door. Peter and Trauma Ambassador Gillian drop by after their morning run. Dana "Mr. Positive" Williams, nicknamed by Steve, catches us after a neighborhood walk. Ross and Erin swing by with a bouquet of flowers from their backyard. Kristin drops off her delicious, gluten-free bread from Juice Girl, a gift from Karen, the owner. There is nothing more uplifting and joyful than being surrounded by so many loving souls, no matter what state my home life is in.

Aria walks in the door and beams, "Mommy! I met Grace!"

I wrinkle my brow. "Grace?"

She blurts, "From the movie! The lady who got hit on the Golden Gate Bridge."

Dr. Grace Dammann was a prominent HIV/AIDS physician who was honored by the Dalai Lama for her extraordinary work during the height of the epidemic. In 2008, while driving on the Golden Gate Bridge, another driver hit her head-on. Grace spent more than a year in rehabilitation hospitals, including Steve's. My friend Natasha, who knows of Grace's story, recommended her documentary *States of Grace.* Grace now lives around the corner from us and Aria ran into her at the coffee shop. After confirming she was the famous Grace, Aria said, "My name is Aria. It's so nice to meet you. We know about you because my Dad was in an accident too. My mom wants to talk to you. May I have your number?" I call Grace this evening. I bet she knows the perfect person for Steve to talk to. It may even be Grace herself.

DAY 133. It's 3:36am. I hear the faint sound of Steve exhaling. I feel a wisp of wind against my face. I ask, "Steve, what are you doing?

"I'm blowing on you."

"Why?"

"You're hot and sweaty."

I've been sweating in my sleep the past few nights. Steve cooling me off makes the fact that he's up in the middle of the night less annoying. Steve blames me regardless; my sweat somehow makes him cold. Steve's blood thinners and TBI make his entire body perpetually cold.

At 4:43am I find Steve in the kitchen. "Steve, what are you doing?"

"Eating ice cream."

I am researching how to best help Steve. He wears a rosary and clutches a wooden cross in his hand 24/7, even while sleeping. He needs someone who is both spiritually and medically astute to unravel his sadness. Conventional physicians who treat Steve offer medication as the answer to his woes — but he's already on a host of medications. I want Steve to access his mind via words, meditation, prayer, the right foods and vitamins, and alternative therapies like Bowen and EMDR. I believe Steve needs to be grounded to the earth.

Steve and I drop off Payton at school. To my surprise, The Phenom wants to see the teachers, including the headmaster. Steve asks, "The small European woman — what's her name?"

I answer, "Meinir."

Steve exclaims, "Meinir!"

But the first person we see is Chako San, who recognizes Steve and seems flooded by emotion. As Steve slowly shuffles toward the big room, where teachers, parents, and students gather each morning in a circle, he's unraveling each teacher or parent one-by-one. Parents approach me crying, so overcome with feelings by the living Steve. When we arrive in the big room we spot Meinir, casually seated at the pink piano, playing with her back to us. She's wearing white flowing linen pants and a matching shirt with a blue scarf around her neck. Her short dark hair is wrapped in another scarf. Steve walks up to the piano and lays his hands next to Meinir's. She stops playing and springs up stunned, a huge grin on her face and her hand on her chest. "I can't believe what I'm seeing," she gasps.

Steve smiles and says, "Hello Meinir. I'm here."

We join morning circle — a spiritual occasion on any day, but especially today when Meinir announces our guest. Steve responds, "This is what resurrection looks like." He glows, looking over the sea of inspired faces. Meinir initiates the morning ritual, whereby teachers and students greet one another. Each teacher says something heartfelt about Steve. Meinir suggests the children sing the special song they sang many times before, including during Grace's gospel prayer service. It's called *"Come to Me."* I never imagined hearing this song with Steve in the room. I remember that my friend Angela dreamt of this very moment. This is surreal.

Heading home, I feel moved by Steve seeming so joyful, ener-gized, full of life this morning. Anything feels possible in moments like this. Steve falls asleep and when he awakens, we talk about the visit. He says, "It was very difficult."

I'm confused that he is recalling something different than he expressed. Could it be both difficult and joyful at once? Steve's reshaped mind is a mystery I am devoted to solving.

Tonight, the vegan taco dinner we receive from a generous Mill Valley family is so good Payton repackages the leftovers for school lunch — before I have a chance to eat! He is hiding the food from me. Payton, not a fan of the blog, says, "You'd better write this one up. This is solidly the second best meal we've had during this entire ordeal. Number one, of course, is Lousang's homemade dumplings."

DAY 134. I receive a lovely note from Meinir, reminding me of the blessings of this tragedy. She writes, "When I turned to look and saw Steve, I was blown away. He looks so ethereal — what he has seen is just incredible. And you, beautiful as ever, calm, present — just astonishing. We were all quivering inwardly this morning. It was such an honor to have you both with us..."

Sentiments like this help when the pain of daily life tends to smother the joy. I need to help Steve see beauty again — an enormous challenge for his shattered brain. Today marks one week since Steve's homecoming. It's been wonderful and terrifying, sad and hopeful. Joy and pain are soldered together, impossible to disconnect. I repeatedly tell Steve I love him and am grateful for his life. I can't stop saying it because I can't stop feeling it.

Steve complains so little about his pain that when it's released, like after Bowen therapy, I realize how unaware I am of his quiet suffering. The same is true for emotional pain, which seeps out unexpectedly. When Steve describes traumatic childhood events that sound like fiction, I call his brother for validation. We carry so much around in our heavy bodies; I long for my husband to feel weightless.

People often ask me how I do it all. The answer is I don't. I do only what I can and I'm well aware of the long list of things I am *not* doing. This tragedy happened at a challenging developmental time for my children. Payton became a teenager when Steve was in a coma. Aria started middle school, which is essentially the same thing. I am not the present mom I want to be. They feel it and are having their own reactions to it. Meeting everyone's needs is hard.

I am out at night for the first time, a party for middle school moms. The conversation quickly goes dark: drugs, sex, kidnapping. I cannot fit the terrifying information about what kids are facing into my already overflowing mind. A tall, beautiful woman with short, curly auburn hair shyly approaches me. She carries me away from the darkness with her charming British accent. She says, "Hi Jenna. My name is Sarah. I've been following your blog. I am so sorry about Steve."

Sarah explains that our daughters were in class together last year and she's made something for Steve but has been afraid to come over. Her blessing is that she distracts me from the tailspin the group conversation tempted me with. Sarah and I get lost in our own conversation, focusing on love versus fear. It's moments like these — when someone reaches out with a kind word, gives me exactly what I need the moment I need it, sends me the perfect book in the mail — that enables me to get through this wackadoodle life without falling apart.

*"Go to your fields and your gardens, and you shall learn that
it is the pleasure of the bee to gather honey of the flower,
But it is also the pleasure of the flower to yield its honey
to the bee. For to the bee a flower is a fountain of life,
And to the flower a bee is a messenger of love, And to both,
bee and flower, the giving and the receiving of pleasure is
a need and an ecstasy."*

— Kahlil Gibran

CHAPTER 29

"Peanut Butter"

DAY **135.** Steve says, "I can't believe it."

"You can't believe what?"

"That I can take a shower."

"Yes, you can and that's great… Wait a second! How did you get *out* of the shower? Please don't leave the shower without me present!"

DAY 136. It's 6:30am and I find Uncle Mario awake on the family room sofa. He arrived at 2am but no one answered the door, so he slept in his rental car until Lola found him at 4:30am. *How did I not leave a key for him?* I forget to do the simplest things. Because he's Uncle Mario, he woke up happy. I say, "You're used to being up 'til 4am, Uncle Mario. You're a Colombian from Miami! I know how you roll."

He laughs and says, "Those days are over!"

Nicknamed Uncle Mario, he was married to Steve's mom and raised him and his brothers when they moved to the U.S. He considers Steve, who he calls *Cocoy*, his son. Uncle Mario last saw Cocoy on Day 7 in the ICU. The reunion between him and a walking-talking Steve is tender and heartwarming. While embracing his son in the kitchen, Uncle Mario retells his last words to Steve in the ICU: "The next time I see you, Cocoy, you will be on your way to a full recovery." His prediction is coming true.

For days, it's been over one hundred degrees. Twice, Steve has unsafely escaped our home unaccompanied, to cool off on the front porch. He feels miserable, barely speaks and stares into space. Desperate, I drive Steve to Safeway to walk inside the cool air. It's refreshing but overstimulating.

We return home to a full dinner served by Dr. Beth — home-made Tom Ka Ga soup, a tangy salad with lime, cilantro dressing, and a cool corn and red pepper salad. The fresh and flavorful meal distracts us from the heat. Afterward, we eat ice cream on the front porch. As I'm thinking about what to write in today's blog, I realize that today is the first more-or-less normal day in over 130 days!

DAY 138. Several friends surprise us at church. It's exciting to be surrounded by so many people we care about, sharing our journey of giving thanks to God for our blessings. Steve stays the entire service, despite its difficulty for him. I say, "Honey, if you need to rest, tell me. What you need comes before pleasing others."

Steve wakes in the middle of the night and if I don't, the adventures are endless. Last night he ate truffles, made a bowl of ice cream Payton confiscated at 4am, went outside by himself and who knows what else. We remind him of the dangers of a secondary injury and that he needs to stay in bed at night, but self-control is wishful thinking. As we cope with the stressors of keeping The Phenom alive, the question of what to do with this tragedy to create something meaningful, especially for Steve, is starting to focus.

Notes, conversations and appointments from Steve days before the accident are surfacing. Each revelation is a clue. It all points to this statement Steve posted on Facebook seventeen days before the accident:

"... I want to lead a non-profit— to be financially successful— to earn and share. I want to mentor disadvantaged kids, because I was one and be a role model to my own kids and give back..."

This is where Steve was headed, but apparently he had a few brutal checkpoints to clear before he could arrive.

I ran into my neighbor Micaela the other day. We don't know each other well, mostly running into each other at yoga. Micaela commented how alive and glowing I am now. She said I'd looked lost, before the accident. I'm surprised someone who barely knows me picked up on that. I did feel lost. It's almost as if this accident happened so I could find my way too — not just Steve.

Every day I look at Steve, I can't believe he's alive. Sometimes I ask, "Are you real, Steve?" I feel blessed that he lived but I struggle with his constant pain. Steve hardly complains but I see the pain in his face constantly. He's in agony much of the time and I wonder how I can help him. Then, I think of what Grace from the documentary *States of Grace* says: "I think I would have died early on if it weren't for my Zen practice. I learned that nothing lasts forever, including great pain, great sorrow, great helplessness. Nothing lasts forever... Who am I really now? Who do I want to be now? We'll see."

DAY 139. Alexis, from the life-saving father-and-daughter team of Alexis and Otis, is here with another dinner. She keeps feeding us! Steve knows Alexis and Otis as his first responders but doesn't know the details. Today, Alexis shares them. The accident is a puzzle with many missing pieces that we are slowly finding. As we place each piece the picture emerges, but do we really want to see it? Alexis says she has tried to get the picture of Steve lying on the road out of her mind, but can't. The conversation shifts and Steve asks, "What can I do for you, Alexis?"

Alexis explains, "You are giving people hope."

Steve's face wrinkles. She explains that whenever someone miraculously survives something tragic, it makes people feel hopeful about the world.

She says, "Steve, you survived for a reason. You are meant to be here. You just have to find out what that reason is."

Steve says, "It was overwhelming listening to the details of the accident — that the driver thought I was dead and that Alexis thought I wasn't going to make it."

I apologize. "I should have redirected the conversation, honey." Alexis suggests Steve develop a safe word.

I exclaim, "Great idea! What should it be?"

"How about brachial plexus?" Steve suggests.

I say, "That's a mouthful. How about peanut or bubble gum?"

"How about, 'I want to eat peanut butter?'"

"That's confusing because you do always want to eat peanut butter. How about just 'peanut butter'?" We settle on that. Whenever Steve feels like he needs to get out of a conversation or situation, he says "peanut butter."

Today, we plan to spectate Aria's soccer tournament, which is walking distance from our home. Going out with Steve is like getting out of the house with a toddler. It takes forever so we leave later than planned. There are countless false starts. And, he has to back up to the bathroom as soon as his foot crosses the threshold.

Then, once we are out, we move painstakingly slow. I am acutely aware of the bumps in the sidewalk, distractions, roads, lights, cars, people, our direction, walking straight, having good posture, being present and calm, and the need for rest.

By the time we see the soccer field, Aria and Amelia are coming toward us. We missed the first game entirely. Good thing it's a tournament.

I vow to improve for the second game and do. We arrive just as the halfway horn is sounding. It's so stressful. The notion of a rogue soccer ball hitting Steve is my primary concern, instead of watching the girls play. I've never noticed the chaos of a soccer game — fields and balls everywhere. I imagine how Steve feels and I am frightened too.

Getting ready for bed, we barricade the front door with boxes so if Steve tries to escape, we can hear the kerfuffle. I wake up at 3am and Steve is gone anyway. I follow the light to almond butter and ice cream. I tell Steve it's exhausting getting up in the middle of the night and he apologizes. He doesn't want to behave this way; his mind can't help it. We are working on sleep strategies like exercise. He rode the Peloton today but complained about it being too hard. Alexis figured out that it's the screen that's challenging, not the pedaling. It's too stimulating. Alexis suggests Steve ride the Peloton without the screen and listen to music instead.

Simple things are a struggle and a puzzle for Steve and me now. It's trial-and-error all day long. I hear my friends' voices in my head telling me to take care of myself, let go of things, worry less. I keep meaning to write things down and post them on the wall like they do at the hospital. Filling out a form, booking a dental appointment, printing a note are challenging for me these days.

It's a strange feeling to have a hard time doing little things, but I let it go. My strategy for getting things done is to allow what's important to rise to the top on its own.

Day 140. Every time I say the word "meeting," Steve puts on a sport coat. It's endearing and symbolic — Steve desperately wants to be whole again. He knows how to look the part, he just can't play it.

Aria is raging around the kitchen, shouting about something in front of a mousy Steve. I hold my line, remain cool and keep the peace. This is a new strategy because when temperatures rise, I typically rise with them. But screaming is not a TBI protocol so I'm learning to be a "mindful mom." This is not my strong suit.

Ironically, one of several angels Marc Benioff sent me to help with the kids calls this morning. I catch her up to speed and prepare her for our meeting this afternoon. I'm finally doing more for my family than for Steve.

Meanwhile, Payton is upset with me and repeatedly raises his voice as Steve slowly backs away, retreating. Then he sits on the sofa with a sullen face, slumped shoulders and sad eyes. I ask Payton to sit on the front porch until he composes himself "in front of my husband." I pull rank, scolding: "You are hurting my husband with your harsh words."

We have all changed. Our children are drowning in trauma and it's challenging to support their grief while keeping their behavior and responses in check. We all have impulse control issues; the answer to that is mindfulness. Unfortunately, we need a crash course because time is of the essence.

Steve was exponentially happier in the hospital than he is

at home, even though he wants to be here. He doesn't smile and laugh like he did in the North Tower. He's afraid, worried, and sad around the clock. I hope it's temporary but fear that it's rooted in the family dynamic. The kids are tough to manage and when they argue with each other or me, it overstimulates Steve.

Steve wants to be with me non-stop. He lets me leave the house but when I do, he lashes out against his mom asking, "Why is Jenna still out?" I feel pulled in opposite directions. On the one hand, Steve is no longer in an acute medical phase, so I should be free to hang out with friends and take the kids to fun places. On the other hand, Steve is housebound, can't enjoy the same pleasures we do, and feels abandoned when we leave. I need to leave him with close friends who can take his mind off me when I punch out of TBI Headquarters.

I ask permission to take Aria and her friends to Trauma Ambassador Gillian's pool. I tell Steve it's a five-minute drive and the girls want to swim for an hour. He reluctantly says okay but when I try to throw in dropping off laundry at the neighbors, he draws the line. I take what I can get.

These California cutie pies have so much fun. Gillian's sweet eighth-grader son, Alex, hops in the pool too and gives the girls middle school advice. Alex initiates Marco Polo, a summertime fave. While staring at a giant palm tree, listening to the sounds of laughter and water splashing, I think how happy I am to be here… what a privilege it is to be relaxing at a pool in the summertime.

Day 141. Steve has a warning: "*Malcolm in the Middle* is a scary show, Bina."

Payton watched it yesterday. Common Sense Media says: "This

comedy series pushes the envelope on irreverence and the humor can be crude and/or risqué…The show puts family dysfunction and sibling rivalry in the spotlight."

"Irreverence," "family dysfunction," and "sibling rivalry" are hallmarks of TBI Headquarters. No wonder Steve is scared. Reality versus fiction is blurred for him. It's why my husband questions who the models are in magazines and books, and thinks he knows everyone on the street. When Steve sees our kids get upset with each other he knows it's wrong and wants to help but sits motionless, as if he is watching them on television, powerless to respond.

Steve's best friend Ray is here to visit and says, "Hi Steve! I made you a beet smoothie."

"Come on man. I thought you were my homey? Beet juice? That's what you're bringing me?"

Ray laughs and says, "Okay. Next time I'll bring you contraband."

Steve moans, "You've been talking to Jenna."

Steve could not wait for today. He is seeing Meghan again for Bowen therapy. Afterward, when I return, he is awake. Meghan is tweaking the work she did and I am about to witness the transformation.

Before Bowen, it looked like Steve was dragging the whole right side of his body around with him, barely able to lift his right hand. If you shake Steve's hand, he uses his left hand to lift up his right hand just a few inches, so he can latch on. It's cumbersome and painful but he does it wordlessly.

Meghan asks Steve to move his right arm as she examines his body, making micro-adjustments. All three of us see the transformation after Meghan gently pokes Steve's left shoulder, then his neck area, and then his right armpit. After those subtle motions, Steve raises his right arm and hand to the center of his chest. Meghan grins ear to ear. Steve cannot stop flapping his arm and hand. My jaw is on the floor.

Immediately I go to video, via my iPhone. "Breaking news from downtown Wonderland. Steve, tell me, what's happening?"

"I'm moving my arm."

"Is that something that's happened before?"

"No."

"How do you feel?"

"Amazing. I feel solid. Thankful."

"Why?"

"Because I can move my arm on my own."

"What are you thinking?"

"How the hell is this possible?"

I say, "It's because of Bowen Meghan. What do you want to say to her?"

Steve smiles and says, "Thank you, Meghan...What the hell? All this stuff happens when I'm here with Meghan. I need to spend more time with her." Thanks to Meghan's generosity, he will.

After Bowen, I ask Steve if we can stop by the Clear Center of Health so I can turn in my forms and book an appointment. I reassure Steve: "It's around the corner, up one flight of stairs." Steve is reluctant but gives it a go.

Steve is tired after Bowen therapy. When we enter the building, I point to the staircase and say, "Take your time." Like a race-horse hearing the gunshot, Steve is off. Only it isn't the sound of a pistol that fires up Velo Biscuit. It's the sighting of a little old lady. As soon as Steve sees the hunched-over 90-year old wobbling her way up the stairs with a cane, he hightails it to the top, almost running. *Did he just pass an old lady on the stairs to inflate his ego?* When Steve summits he turns around to check out the granny and I nearly pee my pants. Steve just gave a little old lady the cyclist's "glance back"! The competition has changed, but the athlete has reincarnated.

CHAPTER 30

The New IKEA Husband

DAY 142. The construction work will reconfigure our home office into a spare bedroom for Steve's mom, who is scheduled to live with us for a few months. Having Lola here is a blessing. It's so nice to have help caring for Steve. I am his primary person and it's a lot of weight on me. Am I doing everything right?

"How could Jenna and Claire talk about our bedroom for four hours?" Steve complains to his mom. Steve is worried that Claire, a high-end interior designer, is convincing me to purchase luxury furnishings. While all of us are seated in the kitchen, Steve nonchalantly slides an IKEA catalog across the table toward Claire. I miss the hint but Claire catches it. She immediately flips to the Malm dresser — $179 — and says, "Steve, this is your new dresser." After throwing away my last IKEA dresser, I have been lured right back to their cool, minimalist designs. One of my contractors explained that the trick to keeping an IKEA dresser from breaking is you build it, secure it to the wall and never move it again.

A kind neighbor drops off cookie bars. Before I can hide them, The Phenom has one in his good hand and another in his mouth. Claire moves at breakneck speed to offer a trade. "Steve, may I prepare a plate of fresh fruit for you?" I have never seen anyone slice and plate a cantaloupe so quickly.

Recalling the bait-and-switch, Steve says, "Claire used a steak knife and didn't even have a cutting board."

I ask, "Steve, wanna go for a ride? I need to drive Aria ten minutes away to her friend Amelia's house." Car rides are an opportunity to trigger memories and get fresh air. As we approach Amelia's home, Steve says, "I've been here before."

I correct him saying, "I don't think so, honey. I've never been here."

As I am pulling out of the driveway, Steve insists, "Turn onto that road." I humor him.

Thirty seconds later I see it and shout, "Steve! That's the house we wanted to buy! Great job remembering!" My brain-injured husband already recalls things I don't.

He points to another road and says, "I used to ride my bike up that road."

As we head home Steve says, "We could go that way, to return to Aria's friend's house." I nearly pull over and hand him the keys. He's been overstimulated since coming home, reversing his upward trend the past few weeks. I needed to see a burst of progress, and I receive it in spades.

Our generous friend Virgine is here to lead another trauma therapy session. She reminds me of a Disney princess; I swear her eyes are made of stardust. As the shimmering Virgine tells Steve his therapy today will involve riding the Peloton, he tenses up. I say, "Before the accident, I couldn't get this guy off the bike. After the accident, I can't get him on it!"

"That's because I'm your IKEA husband now," Steve counters. "If you move me a lot, I'll break."

Virgine's therapy sessions with Steve are solo but she debriefs us afterward. She unravels many mysteries. For example, she suspects the sugar cravings are from low dopamine levels, which elevate during exercise. Since Steve used to exercise like crazy and is now sedentary, his levels are down. I learn that when I leave Steve, he misses me because he needs an oxytocin release, aka the "love hormone." One way to compensate for that is to give him a transitional object, like a pregnancy body pillow.

Virgine reveals that while we all understand Steve's shoulder, arm and hand are vastly improving, he sees things differently. Steve is afraid his shoulder injury is just *beginning* and he's on his way to being paralyzed! That never crossed my mind. Virgine teaches me how to speak to Steve. First, validate his fears. Next, do a "fact-finding" excursion to see if his concerns are real. Then, using reasoning instead of emotions, we can alter the perception.

DAY 143. Today is the Frances England benefit concert at church. We invited everyone we know to listen to Frances sing, eat Chez Pay desserts and celebrate. Payton could not bring himself to make the sugar-free "desserts" we eat at home: "I know what kids want, Mom. They don't want your date paste." Like father, like son.

When I leave for church with Chez Pay and his mountain of baked goods, Steve is sound asleep. I am not certain he will wake up for the celebration, but he does eventually and slowly meanders to church with his mom. We usher him into the church office, his safe room, where he rests before call time. David, the tall, bald usher, estimates there are 250 people here! Guests are mingling outside, ordering desserts, checking out the raffle prizes and buying tickets. Steve says repeatedly in disbelief, "There are so many people here. I can't believe they are all here for me?"

Frances' husband Funke gives a heartfelt welcome. We are humbled by this couple's generous offer to host an event of this magnitude. Funke pitched his idea when Steve was comatose at Stanford. At the time, I couldn't wrap my head around it but agreed nonetheless. I say to the crowd, "What's happening here today is not what I envisioned when Funke suggested it. This day has turned into a welcome home party for Steve! How is that possible?"

I feel like I'm dreaming. Just over 140 days ago I stood in this same spot, praying to these same people to bring my dying husband back to life. Steve joins me on the altar and says these words, which he spent weeks practicing:

"Thank you for your help. I am alive today because of your kindness. Four months ago I was clinging to life. I was given one day to live. But I had a strong WHY for coming back to life. 'He who has a *why to live for can bear almost any how.*' I learned this lesson from Friedrich Nietzsche, quoted in Viktor Frankl's book *Man's Search for Meaning.* My WHY is my wife, Jenna; my son, Payton; and my daughter, Aria. I love all of you here today. Thank you again." Steve receives a standing ovation.

Frances opens the concert singing *Come Back to Me.* My heart can hardly take it; the last time she played that song for us, Steve was comatose. When the concert ends, we stay in our pew as a stream of loving faces line up to greet Steve. People came from far away, years ago and around the corner. Before long I hear Steve mutter "peanut butter" and we quickly gather a team to gently usher him to the safe room. He passes out for an hour with his loving mom by his side.

When Steve awakens, he returns to the party, which has moved outside. He sits in a chair next to the grassy field, buzzing with throngs of people. Guests line up to connect one-on-one, filled with wonder after a precious moment with The Phenom. It dawns on me that this is the "big party" on the "grassy field" my beloved described when Alice spoke on his behalf on day 59.

The celebration ends and we head home for the after-party. The house fills up and life feels joyful but I sense we are on borrowed time. It doesn't take long for Steve to say "peanut butter" again. I give him some water, do some tapping, guide him to say his mantra and kiss him goodnight.

The house eventually becomes quiet. The concert flew by. I didn't eat any cake. And as I sit reminiscing, I long to be back there. I wish I could have told each person how much they mean to our family. I open up my laptop to do just that.

I tell the blog, "We are overwhelmed by your love and generosity. From the deepest center of our being, we thank you all for filling our hearts at the Frances England concert. From the incredible turnout and your enormous generosity, to the emails, cards, notes, gifts, meals, GoFundMe page, massive donations of time from our contractors, raffle donations, efforts of neighbors maintaining our house, rides for our kids all over town and beyond. Hundreds, if not thousands of people have made a difference in our lives and helped our family. I wish we could thank each of you personally. I don't know how because there are so many of you. – God Bless and Godspeed, Jenna"

As I cull the breathtaking photos taken at the event, one image catches my attention: the butterfly garland. During the prayer service for Steve on April 23rd, people wrote messages on fifty butterflies attached to a thread to hang in the hospital. Today, we hung that garland in the church courtyard. A photo randomly taken focuses on one butterfly in particular on this string of fifty. I recognize the note right away. It's Aria's; it reads: "Dear Dad, I need you to come home."

DAY 146. Steve has a Mr. Rogers chair where he puts his shoes on and takes them off. It's 8pm and Mr. Rogers, Jr. is sitting earnestly in his chair waiting for Millie. Our crew has wanted to see Millie for days now but it hasn't happened. They've banded together and are not budging. "We want to see Millie now!" We are going unannounced to Shanti's, Millie's breeder and caretaker.

Millie was whisked away the same day our pack leader arrived home from the hospital because he could not handle her busy, unpredictable energy. He said, "I am told I love her," but Steve could not find those feelings inside his mangled mind. Before the accident, he was Millie's number one and his sudden disappearance devastated her. She didn't play or eat for weeks and didn't produce enough milk for her puppies after her litter arrived, several weeks after the accident.

Shanti welcomes us and Millie jumps and plays. She is happy to see us! Steve calmly sits on the sofa and is not bothered by her. We put Millie on Steve's lap for some skin-on-skin. She snuggles for a moment before running around. Steve throws the ball a few times but his lats cramp and it's time to leave. Walking to the car, he says, "I love her. I want her to come home."

Before sleeping, I discover Steve in bed with both arms over his head — as in the cyclist's finish line salute. I exclaim, "Does that hurt?"

"Yes."

"Why are you doing it?"

"To stop my lats from cramping." Last week, this arm was glued to his side. Two words explain this feat: Bowen Meghan.

Not all Bowen therapists are alike. Ours is special, a gifted, angelic healer who has been key to Steve's survival and recovery, as well as my own. A big reason I am handling this tragedy with grace and ease is because of Meghan's guidance. She's been my connection to my beloved's soul from the coma days to the present. She has called or texted me countless times with strange messages from Steve that I can always decipher. He was giving me advice and sharing concerns from a coma! I can't imagine I'd have been doing as well as I have been without this precious connection.

After a session with Meghan, there are many changes and sensations as the body reconnects. Recalling my own, I can only imagine Steve's. After Steve's session Meghan notices, "He has a look of determination in his face that is not hidden by a childlike essence, now.'" Each day, glimmers of a more awakened Steve appear.

My husband speaks slowly and quietly with a rasp, as if he were in his 90s. Out of the blue, he mentions God or offers a pearl of deep wisdom about our children. He floats in and out of his physical realm on earth and his soul's state on the other side. Meghan says, "This time that our soul is living as a human is just a little but wonderful part of it all." If we all lived our lives with that celestial premise, I wonder what we would focus on and how we'd treat one another?

DAY 147. Steve's cramping lats ruin his sleep. I think, *He needs rigorous exercise to knock him out!* Back from yoga, I am shocked to see Steve riding the Peloton. While reminding me he didn't sleep, a friend from Payton's school, Tara, calls. After reading my post about Vasper Systems, Tara located a studio, Vitality for Life, ten minutes from Mill Valley. It's Divine timing.

I need approvals from Meghan and Steve's physiatrist, Dr. Rome. Meghan says Steve can try Vasper as long as he is monitored by a physical therapist and takes it slow. Steve has an appointment with Dr. Moser; I'll try to visit Dr. Rome since they're in the same medical building. While walking in the lobby, who do we run into? Dr. Rome gives us a huge smile and hugs Steve. "I'm riding a stationary bike now, Steve. It's so boring. How did you do it?"

After Steve talks about cycling I can hardly contain myself. "Interesting you should mention that, Dr. Rome. Have you heard of Vasper Systems?" I recommend the technology and get approval for Steve.

We head to the North Tower and reunite with Steve's old therapists and nurses, one of whom suggests he remove the eye patch so his eye can relearn how to function properly. I had a feeling it was bad. On our way home, Steve enters Bi-Rite Market for the first time—my TBI grocer, a few blocks from the North Tower. I treat him to salted caramel, malted vanilla, toffee ice cream. In exchange, he grabs the beet and peach salad — a fair trade.

DAY 148. My boyfriend asks, "Where were you tonight, Bina?"

"I took Millie for a walk and picked up laundry at the neighbors."

Steve responds, "Our neighbors are great." I add, "It's like this entire neighborhood is caring for our family." We even learn from each other and gain different perspectives on our kids. Payton recently spent several evenings baking at our neighbor's house when our oven broke. Payton's alone time with the neighbor paid off. He received an outsider's perspective on his mom. His attitude at home shifted and I didn't know why. When I heard about their talks, I pieced it together. Payton learned to appreciate his mom.

Steve loves listening to romantic songs, using the lyrics in conversation. He loves telling the kids, "I'm just a phone call away. Superman's got nothing on me."

Today, he says, "When we fight, I know it's okay."

I laugh. "Steve, we don't fight."

"That's because I'm stupid."

I object, "You're not stupid, Steve. You have a brain injury and are the most amazing person I have ever met."

Opening mail, I find the non-emergency ambulance bill for driving Steve to Stanford from Kentfield, for the appointment I'd canceled — ten thousand dollars! Ambulances are always out-of-network. Because of this, providers charge whatever they want, insurance pays what they want, and the patient is stuck with the difference. I am not paying for a service I canceled, so I hunt down the hospital's CEO and pray she'll take care of it. Now I need to call the insurance company.

I reach a helpful service rep who goes through every bill as I manually enter the charges into an Excel spreadsheet. I say, "What's your name and number in case we get disconnected?… Hello? Hello? Are you there?" Crickets. We got disconnected. I take a deep breath and reassure myself, *I'm not supposed to be on the phone with that lady.*

I reach a new rep who teaches me to download the bills into an Excel spreadsheet within seconds. I make progress on the bills and more importantly, I am no longer afraid of them. Turns out I am not the only one releasing fear. Steve says, "I'm no longer afraid of my therapists." Fear is leaving our household and joy is returning; Joy's name is Millie. Our family dog is home for good and Steve is no longer tortured by her.

DAY 149.

Our entire family is together again.

CHAPTER 31

Can We Afford This?

DAY 149. Steve feels guilty for not working. I explain that we are fine financially. I say, "Your job is to get better, which involves sleeping, eating healthy, participating in therapy and exercising. I have everything else under control."

I take Steve to Equator Coffee and as I approach the register, he whispers, "Can we afford this?"

I'm incredulous. "A cup of coffee and a croissant?" The look on his face makes me feel like I'm about to buy a vacation home, not a pastry.

Steve initiates three walks outside today with Millie, a new record from *before* the accident. Afterward, they snuggle on the sofa. Steve says, "Something must be wrong with me."

"Why?"

"The way Millie and I are sitting on the sofa, I feel like she's a person, not a dog."

"That makes sense. Millie is like a person and you both are healing from deep pains. Millie loves you."

Today is Steve's third EMDR session with Virgine. Recalling last week's session, Steve says, "I remember biking on the Peloton is important and hugging is for oxytocin." Virgine smiles. She wants to uncover the root cause of his problems. They may not be derived from physical trauma; it could be the reverse. The physical trauma may be igniting emotional pains, creating a continuous loop. I think of Kerry saying trauma stays lodged in the body until it squeezes out in places you don't expect.

Steve says what's physically bothering him today are his right shoulder, lats and knee. When Virgine places vibrating pulses on him, his left shoulder hurts. Virgine wonders if Steve's left shoulder is overcompensating for his right one. Steve and Virgine are co-processing his trauma, trying to determine what to focus on. Virgine explains to me that the physical pain Steve experiences reveals what's most alive in him and can be linked to a trauma network. To understand a trauma network, imagine you are a tree. The roots are your childhood and past. The accident triggers an electric charge in the tree branches. That charge travels down the tree, to the roots, electrifying what's in them. So, the physical pain in Steve's body may connect to something else — emotional pain in his heart and mind.

Virgine asks if Steve is ready for the darker side — the shadows. To my surprise, Steve replies, "Yes."

This brings up two questions: "What am I here for? What if I *can't* be a husband and a father?"

When Virgine probes those questions, Steve says, "Jenna says I am helpful because I am alive. How am I alive? How am I a miracle? I am alive because I am strong to deal with this pain? Part of me says I could be in heaven. I was in heaven. But I love my wife so I came back, but it's been hard."

"What's hard about it?" Virgine asks.

"To equalize the work with the family. How can I be a better father for Payton and Aria?"

Virgine asks, "Why do you believe you are not a good dad?"

"I'm slow. I can't physically keep up with the kids. I can't walk down the street with them."

When Virgine asks what he *can do* he says, "I can talk to them. I can kiss them. I can hug them."

"What do the kids need most from you?"

"My spiritual attention. I can pray with them and be a listening board."

When Steve speaks about how he can be a good parent in his current state, his physical body responds. The pain on the left side goes away; his right side starts to feel warm. The numbness and knee pain both disappear. But Steve's thoughts return to: "When am I going to get better?"

Virgine says Steve's body is expressing the terror he feels in his brain. "Our shoulders are our heart chakra," she clarifies. When they are opened, the release comes.

Virgine recommends placing a bowl of strawberries next to the bed so Steve doesn't have to travel for comforts in the night. She explains that going from an unconscious state to a conscious state is overwhelming. When Steve wakes up in the middle of the night, he's startled, like a child frightened by a nightmare. My poor husband's driving forces are fear and love. What is more tender than that? I am amazed by how much I am learning about the vulnerable human spirit and body.

DAY 150. I say, "Steve, give me three words to describe how you feel."

"Annoyed. Unsatisfied. Irritated."

A couple months ago I received an invitation from Trauma Ambassador Gillian to attend her husband Peter's 50th birthday party. I optimistically RSVPed yes for myself but thought the odds of attending were slim. On the day I said yes, day 44 of Steve's recovery, he was minimally conscious. Despite the intensity of that day, I set the intention of attending Peter's 50th. I never imagined this moment because it never crossed my mind. The party is today, and I am attending with Steve.

I tell Steve the plan. "The party starts at 7pm. Let's arrive at 6:45pm, give Peter and Gillian a hug and kiss and leave around 7pm, maybe 7:15, depending on how you feel. Say 'peanut butter' when you're ready to bolt." Steve agrees.

Peter's wife is "Trauma Ambassador" Gillian. Steve found footage of Day One at Marin General with Gillian doing her thing and has watched it repeatedly the past several days, mentioning her constantly. The video shows Gillian making sure Steve receives the best care. She asked the doctors questions like, "If Steve were your brother, would you put him on the helicopter now?" We will never forget Gillian's tireless efforts to save Steve. Her husband, Peter, a Kaiser ER physician, is no stranger to helping people either. Going above and beyond the call of duty is a hallmark of this family.

We arrive at the party at about 7:20. By now, it's a full-fledged party with a rager on the horizon. I am concerned about the number of people here but figure we made it this far. I suggest, "Let's give it a go, Steve!" The Phenom is wearing eyeglasses with his eye patch centered on his forehead, not covering his eye — like a security blanket patch. His sunglasses are perched on his hipster haircut. Only Steve can pull off this look.

When Steve wobbles into their home he spots a life-size cardboard cut-out of Peter. Steve says, "That's Peter"—a successful identification. We easily track down the real deal and his radiant wife, squeeze them both and extend our birthday wishes. To my surprise, Steve wants to climb a set of steep outdoor stairs to the pool area, where the band is about to play. I feel like we are climbing El Capitan. Steve summits the top with throngs of people, and I don't let him out of my sight.

Steve listens to one song and talks to Heather and Teg, old San Francisco friends who also moved their family to Mill Valley. It doesn't take long for me to hear 'peanut butter.' I ask if he wants to go home and he says no, so I suggest we eat dinner at the kitchen table where it's quieter.

A few friends join us and Trauma Ambassador Gillian says hello before heading upstairs to sing another song with the band. To my surprise, Steve wants to go back up the stairs to watch Gillian perform, which he does. But our carriage quickly turns into a pumpkin and it's time to bolt. For the journey down, I suggest we enter via the house and use the internal carpeted stairway. I am in the lead holding Steve's hand when he suddenly loses his balance and falls. Thankfully, he lands softly on his bottom.

I nervously ask, "Steve, are you alright?"

"Yes."

"Why did you fall?"

"I was not balanced. You were in the way. I need to grab onto the railing."

"I see. Next time, please tell me what you need. I thought I was helping you by holding your hand. I'm sorry."

"You're not strong enough, Bina."

"I am strong enough," I argue, "when I know what I need to do."

Steve is okay but it's clearly time to go. We make it to the car, at which point I start breathing again. Not only did Steve attend Peter's party, but he stayed for an hour and a half. After witnessing his fall, I get why Steve is shocked that he is alive and constantly worries about "not making it." I place a bowl of sliced plums next to Steve's bed and tell him if he wakes up in the middle of the night to stay put and eat the fruit. He agrees.

It's morning and I see an empty bowl. What I didn't realize was how taxing that hour and a half at the party was for Steve. We pay the price today, as Steve falls asleep in the middle of church. I suggest he rest in the pew or go home. He chooses neither, which means he is banking overstimulation hours. The rest of the day he is irritated, repeats stories, asks the same questions and slurs his speech. He naps but not enough. It's been a while since Steve has been this overstimulated.

DAY 152. "Steve, give me three words to describe your feelings after Vasper today."

"Cold. Too easy. I want it harder."

I see exactly what Vasper will do for Steve. He will find his cadence, his passion, his endorphins. But today is a gentle trial. He can only *imagine* what's in store for him. Steve is still locked inside his broken body, sorting it out on this machine. Vivian, the kind, generous, and knowledgeable owner of the Vasper studio near our house takes it slow.

Vivian is a stunningly attractive, petite woman with long locks of silver hair and a radiant smile. She assures Steve, "Hang in there.

I know you want to do more. We will get there in time." The Phenom cannot wait to get there; the pilot light is lit.

Vivian floats around her cozy studio, exuding beauty and grace. A former opera singer, I secretly hope Vivian will sing for us while we workout. Vivian shares her own story of working through pain via Vasper and the myriad benefits of this NASA developed technology. She no longer medicates for her arthritis.

What happened after my 21-minute Vasper session? I have a runner high. I sleep soundly for seven hours.

DAY 153. If God talks to me through raindrops, he downpoured today.

It's September 18, 2017, and Steve laments, "Being a miracle is so painfully hard, God. I need some of your angels to help me get through this. Dying is easier."

I ask, "What's hard about it, Steve?"

Steve whimpers, "Everything. Getting out of bed is hard. I am lying in bed nailed to a cross. To get out of bed I have to pull the nails out, one-by-one."

This morning, Steve has an ultrasound appointment for his leg to confirm the blood clot is gone. If so, the blood thinners will be gone too — one less drug in his massive pillbox. The appointment is at Marin General, the hospital that brought Steve back to life. Trauma Ambassador Gillian happens to be working and is rounding up the available miracle workers for a reunion while Steve finishes his appointment.

During the ultrasound, Steve mentions our engagement. For the first time he recalls the location: Maui.

I ask, "Where did you propose?"

He says, "The beach."

"What did you hand me at the beach?"

After a pause Steve guesses, "A coconut?"

"No — not a coconut."

Silence, then I fill in: "Diary. You handed me an engagement diary. Do you know why?"

"So you could read about my plans for the engagement?"

"Yes!"

He recalls that he proposed to me in a chapel. This memory is a big part of our history and inspired Steve's final Facebook post, eleven days before the accident:

"Aloha. Here's my Hawaiian fairytale. Twenty years ago, a boy asked a beautiful girl to marry him at the chapel in Grand Wailea. The moment she said yes, the Universe set in motion a series of blessed events that has led to this great day. Two beautiful children were born out of the commitment made twenty years ago. Today, this boy, now a man, is back visiting the chapel with not just one but two girls who so completely own his heart. The fairytale is still being written. Life is great. Mahalo."

The ultrasound is complete and we enter the emergency room waiting area, which tugs at my heart harder than I expect. We meet Nurse Jonathan, who was with Steve all day on April 21st, a couple of trauma doctors, the ER medical director, a technician and a few trauma office administrators. The medical director, Jason, states, "We're not supposed to have emotion around our patients but this is what we live for — saving lives." It's what Steve lives for too. We have a tearful reunion, take a few pictures and hightail it outta there. It's a lot.

Steve has been badly overstimulated the past two days so I put him to bed right after. Rich Landry, who would have been Steve's new boss at Salesforce, is on his way. When told post-coma that he was going to work for Rich, Steve went ballistic with joy. He's still in bed when Rich arrives, so Rich climbs into bed with Steve and hugs him. How many bosses do that?

Steve says: "Rich came here like I was in charge. He said, 'Tell me what your purpose is and we'll figure out how to make you successful.' That is powerful. He left me T-shirts that say 'Believe there is good in the world.' I do."

Kara and Jamie are here with dinner and a dose of California sunshine. Steve says, "Jamie is like my brother and Kara is beautiful like you, Bina." I mention Alice to them, whom they've read about in the blog; they are intrigued. I say, "Hang around until 8pm and you'll meet Alice in the flesh." Before Alice sits down Kara and Jamie are booking readings and before I know it, Alice is reading Steve awake for the first time.

Since Steve has a kind of soul amnesia, he can't answer the burdensome questions that linger: "What's it's all for? Why did this happen to me? Alice comes with a powerful message: "Your spirit guides want to talk to you about your calling." Steve is finally ready to hear it.

C H A P T E R 32

Steve's Calling

Day 154. It's September 18, 2017, and Steve's Spirit Guides say this to Steve through Alice:

"You're in a lush garden surrounded by butterflies. In your life, you've been inspired by everything around you in a non-linear way. You follow something until it's no longer interesting — not caring if you go to completion. You look at this butterfly or that butterfly, having reverence for the beauty of the moment. This is what makes you special and what people love about you. It's also their frustration with you. You are easily taken off course. You have evolved through this tragedy. Before, you received beauty and enjoyed it. Now, you want to give beauty away. The desire and capacity to give are what's new."

This calling maps to Steve's behavior since he began speaking after his coma. Steve agrees and says, "I know I am supposed to help people. The question is how?"

Spirit Guides: "You want to take the butterflies surrounding you and place them in people's hearts. You want to help people authentically live their most fulfilling lives. You will tell your story to help others. You already went through something challenging that woke you up with your first brain injury. So, why did this happen again? Your Spirit Guides say the answer comes in three parts.

"First, you received the butterfly experience from the previous brain injury — having reverence for the beauty of the moment. But you couldn't process this understanding. Second, you started understanding how things interconnected, which changed your thinking and you wrote about it. Third, you celebrated your family and people in your community more deeply. Those three things created a new awakening for how you see the world. The whole time you've said, 'I want other people to understand what I'm experiencing so they can learn from it.' The second accident gave you a platform to do something."

"More is being asked of you to fulfill your purpose than most people; know that you are not alone. Every person on this planet can tell you that something incredibly hard had to happen for them to do what they are supposed to do. They know this is hard to hear. You still have a hard road ahead of you. Focus on your victories. You're incrementally getting there."

Then Alice shares *her* perspective:

"For twenty years, I have read for amazing people who have had unbelievable things happen to them. There's nothing I haven't heard. People say to me, 'Literally, it was two years of my life that I wanted to die.' Or they tell me, 'I had ten amazing years that would not have happened if it wasn't for those two painful years.' You're not alone. My job is to help people through their pain by talking for their Guides. This is a common life experience no one talks about. Everyone thinks other people's lives are normal and only their life is hard.

"Your Guides say the most important thing to know is this: You will literally say these words: *'I can't believe what I went through, but for where I am now, it was all worth it.'* This accident was a small price to pay compared to what my life is like now.' I know this is hard to believe, but I see you saying that in two years in front of people."

Two Years Later

September 18, 2019: Today is the last day of the Maui retreat that I have been attending with my girlfriends. We are practicing yoga on the grass of the retreat grounds, facing a Buddha statue and the enchanting mountains presiding over the Pacific. I'm in the downward dog asana with my head upside down, between my knees, facing the sun. The giant hollow Collective Hearts necklace our loving blog community gifted me at Steve's homecoming party dangles down from my neck as sun rays beam through it. I feel a pulsating current of warm, radiant sunlight streaming into my actual heart. I sense an overwhelming but confusing feeling and whisper to myself, *"It was all worth it."* I am referring to Steve's horrific accident.

Tears stream down my face as I picture my beloved and our children. *How can I say such a thing? How could I utter those words in front of Steve, who has suffered so much — or our children who have lost so much and hurt so much? How dare I? And why would I suddenly say this out of nowhere today, of all days?* Then, I remember.

Today is precisely two years from the date of Alice's reading for Steve. Astonished, I realize the person Alice was referring to wasn't Steve — it was me. But still, how can I feel that all that pain was worth it? I close my eyes to bring that answer into focus. I see a bucket with one drop of water in it.

I recall the breathwork meditation yesterday when Alice

began crying uncontrollably. I assumed she was reliving a past trauma; it was the opposite. She was visiting the Kingdom of God in her mind's eye, overcome with reverence. Afterwards, Alice said this: "Everything we experience here on Earth is a mere drop in the bucket compared to God's love in Heaven."

Everything — including great pain and sorrow — is a mere drop in the bucket. That hit home. It answers the question, *"What's it all for?"*

The yoga session ends and I'm crying again. I confess to Tara, Alice and the retreat host, Steph, what happened to me. After retelling my *aha* moment, I admit, "I feel what I am sensing is true. I've experienced so much soul growth. I have a new, guided life's purpose focused on God. I am connected to myself as a spirit living in a human body. I never would have learned those truths without the accident. Knowing that our entire life on Earth — encompassing all the beauty and the pain — is merely a drop in the bucket helps me frame the context of our lives. So I can believe *'it was all worth it'* is true. I can see beyond our pain."

Steph asks me to repeat the words out loud to the group. As I do so, I realize that I am literally saying the accident was worth it, in front of people! It feels surreal but it's true.

All this time, I thought I was waiting for Steve: waiting for him to heal, to tell his story. I had no idea I was waiting for myself. Steve is not the person who can bring me what I've been searching for, because it's already inside me. It's inside *all of us*. Perhaps this story will provide a flicker of healing light in the lives of those who yearn for it. God only knows what that flicker will illuminate. God Bless and Godspeed, dear ones!

Epilogue

To my blog readers: you were a flicker of light when I was engulfed in darkness. You gave me comfort and love, assuring me I was not alone. I scrolled through your names each day, astounded by how many came to the blog, came to pray. Gratitude for how many people care was in my daily prayer. Time and time again you raised me from the cold, hard truth of this gut-wrenching nightmare into a dreamlike state of magic and wonder.

You, dear ones, are the co-creators of the unveiling of all our hearts, not just Steve's. Thank you for saving my life. Without you, I would have perished in the lonely vault of despair. Instead, you lifted me up with your tender loving care. This story is ours; we lived it together. Had you not been there for us, day in and day out, there would be no record of the journey. There would be no magic. There would be no story. From the bottom of my heart, I love you, dear ones.

Writing this epilogue seven years later, much has happened. Before I share where we are today, I'd like to reveal one of my deepest desires. Steve's recovery at four hospitals showed me how desperately we need healthcare reform. In fact, witnessing what I went through to manage Steve's care motivated our son, Payton, to write a 100-page thesis on the perils of U.S. healthcare — in eighth grade! From corn syrup in feed tubes to Steve's $50,000 helicopter transport bill to needing C-level connections to avoid sudden hospital discharge, my weeks were riddled with mind-bending, uphill battles with the healthcare system. Wasn't what we were going through enough?

With all we've seen and endured, if I could choose one cause in healthcare, it would be to support families like ours who are left untreated.

Our entire family suffered in the wake of a horrific cycling accident; not just Steve. I wish we all were identified as patients and shepherded under medical experts' care in a structured, comprehensive trauma recovery program. Had that occurred, the course of our lives could have changed dramatically. All four of us have lasting, damaging, cumulative effects of unhealed trauma that affect us individually and as a family unit. Unfortunately and unbeknownst to me, identifying areas of improvement in trauma care was the tip of the iceberg.

Steve eventually settled down to life at home. Cradling him with love and adoration, obsessed with restoring who he was, I drove The Phenom to endless, cutting-edge brain therapies for well over a year post homecoming. On Valentine's Day 2019, after months of relentless, mysterious back pain, my sweetheart was diagnosed with stage four non-Hodgkin's Lymphoma. We were leveled. I traced the cancer to month four, post-accident. I emailed Steve's doctors about his bizarre, relentless back itching — evidence of tumors on his spine. My concerns were not addressed. My research shows the lymphoma may have resulted from Steve's blood transfusions.

The tumors broke my baby's bones, rendering him lifeless in

a hospital bed at home. I gently sponge-bathed and spoon-fed him, wiped his bottom and cleaned out his urinal, as he withered away from chemo in a family room hospital bed. Steve wanted to live. And he did, beating stage four cancer. We celebrated our twenty-year wedding anniversary in a vow renewal ceremony with Steve down to 130 pounds in a wheelchair. We felt blessed but chemo on top of brain injury further dwindled his life force.

By the time The Phenom could participate in life again COVID hit, along with reality. Caring for Steve was one of the greatest honors of my life. AND, I entirely abandoned myself, barely caring for our children. I had traumatized teens who desperately needed my attention; and, my childlike husband had become worse. As the ever-evolving patient, four years post-accident, Steve was watching television sixteen hours a day alone, barely engaging with his family, disinterested in life. I lost my life partner, identity, sense of self. I was a caregiver, not a wife.

In May 2021, Steve left home to live with his family for a year to give me a desperately needed caregiving break to focus on our children, and to allow me to grieve for the first time. I cried daily for months while tending to our children and myself. I had no idea that I had trauma to heal, and how lonely, worried and confused our children felt.

Steve's physiatrist, Dr. Rome, said the cancer was like being struck by lightning twice. Blog readers swore our family was finished with trauma. Our trauma quota was tapped. Life will get better now, loved ones promised. Just manifest what you want your life to be, Jenna. I thought Steve's accident and cancer was the worst thing that could ever happen to our family — until it wasn't.

Our precious family experienced a third trauma that finally

broke me — my will to fight. It left the kids and me in a spiral of destruction and Steve isolated and lonely. As I write this, tears stream down my face. Steve and I are in the difficult process of being divorced. I am still gathering the pieces, settling into myself, and understanding the truth of what happened, not just to our beautiful family, but to me — the one who thought she could save everyone. How could I — the one who fixes everything — allow this to happen to our family?

If I am not The Phenom's wife, the caregiver, the fixer, the breadwinner, the home manager... who am I? I don't have an answer because I am in a struggle of transformation. Bringing this book to the public has illuminated my internal battle.

My sister Michelle gave me the book title. How about "the phenom's return to life?" I suggested. "No," she said. This book is about the phenom's wife. This is your story." My story? My story. What's my story?

When creating the cover I was drawn to images of me disappearing, lost, fading away. Until my person, Sean, said, "I see your face up close on the cover. The kind of picture that says, 'I've been through something big, it has weathered me, and I survived!'" When I gave the disappearing version of myself to my artist friend, Jen, she came back with not one face on the cover but TWO! And not faded at all. Now I've overprinted my face, my editor warned. It made me second-guess myself entirely and want to disappear again — easier than putting myself out there so boldly and vulnerably. So, I looked at myself in the mirror and asked: What does my face say?

To me it says I made it. I survived. The lines around my eyes. The bags underneath them. My tiny smirk of a smile. Those are imprints of my lived experiences. I am no longer The Phenom's wife but my face carries evidence of that time. It has made me who I am today. But still I struggle with who am I? Why am I here? What's it all for? Ironically, I sound like The Phenom.

I had been writhing in pain the past two years over the divorce until one day, while reading the final edits to my memoir, I felt the real me. I felt drenched in love. Instead of crying out in pain or fear from the past seven years, I cried out for love. And I knew my life's purpose: I am a conduit of love.

But I need to love my true self first. Instead of being a care-giver, I need to give care to her. Instead of being The Phenom's wife, I need to marry myself. My painful life circumstances stripped me to my soul essence. This unleashed the wellspring of love deep within — the place trauma can't touch, the safe place inside me that lives no matter what. This is where I hope to discover my new expression in the world, beyond caring for Steve. I hope this book is the beginning.

Every soul struggles at some point. There is no use in comparing our suffering. I have learned that we are all made of love by relinquishing everything that is not love. It hasn't been easy. I have come close to giving up. But I keep striving to live in the Light — recommitting each day, asking to be shown the way.

Thank you for reading my story, for learning about my life as The Phenom's Wife, and for witnessing the journey of my soul. May you and all beings be filled with blessings and peace. I love you, dear ones. God Bless and Godspeed!

– Jenna Ann Miller
January 2024

A letter from Steve

August 19, 2024

I know that I woke up from a coma and had a happy life but I didn't know how I got to the hospital, how long I was gone, and who to thank. Seven years later, I read Jenna's book, and how I got to the hospital became clear and why I survived. I learned all the challenges that everyone went through and how many people helped me. I want to thank all of you who helped me. I am so thankful to Jenna. She helped me wake from a coma; dealt with my Stage 4 Non Hodgkins Lymphoma; and successfully raised our beautiful children through the trauma. She is an angel.

Jenna voice-recorded the chapters for me to listen to but I only listened at night. It made me sad remembering all the before. I loved Aria's note to God, but it made me sad hearing what the family endured. On days I watched funny shows I could listen to all the difficult chapters. It's an amazing emotional read and it has good laughing moments. The velo biscuit blog is great. The coach story is funny. "I am woman." That made me laugh. I actually don't remember being a cyclist. It was great hearing about my first waking up. Why did I want to leave the room? It's funny that it took four people to restrain me. I can't believe I told Payton I was annoyed; I didn't realize that was a personality trait. I am learning about myself through Jenna's book.

It was hard for me to reconnect with my kids, my dog and the many things I enjoy. I read in the book that Aria wanted to see the old dad, not the hospital dad. Who was I before the hospital dad? That made me feel sad because she's my daughter. She's my R. I want to assure her that I'm back. Chapter 16 was interesting. Every time Jenna mentioned

God, the audio stopped as if God was pausing it himself. Chapter 21 had me laughing — joking with Jenna's dad.

Reading the book and hearing about what happened while I was in a coma made me thankful for all the support. I realize I have plenty of people to thank for my recovery like my mom. Thank you, Mom. My challenges are plenty. I miss the family and I want to help. The book helped me appreciate the life I had to receive that kind of support. I must have done something right. I am learning how much I am loved. Feel free to let me know why you cared so much. Overall I am very thankful and the book helped me realize this.

ACKNOWLEDGMENTS

Countless devoted friends and family supported me and believed in me during the tireless seven years post-accident. There are hundreds if not thousands of you. As the wreckage from the accident got harder for me to endure and I went inward, a small circle of family and friends kept me from going under – Aimee Price, AnneLise Staal, Beth VanStory, Daniel Mudimbe, Elisabeth Yvrot, Jenny Love, John Lewis, Kira Sasaki, Lily Fighera, Matt Cramer, Michelle Miller, Mom & Dad, Nicole Siminoff, Rhiah Kujot, Ryan Kearns, Sara & Greg Stern, Sean Neville and of course, my children, Payton and Aria Pelaez. Thank you for supporting me and helping me not give up.

And, these beautiful souls had a specific hand in bringing my memoir to life. Thank you.

I love you all dearly.

Fearless. AKA D. Patrick Miller (no relation). My Editor & Dream-maker. You gently guided my diary into a narrative, leaving little evidence you did anything at all. You are making my dream come true — sharing my story publicly in the hopes of helping others. Thank you for believing in me at a time when few people in my topsy-turvy world did. I trust you when you say my story is meant to be heard.

AnneLise Staal. Dear Friend. You helped me write my summary and were one of the first people to tell me that this story is not just about Steve, but about what happened to me. And you, my sweet friend, know better than anyone, *what happened to me* — the story that is unraveling and yet to be written.

Molly Humphreys. Professional Photographer. You have been the visual record keeper of our family for nearly two decades. Many of the images I use to share our family's story are your precious works of art.

Jimbo. AKA Jim Hughes. Professional Photographer & second father to Aria. I warned you that I am not photogenic. You made me feel at ease, even giddy, sitting in front of your magic lens. And you gave me not one shot but well over 100 to help me see myself and what I have survived through the contours of my face.

Jennifer Siddens. Professional Artist. Your work as a fine artist moves me. I dreamed of having an artist friend create my book cover. You not only produced something provocative, you looked me in the eyes, described what you see in my soul and my journey, and left no doubt that my face evokes my story. You refused to allow me to fade away.

Swah. AKA Michelle Miller. My Sister & Cheerleader. You named my book. You encouraged me to take ownership of *my story* and *my experience,* even though the book (and 25 years of my life) reflected my devotion to Steve. None of this would be happening if I didn't pull through my darkest hours when you promised me I would.

The Phenom. AKA Steve Pelaez. Thank you for all you are and all you have done for our family. You astound me. Thank you for being excited about me sharing my experience of your remarkable journey. I hope my memoir creates opportunities for you to support others and find the meaning you seek. Please don't ever forget that the four of us are forever family. The love we all share is eternal.

Mom and Dad. AKA Nancy Miller and John Miller. Mom, you told me the book was already written. *"Just print the blog and bind it."* You are my biggest writing champion. Dad, your steady visits to TBI Headquarters gave me potent material for the story and dad wisdom to pull me through.

Big Sean. AKA Sean Neville. My person and father figure to my children. You didn't save me but you sure made the journey of me digging myself out of a 7-year rut hair- raising. Most importantly, you helped me connect with my children again and are by my side, rebuilding our family. I was shuffling through the wreckage of my life when we met, and somehow you instantly knew who I *really* was. You saw my *book cover* before I did. You saw my *return to life* before I did. And you refused to allow me to accept anything other than 100% belief in myself in all aspects of publishing my memoir — a symbol of my life itself.

Goges & R. AKA Payton & Aria. My children. I don't know if you will ever read this. Living it was hard enough. Thank you for giving me permission to share the bleeding of your hearts. For forgiving me. For loving me. For allowing me to focus on mothering you again. With all my mistakes and seemingly horrific choices, in the reservoir of *my* bleeding heart, I *felt* I was doing it all for you.

www.ingramcontent.com/pod-product-compliance
Lightning Source LLC
Chambersburg PA
CBHW072359170726
48002CB00018B/106